I0013969

Amita Agarwal

Impact of Front-End Usability Guidelines on Evaluations of E-Commerce Web Pages

Anshu Agarwal

Impact of Front-End Usability Guidelines on Evaluations of E-Commerce Web Pages

VDM Verlag Dr. Müller

Impressum/Imprint (nur für Deutschland/ only for Germany)

Bibliografische Information der Deutschen Nationalbibliothek: Die Deutsche Nationalbibliothek verzeichnet diese Publikation in der Deutschen Nationalbibliografie; detaillierte bibliografische Daten sind im Internet über http://dnb.d-nb.de abrufbar.
Alle in diesem Buch genannten Marken und Produktnamen unterliegen warenzeichen-, marken- oder patentrechtlichem Schutz bzw. sind Warenzeichen oder eingetragene Warenzeichen der jeweiligen Inhaber. Die Wiedergabe von Marken, Produktnamen, Gebrauchsnamen, Handelsnamen, Warenbezeichnungen u.s.w. in diesem Werk berechtigt auch ohne besondere Kennzeichnung nicht zu der Annahme, dass solche Namen im Sinne der Warenzeichen- und Markenschutzgesetzgebung als frei zu betrachten wären und daher von jedermann benutzt werden dürften.

Coverbild: www.purestockx.com

Verlag: VDM Verlag Dr. Müller Aktiengesellschaft & Co. KG
Dudweiler Landstr. 99, 66123 Saarbrücken, Deutschland
Telefon +49 681 9100-698, Telefax +49 681 9100-988, Email: info@vdm-verlag.de

Herstellung in Deutschland:
Schaltungsdienst Lange o.H.G., Berlin
Books on Demand GmbH, Norderstedt
Reha GmbH, Saarbrücken
Amazon Distribution GmbH, Leipzig
ISBN: 978-3-8364-6467-3

Imprint (only for USA, GB)

Bibliographic information published by the Deutsche Nationalbibliothek: The Deutsche Nationalbibliothek lists this publication in the Deutsche Nationalbibliografie; detailed bibliographic data are available in the Internet at http://dnb.d-nb.de.
Any brand names and product names mentioned in this book are subject to trademark, brand or patent protection and are trademarks or registered trademarks of their respective holders. The use of brand names, product names, common names, trade names, product descriptions etc. even without a particular marking in this works is in no way to be construed to mean that such names may be regarded as unrestricted in respect of trademark and brand protection legislation and could thus be used by anyone.

Cover image: www.purestockx.com

Publisher:
VDM Verlag Dr. Müller Aktiengesellschaft & Co. KG
Dudweiler Landstr. 99, 66123 Saarbrücken, Germany
Phone +49 681 9100-698, Fax +49 681 9100-988, Email: info@vdm-publishing.com

Copyright © 2008 VDM Verlag Dr. Müller Aktiengesellschaft & Co. KG and licensors
All rights reserved. Saarbrücken 2008

Printed in the U.S.A.
Printed in the U.K. by (see last page)
ISBN: 978-3-8364-6467-3

ABSTRACT

This thesis examined the impact of usability guidelines and front-end web site design on consumer aesthetic evaluations of e-commerce web sites and perceptions of the e-retailer. A detailed web site design guidelines framework was developed from an in-depth review of the usability, human factors, and human-computer interaction web design guidelines literature. Four web site design factors (background color, white space, thumbnail image location, and thumbnail image size) were selected and varied using this framework. In addition, as a secondary research focus, this study explored the impact of these front-end web site design factors on consumer trust, product preference, and purchase intention. Based upon the literature, a conceptual model was proposed which integrated usability and web site design with consumer web site evaluation, trust, purchase intention, satisfaction, and loyalty. Conjoint analysis methodology was then used to design web page prototypes. Results showed that subtle front-end web site design elements impacted consumer aesthetic evaluations of the web page and subsequent e-retailer evaluations, although individual-level analysis showed a high level of heterogeneity across respondents. Results also provided support for the conceptual model developed.

BIOGRAPHICAL SKETCH

Anshu Agarwal is a graduate student in Cornell University's department of Design and Environmental Analysis, concentrating in Human Factors and Ergonomics. She was awarded the Flemmie Kittrell Fellowship for her graduate studies at Cornell. Anshu completed her high school education in 2002 from Vestal Senior High School (Vestal, NY). Selected as an Outstanding Senior in the College of Human Ecology, she graduated with a Bachelors of Science with Honors from Cornell University in 2006. During her undergraduate years, Anshu worked as a research assistant to Professor Alan Hedge, which resulted in three published conference papers. She presented her Honors thesis research, "Volumetric Deformation: A New Objective Measure to Study Chair Comfort," at the 2006 Human Factors and Ergonomics Conference in San Francisco, CA. She has also interned in the Statistical Research Division's Usability group at the U.S. Census Bureau (Washington, DC) and with the User Centered Design team at Intuit, Inc. (Mountain View, CA).

For my family, who provides infinite support, motivation, and encouragement. This thesis is especially dedicated to Papa, Professor Manoj K. Agarwal, whose passion for academia and new ideas instilled in me a love for research.

ACKNOWLEDGMENTS

First and foremost, I would like to thank my adviser, Professor Alan Hedge, for his steadfast support and invaluable guidance during my undergraduate and graduate years at Cornell. The numerous opportunities that he provided for research, projects, and internships were essential to the gradual development of my interests and skills. An additional thank you is extended to Professor S.P. Raj for his input and direction.

Finally, I sincerely express my gratitude to the College of Human Ecology, the sponsors of the Flemmie Kittrell Fellowship, as well as the department of Design and Environmental Analysis of Cornell University for their generous funding of my graduate studies. To each of these, I extend my deepest appreciation.

TABLE OF CONTENTS

LIST OF FIGURES

LIST OF TABLES

1. INTRODUCTION

In many developed world regions a substantial percentage of the population has access to the internet, such as in North America (69.7%), Australia (53.5%), and Europe (38.9%) (Miniwatts Marketing Group, 2007). As the internet has become increasingly prominent, it has transformed into a new market place for consumer goods and services (Haig, 2002). This transformation of the internet into a new buying and selling arena has been termed electronic commerce, or 'e-commerce.' A key value proposition of business to consumer (B2C) e-commerce web sites is that the design has the ability to "transcend physical barriers" in reaching new customers and in broadening the company's customer base (Venkatesh & Agarwal, 2006). This proposition however, is built upon the assumption that consumers will be willing and able to successfully interact with the e-commerce web site (Venkatesh & Agarwal, 2006). Although the amount of US dollars spent every year in e-commerce sales has been steadily increasing, the overall adoption rate of consumers purchasing online remains lower than anticipated (Scheleur, King, & Shimberg, 2006; Cheung & Lee, 2006; Nua, 2002). Research indicates that poor web site usability and inadequate consumer trust are the crucial obstacles to e-commerce acceptance and success (Nielsen, 2001; Green & Pearson, 2006; Lais, 2002; Boston Consulting Group, 2000; Forrester Research, 1999; Mariage, Vanderdonckt, & Chevalier, 2005; Cheung & Lee, 2006; Lee & Turban, 2001).

Research studies confirm that user success rates in completing a purchase transaction in 2001 were only 56% on e-commerce web sites and that most e-retailers followed only one-third of prescribed usability guidelines (Nielsen, 2001). According to Nielsen (2001), improvement in the usability of an average e-commerce web site could increase its current sales by 79%, which was calculated as the 44% of its

1

potential sales relative to the 56% of cases in which users succeeded. Further research has demonstrated the direct link between usability and sales revenue; consumers visiting e-commerce web sites with intention to purchase often abandoned their goal due to poor usability that prevented them from accomplishing their task (Boston Consulting Group, 2000; Forrester Research, 1999; Mariage, Vanderdonckt, & Chevalier, 2005). Users are less likely to stay on a badly designed web page long enough to make a purchase (Nielsen, 2001). Web site usability reflects on the company image (Nielsen, 2000), is used as an indication of company capability, and as a means to predict consumer post-consumption satisfaction (Alba, Lynch, Weitz, & Janiszewski, 1997). Development of web sites with high usability that encourage purchase and repeat visits are crucial for e-retailer survival and success (Vassilopoulou, Keeling, Macaulay, & McGoldrick, 2001). As stated by Green and Pearson (2006), "e-commerce experts agree that poor website design is one of the major reasons for recent dot.com failures, and over half of online traffic was driven away due to poor website design." Even well-known, successful web retailers may be capturing only half of potential new customers because of inadequate web site usability (Lais, 2002).

Consequently, web site usability has become an effective source of competitive advantage in the online marketplace. Web site usability is increasingly important in e-commerce, where a low switching cost allows consumers unimpressed by web site design to easily switch to another e-retailer. As e-commerce grows, an increasing number of companies are investing in the development of their internet storefront; empirical evaluations of what exactly makes e-retailer web sites effective and successful is in high demand (DeLone & McLean, 2003). Moreover, development of usable and easy to use web sites may accelerate the acceptance of e-commerce web sites as a new online marketplace through the alleviation of cognitive effort (Henneman, 1999; Venkatesh & Agarwal, 2006).

While usability goals provide a benchmark for good web site design and may be a key source of competitive advantage, numerous other characteristics may also impact the success of an e-retailer. Two of these important factors are: (1) e-retailer web site attributes (i.e. refund policies, security and privacy policies, product selection, community chat, etc.) (Bart, Shankar, Sultan, & Urban, 2005; Schlosser, White, & Lloyd, 2006; Fogg, Soohoo, Danielson, Marable, Stanford, & Tauber, 2002), and (2) brand equity (i.e. brand name, recognition, awareness, and loyalty) (Chaudhuri & Holbrook, 2001; Gommans, Krishnan, & Scheffold, 2001; Morgan & Hunt, 1994). The strategic use of the three components of web site design, web site attributes, and brand equity by an e-retailer may engender positive consumer evaluations and increase consumer trust in the e-retailer, therefore increasing its success in the marketplace (Everard & Galletta, 2005; McKnight et al., 2002; Sillence et al., 2004; Toms & Taves, 2004). Increased consumer trust has been proven to be related to consumer purchase intention (Schlosser et al., 2006; Yoon, 2002; Jarvenpaa et al., 2000), which is then associated with consumer satisfaction (Harris & Goode, 2004; Gommans et al., 2001) and loyalty (Sirdeshmukh et al, 2002; Ganesan, 1994; Morgan & Hunt, 1994).

The e-commerce web site is a full representation of the store to the consumer; the home page is the new store front. The look-and-feel of the web site is equivalent to the carefully constructed ambiance and window displays of any three-dimensional retailer; exceptional web site design may lure potential customers into the store and encourage browsing and product purchase. Although several studies have assessed the features of an e-commerce web site that promote success (i.e. Sultan, Urban, Shankar, & Bart, 2002; Page & Lepkowska-White, 2006; Urban, Sultan, & Qualls, 2000; Cheung & Lee, 2006), very little research has focused on the impact of front-end web

3

page design on the consumer. Furthermore, web site usability guidelines are often conflicting and lack supporting empirical evidence; limited research has been conducted to compare varying web page design recommendations available in the literature and how their implementation impacts consumer evaluations of the web page.

Therefore, the primary research goal of this thesis is to examine the impact of usability guidelines and front-end web page design on consumer aesthetic evaluations of e-commerce web pages and higher-level perceptions of the e-retailer. Four web page design elements (background color, white space, thumbnail image location, and thumbnail image size) were selected and varied based upon the usability, human factors, and human-computer interaction web design guidelines literature. Donald Norman (1998) wrote that successful products rest "on the foundation of a solid business case with three supporting legs: technology, marketing, and user experience." In addition, as a secondary research focus, this thesis explores the impact of web page design and usability on consumer trust, product preference, and purchase intention. This thesis aims to study the relationship between two of Norman's (1998) supporting legs: user experience and marketing. A conceptual model is thus developed which incorporates usability and web site design as a strategic component of the e-retailer.

This thesis is organized as follows: Chapter 1 provides an introduction to e-commerce (1.1), presents a conceptual model in which usability guidelines and web site design are postulated to be strategic components of the e-retailer (1.2), then provides an in-depth literature review on usability (1.3), usability, aesthetics, and web site design (1.4), web site design as an e-retailer strategic component (1.5), consumer trust (1.6), web site attributes (1.7) and brand equity (1.8) as additional e-retailer strategic components, and introduces a web site design guidelines framework developed for this thesis (1.9). Chapter 2 then presents the methods, Chapter 3 reports the results, and Chapter 4 provides a discussion about the implications of the findings, opportunities for improvement, and avenues for future research.

1.1. Electronic Commerce

E-commerce may be loosely defined as conducting business over the internet to "simplify and accelerate the stages in the business process" (DTI, 1999). Buyers and sellers can be directly connected in this new arena, which Bill Gates has coined "friction-free capitalism" (Palmer & Griffith, 1998). As described by the U.S. Department of Commerce, "Both the new Internet-based companies and the traditional producers of goods and services are transforming their business processes into e-commerce processes in an effort to lower costs, improve customer service, and increase productivity" (Henry et al., 1999). Internet shopping also provides numerous advantages for the customer compared to traditional shopping channels. E-commerce enables consumers to shop twenty-four hours a day, all year round, in any store, and from any location. Furthermore, e-commerce web sites often provide greater selection and allow for easy comparison between both products and web sites.

According to the U.S. Census Bureau, the adjusted estimated retail e-commerce sales for the second quarter of 2006 were approximately $26.3 billion dollars (Scheleur, King, & Shimberg, 2006). Although the amount of US dollars spent in e-commerce sales has been steadily increasing every quarter, e-commerce represented only 2.7 percent of total retail sales in the second quarter of 2006 (Scheleur et al., 2006) (Figure 1.1.1).

Recent surveys have further demonstrated that the penetration rate of Internet shopping remains low; the percentage of consumers purchasing online has remained at 15% since 2001 (Cheung & Lee, 2006; Nua, 2002). Poor web site usability and lack of trust are often cited as the main reasons for the slow adoption rate of e-commerce web sites (Nielsen, 2001; Green & Pearson, 2006; Lais, 2002; Boston Consulting Group, 2000; Forrester Research, 1999; Mariage, Vanderdonckt, & Chevalier, 2005; Cheung & Lee, 2006; Lee & Turban, 2001).

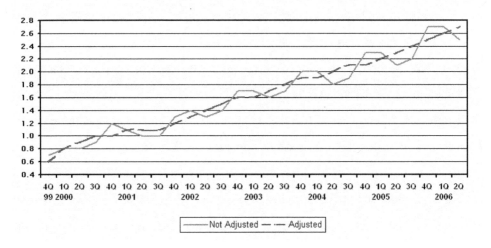

Figure 1.1.1. Estimated Quarterly U.S. Retail E-commerce Sales as a Percent of Total Quarterly Retail Sales: 4th Quarter 1999–2nd Quarter 2006

1.2. A Conceptual Model

Based on an extensive review of the human-computer interaction, usability, marketing, and electronic commerce literature conducted for this thesis, a conceptual model was developed that incorporates usability and effective web site design as crucial components that may impact the success of an e-retailer. While previous models have been presented in the literature, this thesis emphasizes and aims to empirically demonstrate the influential power of front-end web page design elements on consumer evaluations of a web site.

6

In this model (Figure 1.2.1.; Appendix 1.1), it is proposed that the web site leverages three main strategic components: (1) web site design (i.e. front-end design elements and interaction design features), (2) web site attributes (i.e. refund policies, privacy/security statements, product selection), and (3) brand equity (i.e. brand name, logo, reputation, awareness). These three strategic components may constitute the e-commerce web site, which consumers then evaluate based upon their first impressions and interactive web site experience. Although the conceptual model utilizes the broader terminology of "web site strategic components," the focus of this thesis is on the e-commerce web site. Therefore, strategic components are subsequently referred to as e-retailer strategic components.

Upon arrival at an unknown e-retailer web site, consumers immediately evaluate the e-retailer web site based on its front-end design and aesthetic qualities such as perceived usability and attractiveness. However, as the full representation of the store to the consumer, superficial evaluations of web site design can then become the foundation for, and potentially bias, higher-level judgments about the e-retailer itself (i.e. credibility, professionalism, reputation, and quality) (Pitkow & Kehoe, 1995; Toms & Taves, 2004; Sillence, Briggs, Fishwick, 2004; Fogg et al., 2003; Everard and Galletta, 2005). Research has shown that aesthetic evaluations are affective in nature, occur almost instantaneously, and may influence subsequent higher-level cognitive processes (Tractinsky, 2004; Fernandes, Lindgaard, Dillon, & Wood, 2003; Norman, 2004; Pham et al. 2001; Zajonc and Markus 1982). Positive consumer evaluations of the web site design may therefore result in a positive evaluation of the e-retailer, which encourages the development of consumer trust (Schlosser et al., 2006). Trust consequently can lead to consumer purchase intention (Schlosser et al., 2006; Yoon, 2002; Jarvenpaa et al., 2000); successful order fulfillment from the ecommerce web site will encourage varying levels of consumer

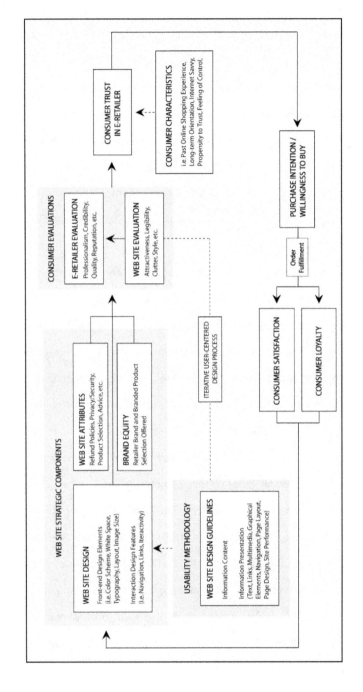

Figure 1.2.1. Conceptual Model

satisfaction (Shankar et al., 2002; Harris & Goode, 2004; Gommans et al., 2001) and loyalty (Sirdeshmukh et al, 2002; Ganesan, 1994; Morgan & Hunt, 1994). Consumer characteristics such as past shopping experience and propensity to trust moderate their web site evaluations and the subsequent impact of consumer evaluations on trust and purchase intention (Sultan et al., 2002; Shankar et al., 2002; Jarvenpaa et al., 1999; Lee & Turban, 2001; Dayal et al., 1999). Finally, consumer impressions and beliefs about their initial shopping experience with the e-retailer feed back to the beginning of the process model, reinforcing or diluting preexisting e-retailer brand equity.

A rigorous usability methodology is shown in the conceptual model as the foundation upon which the e-retailer strategic component of web site design rests. Effective web site design is dependent upon the usability literature and empirically tested web site design guidelines. Usability, however, must be integrated in an iterative user-centered design process to be successful; this process is portrayed as the cyclical route between usability, web site design, and consumer web site evaluations. The following chapter provides an introduction to usability, its dimensions, and a detailed description of the user-centered design process.

1.3. Usability

In simple terms, usability assesses the user's experience following an interaction with a product or system in the hopes of making it easy to use and a better fit for its users (U.S. Department of Health and Human Services, 2007; UPA, 2007). Usable products are appropriately complex based upon the task and the end-user's capabilities (Norman, 1998). Usability as a field has flourished under the larger discipline of human-computer interaction (HCI), which studies how humans interact with computer interfaces and other computer technologies. Both HCI and usability are grounded in theories from cognitive psychology, ergonomics, human factors, and computer science (Udsen & Jorgensen, 2005). As a multidisciplinary field, usability practitioners may have formal training in any of these areas of study.

Usability is a multidimensional construct for which numerous attributes and measures have been provided in the literature. These include ease of learning (learnability), efficiency of use, memorability, errors (frequency, severity, control of), and user satisfaction (U.S. Department of Health and Human Services, 2007; Green & Pearson, 2006; Nielsen, 1993). Quesenbery (2004) developed the Five E's to explain the dimensions of usability in web site and software development: effective, efficient, engaging, error tolerant, and easy to learn. Additional factors such as usefulness and cost-effectiveness may also be considered in the usability process (U.S. Department of Health and Human Services, 2007). Although different models and terminology have been presented in the literature, the three pillars of usability are those of effectiveness, efficiency, and user satisfaction. Effectiveness is the ability of users to complete a task accurately and completely; efficiency relates to the resources utilized to completing the user's goals; and satisfaction is the comfort and acceptance of the product by its target end-users (Henneman, 1999). The dimension of satisfaction has been criticized by many as an inadequate design ambition and as an ambiguous construct that is difficult to assess; recent usability literature has expanded its definition to encompass a user's positive emotion following product usage. This shift is evident in the recently coined terms of emotional design (Norman, 2004), hedonics (Hassenzahl, 2001), and pleasurable products (Jordan, 2000).

Two international standards currently exist in regards to usability and human-centered design. ISO 9241-11 was developed in 1998 by the International Organization for Standardization (ISO). It defined usability as "the extent to which a product can be used by specified users to achieve specified goals with effectiveness, efficiency and satisfaction in a specified context of use" (Usability Net, 2006). The second international standard (ISO 13407) defined human-centered design as "the active involvement of users and a clear understanding of user and task requirements; an appropriate allocation of function between users and technology; the iteration of design solutions; and multi-disciplinary design" (U.S. Department of Health and Human Services, 2007).

The appropriate allocation of function between users and technology as stated in ISO 13407 for human-centered design is a critical issue for usability and HCI practitioners. As technologies become more advanced, developers must decide which aspects of the system should be controlled by the human and which should be afforded and automated by the technology. With the advent of computers, a thorough understanding the user's tasks and needs is required in the design of web sites and interfaces. Usability problems often arise due a purely technology-centered approach in the product development process; this approach emphasizes the functional but overlooks the human as an essential factor in the system (Henneman, 1999). Product development teams in organizations often assess and analyze product attributes such as functionality, reliability, compatibility, and manufacturability; the crucial attribute of product usability, which may help determine product success, is frequently overlooked or eliminated due to additional costs (Henneman, 1999). In contrast to this technology-centered approach, usability is an essential component of user-centered design, a product development process in which end-user feedback is actively solicited to ensure that user needs, limitations, and preferences are taken into consideration (U.S. Department of Health and Human Services, 2007; UPA, 2007). Organizations that integrate usability and necessitate a user-centered design process are better equipped to develop products, interfaces, and web sites that accurately address their end-user's needs.

Due the inherent advantage resulting from a well-supported user-centered design process, the discipline of usability has quickly gained increased attention in the past few decades and has become an integral part of the product development process in a multitude of large corporations. Successful adoption of the usability methodology has been associated with increased productivity and decreased task completion time, lower error rates, increased sales and revenues, decreased training and support costs, reduced development time and costs, reduced maintenance costs, less user frustration, and increased customer satisfaction (Henneman, 1999; UPA, 2007). In order for usability to be effective, however, it must be part of an iterative user-centered design process. It is through this feedback oriented iterative process that usable products, web sites, and interfaces are successfully developed.

1.3.1. The Iterative User-Centered Design Process

In the conceptual model developed in this thesis, a strong usability methodology, including empirically validated web site design guidelines, provide the foundation for effective web site design (Figure 1.3.1.). Web site design is made up of both front-end design elements (i.e. color, layout, typography) as well as deeper interaction design features of navigation, interactivity, links, etc. The circular route between usability, web site design, and web site evaluation portrays the iterative user-centered design process; development of exceptional web site design often requires several iterations with extensive usability testing and continual user feedback.

Gould and Lewis (1985) describe the four crucial characteristics of user-centered design, which are as follows: (1) early focus on users, (2) integrated design, (3) user testing, and (4) iterative process. First, user-centered design should have an early focus on users, in which the development team has direct contact with their

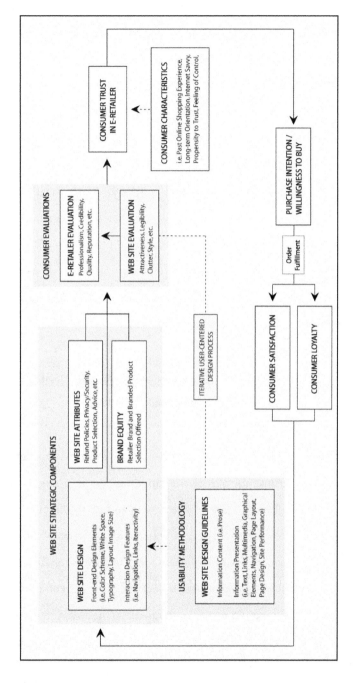

Figure 1.3.1. Conceptual Model: The Iterative User-Centered Design Process

13

target end-users through interviews, surveys, observations, etc. The goal of this early focus is to fully understand the end-user, the tasks they complete, their needs, and preferences prior to any product development work. Second, user-centered design has a characteristic of integrated design; usability efforts should occur in parallel and not sequentially in the organization and should be involved in the total customer experience from purchase, to installation, to use, to maintenance. Third, there should be early and continual user testing of design prototypes in order to keep the designs "on track" in the development process and consistently aligned with user needs. User testing should also be conducted following product deployment to gather product usage information in the user's natural environment. Finally, Gould and Lewis (1985) write that user-centered design is an iterative process, in which the results of usability testing feed back into a redesign of the product or system. Design iterations continue until the product "meets or exceeds user expectations" (Gould & Lewis, 1985). User-centered design is most effective in organizations when it is applied early in the product development process, before recommended changes based on usability testing become too expensive to implement (Henneman, 1999).

Both the standard for human-centered design provided earlier (ISO 13407) and Gould and Lewis (1985) describe an iterative design process as essential to the user-centered process; an illustration of the iterative process is provided in the diagram below (UPA, 2007) (Figure 1.3.2.). The four steps of the human-centered design process recommended by the ISO are to (1) specify the context of use, (2) specify requirements, (3) produce design solutions, and (4) evaluate the designs. If it is decided in the evaluation stage that the product satisfied the requirements determined in step two, then the iterative cycle is complete. If however, requirements are not adequately met, the cycle begins again with prior work feeding into the next iterative product design.

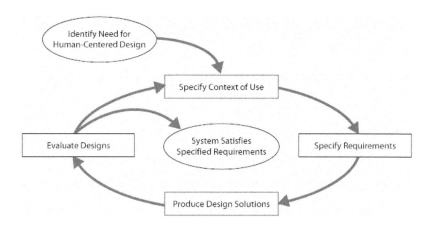

Figure 1.3.2. ISO 13407 Human-Centered Design Process

Although adequate, the human-centered design process recommended by the ISO does not provide guidance as to the more specific steps or methods utilized by usability practitioners in each phase of the iterative user-centered design process. Although various design models exist, the majority of usability literature presents an iterative user-centered design paradigm with four key phases: (1) analysis, (2) design, (3) evaluation, and (4) implementation (Henneman, 1999). A detailed explanation and description of each of these four phases is subsequently provided.

1.3.2. Phases of the Iterative User-Centered Design Process

1.3.2.1. Analysis (Predesign)

The analysis phase aims to fully understand "who the users are, their tasks, the environment and context of use, and the technology" (Henneman, 1999). Much of the analysis conducted in this stage may be accomplished by the marketing groups if management has integrated marketing and usability activities within the company

(Nielsen, 1992). Designers and developers should first and foremost understand the individual user's characteristics (i.e. work environment, age, education level, computer experience, social context), analyze the user's current task (i.e. current user approach, information needs, mental schemas, pain points in the task), conduct a functional analysis (i.e. underlying functions, sequence of typical tasks), and predict the potential evolution of the user (i.e. future users and unforeseen uses of the product) (Nielsen, 1992). The UPA (2007) cites following activities as characteristic of the analysis phase: meet with key stakeholders to set vision, include usability tasks in the project plan, assemble a multidisciplinary team with broad expertise, develop usability goals and objectives, conduct field studies, examine competitive products, create user profiles, develop a task analysis, document user scenarios, and document user performance requirements. Thorough analysis of competitive products available on the market should also be conducted using empirical usability testing and heuristics (Nielsen, 1992). According to Chignell and Hancock (1992), the most basic design "triad" of user-task, user-artifact, and artifact-task are the basis for design concerns in the analysis phase. Exploration of both the user-artifact (i.e. task analysis) and artifact-task relationships are central to the discipline of ergonomics and human factors (Chignell & Hancock, 1992). Design requirements may also be generated during analysis to ensure that specific user needs and goals are met throughout the entire design process; results from usability testing later in the process may then be measured against these user requirements. Usability goals and objectives should be set by the end of the analysis stage based upon prioritization of key usability attributes (Nielsen, 1992).

Methods used by usability practitioners in the analysis phase include interviews, surveys, questionnaires, focus groups, direct observation, and competitive product analysis (Henneman, 1999). The initial analysis phase is the most crucial stage of the iterative user-centered design process; the remaining three phases build on the foundation and understanding gathered during this first phase.

1.3.2.2. Design

The main objective of the design phase is to "translate design requirements derived from knowledge about users, their tasks, the environment of use, and the platform technology [from the analysis phase] into prototype interface designs" (Henneman, 1999). Usability teams in the design phase begin to brainstorm design concepts and metaphors, develop screen flow and navigation models, conduct design concept walkthroughs, and begin prototyping from low fidelity (paper and pencil) to high fidelity prototypes (UPA, 2007). Prototypes created in the design phase have two purposes: (1) for evaluation to unveil usability issues and end-user needs and preferences, and (2) for exploration of the actual viability and feasibility of the product and concept (Henneman, 1999). Prototypes may be low fidelity (i.e. paper mockups, mock three-dimensional models) or high fidelity (i.e. fully functioning, interactive software). Use of low or high fidelity prototypes in the evaluation phase are dependent on the number of iterations previously completed; generally, as iterations increase, so does the fidelity of the prototypes. Additionally, frequent prototyping in early iterations with low fidelity prototypes is recommended rather than in later iterations with more complex, higher fidelity designs.

Actively solicited user feedback about design concepts and prototypes is an essential characteristic of the user-centered design process. In participatory design, representative user groups may be recruited to critique and to encourage discussion about design ideas and initial prototypes (Nielsen, 1992). The design phase within itself is often iterative, with multiple designs created in quick succession based upon findings from prior analysis and evaluation stages.

1.3.2.3. Evaluation

The third evaluation phase aims to "assess the extent to which the system design solves the user's problems, whether or not organizations/individuals will use the system, and the extent to which the benefits of system use are sufficiently greater than its cost" (Henneman, 1999). Evaluations of the prototypes created in the design phase are conducted to assess product functionality, layout, terminology, media use, and usability issues (Henneman, 1999). Methods in the evaluation phase vary based on the depth of analysis needed, from subjective interviews in early stages of the iterative process to in-depth usability testing with quantitative measures of error rate and task time at later stages. Usability may be assessed through usability testing methods, questionnaires, and focus groups (Henneman, 1999). Two basic forms of empirical usability testing exist: (1) quantitative testing of a finished product to see if usability goals have been achieved, and (2) formative, qualitative evaluations of product to understand what aspects need further refinement (Nielsen, 1992).

The process of usability testing exposes possible problems users have in their interactions with the product or system (Green & Pearson, 2006). Think-aloud usability testing is commonly used by practitioners; in this process, participants are asked to verbalize their thought processes and perceptions of the product during their interaction experience (Nielsen, 1992). Think-aloud processes are valuable for adult users but may be applicable for children or special populations. In constructive interaction usability testing, two users work together to figure out and perform a task using a newly developed product. Compared to think-aloud methods with only one participant and in which prompting by the experimenter is common, constructive interaction methods are often considered more 'natural' and conversation-like (Nielsen, 1992). With the advent of technology, automatic computer logs of user actions (i.e. clicks, errors, recording of the session) may also be conducted during any testing session for later quantitative analysis (Nielsen, 1992). Usability practitioners may also observe representative users in their interactions with the product in either a laboratory or natural environment. During the evaluative process, practitioners should document standards and guidelines and create design specifications which may be used to measure prototype success in the following iteration (UPA, 2007).

Until evaluative results fulfill product objectives and end-user needs, results from the evaluation phase are fed back into the iterative design process to improve the subsequent prototype design of the next iteration. The duration of the iterative stages of design and evaluation varies based upon the product and the effort required to prototype; web site and software development processes are generally characterized by a shorter, more rapid iterative cycle than in product development.

1.3.2.4. Implementation (Postdesign)

Once a design has been selected, tested, evaluated, and approved through the iterative user-centered design process, usability teams may continue onto the fourth and final step of implementation. The implementation phase ensures that "the final product is consistent with the validated prototype and, ultimately, with end-user needs" (Henneman, 1999). Collaborative, multidisciplinary teams made up of interface designers, usability analysts, human factors specialists, engineers, and other members of the development team are a key to successful implementation. Follow-up usability studies of the product in the field should be conducted to gather data for successive product versions, practitioners should send out surveys to get user feedback, support calls should be logged, and economic data on the impact of work quality and costs to the user should be documented in this implementation phase. Testing of product acceptance by the target user group as well as development of

19

training and installation programs should also be completed during this final phase (UPA, 1997; Henneman, 1999).

1.4. Usability and Web Site Design

Although user-centered design and usability methods may apply to a multitude of products, systems, and interfaces, in the context of this thesis usability is discussed primarily in terms of the web site. In contrast to early computers, which were used by an exclusive set of users who had been explicitly trained, modern-day computers are designed for easy use by a diverse set of users who often lack any training (Chignell & Hancock, 1992). The evolution of fundamental usability issues regarding the computer and its interface parallels the evolution observed in other technologies. The initial design focus during the technological evolution of the automobile was on basic issues such as reliability, speed, and safety. As the automobile technology advanced, these basic usability concerns gradually become taken for granted and a refocus onto finer design attributes and usability issues occurred (i.e. style, ease of use) (Chignell & Hancock, 1992). Likewise, as computer technology has advanced, the design focus of computer applications, software, and web site development has now become usability issues of effectiveness, efficiency, and satisfaction. A similar argument has been posited by Norman (1998), who explained that as technology advances and the functionality of products successfully meet or exceed the users' needs, competition in the marketplace gradually becomes focused on improving the user experience rather than basic functionality. Essentially, the evolution of user design concerns mirrors that of Maslow's self-actualization hierarchy (1970); once lower order, basic user needs have been fulfilled, higher order needs regarding aesthetics and usability become primary. Furthermore, unlike lower order needs which are satiated once fulfilled, as

20

higher order needs are satisfied they are also increasingly desired (Maslow, 1970; Tractinsky, 2004). Implications of this theory on e-commerce are immense; consumers who have experienced exceptional aesthetics and web site design will refuse to settle for an e-retailer whose web site design they deem unappealing.

This section will first discuss the impact of usable web site design on the consumer and on e-commerce success, then the relationship between aesthetics and usability, and finally provide an introduction to usability web site design guidelines.

1.4.1. The Impact of Usable Web Site Design

Research has demonstrated the positive impact of usable web site design on the consumer. In a study of 750 corporate websites in three years, it was found that those websites that addressed usability issues and incorporated design criteria such as navigability and interactivity had higher traffic, increased repeat visitors, and higher consumer satisfaction ratings (Palmer, 2002a; 2002b). Increasing web site usability has also been associated with positive consumer attitudes toward the e-retailer, consumer retention, visit frequency, and purchase intention (Becker & Mottay, 2001). Usability testing and the resulting redesign of the Staples web site resulted in a decrease in consumer abandonment rates during the registration process by twenty-five percent (Green & Pearson, 2006).

A recent study by Kuan, Bock, and Vathanophas (2005) examined the impact of usability on consumer conversion, retention, and purchase intention. Three multidimensional usability dimensions were tested: system quality, information quality, and service quality. System quality referred to the usability attributes of navigation, layout consistency, visual appeal, accessibility, check out, and download delay; information quality comprised of relevance, accuracy, timeliness, content, format, completeness, and understandability; and service quality was related to the usability issues of search, interactivity, responsiveness, security and privacy, assurance, and empathy. According to the structure provided by Kuan, Bock, and Vathanophas (2005), layout and visual appeal, aspects of front-end web site design, were components of the usability dimension system quality. Although studied in conjunction with additional web site attributes such as download delay and accessibility, system quality was most significant for customer conversion. Service quality, however, was most significant for consumer retention (Kuan, Bock, and Vathanophas, 2005). Furthermore, Kuan, Bock, and Vathanophas (2005) found that the three dimensions of usability (system quality, information quality, and service quality) explained approximately 70% of the variance for both consumer purchase intention and future purchase intention. This thesis examines the impact of front-end design elements on consumer evaluations of unknown e-retailers; during an initial interaction with an unknown e-retailer, consumer conversion is a primary objective necessary for development of the e-retailer's customer base. Based upon the finding from this study, front-end web page design elements may be a key component of system quality to encourage consumer conversion.

Additional research has explored specific web site usability factors that relate to e-commerce success; these included download time, navigation, interactivity, responsiveness, and quality of content (Palmer, 2002b), learnability, playfulness, system quality, information, and service quality (Kuan, Bock, & Vathanophas, 2005; Liu & Arnett, 2000), search mechanisms (Koufaris, Kambil, & LaBarbera, 2001), and web site design, security, and privacy (Raganathan & Ganapathy, 2002). The usability constructs of navigability and interactivity have also been studied in relation to online consumer satisfaction (McKnight, Choudhury, & Kacmar, 2002a; Szymanski & Hise, 2000). As indicated by the list of web site usability factors provided, the impact of usability literature and front-end design elements on e-commerce success has not yet been adequately addressed.

Usability irrefutably provides developers the foundation for good web site design. From usability's functionalist perspective, superior web site design should be efficient, effective, and satisfying for the user in order to be truly usable. However, increased realization of the importance of aesthetics in interface design and the exploration of how aesthetics may impact perceptions of usability, human-computer interactions, and the user experience are an emerging trend in the literature (Udsen & Jorgensen, 2005). Recent research indicates an inherent interconnectedness between user perceptions of aesthetic design and perceptions of usability.

1.4.2. Aesthetics and Usability

Norman (2000; 2004) has developed a model for human information processing, in which humans utilize two connected processing systems (affective and cognitive) to evaluate (affect) and interpret (cognitive) the world. Affect occurs at the lowest, most primitive level of response and may influence "subsequent cognitive processes because our thoughts normally occur after the affective system has transmitted its initial information" (Tractinsky, 2004). Research has indicated that aesthetic impression formation was (1) affective, (2) formed almost immediately, and (3) preceded cognition and interpretation (Tractinsky, 2004; Fernandes, Lindgaard, Dillon, & Wood, 2003; Norman, 2004; Pham et al. 2001; Zajonc and Markus 1982). Based upon Norman's human information processing model, this thesis utilizes the terms "lower level" and "higher level" to characterize rapid, primitive, affective (lower level) evaluations and subsequent cognitive (higher level) evaluations of the web page and the e-retailer.

23

Support for the impact of attractiveness and aesthetics on human evaluations can easily be found in the social sciences literature. Two of the most well-known experts in usability have acknowledged the importance of aesthetics in design: "attractive things work better" (Norman, 1998), and "what is beautiful is usable" (Tractinsky, 2000). A study by Dion, Berscheid, and Walster (1972) found that subjects trusted attractive people more than those who were unattractive, which they coined the "what is beautiful is good" stereotype. More attractive people also earned more (Hamermesh and Biddle 1994) and received higher evaluations on their teaching skills (Hamermesh and Parker 2005). The "what is beautiful is good" stereotype was also corroborated by Hassenzahl (2004), who found that perceived beauty was significantly related to perceived goodness of system design. Aesthetics have also been shown to significantly impact new product development, marketing strategies, and the retail environment (Kotler and Rath 1984; Russell and Pratt 1980; Whitney 1988). In a study on product design, Bloch (1995) concluded: the "physical form or design of a product is an unquestioned determinant of its marketplace success." Physical appearance and attractiveness clearly human impact impression formation; research has further demonstrated the influence of aesthetic design on a variety of constructs in relation to the web site.

A study by Fernandes et al. (2003) exposed users to web pages for a period of 500 milliseconds; results found that attractiveness evaluations made in the 500 millisecond condition were significantly associated with attractiveness evaluations of the same web pages under conditions of unlimited exposure time. Aesthetic web site design has been shown to significantly influence consumer perceptions of web site usefulness and value (Pitkow & Kehoe, 1995), web site preference (Schenkman and Jonsson, 2000), consumer satisfaction (Lindgaard and Dudek, 2003; Szymanski &

Hise, 2000), web site reputation, and consumer trust (Toms & Taves, 2004; Sillence, Briggs, Fishwick, 2004).

The interconnectedness between aesthetics and usability has also been supported by the literature; aesthetic design increases perceived usability of products, interfaces, and web sites (Udsen & Jorgensen, 2005). Kurosu and Kashimura (1995b) studied the "appearance" of inherent usability and its determinants. Termed apparent usability, apparent usability was a distinct construct from inherent usability and its visual determination was based upon the interface aesthetics (Kurosu & Kashimura, 1995b). Users attempting to assess the inherent usability of an interface were strongly influenced by its aesthetic characteristics (Kurosu & Kashimura, 1995a). The findings of Kurosu and Kashimura were further explored in research conducted by Noam Tractinsky (1997). In an initial study examining cross-cultural differences, Tractinsky (1997) validated the Kurosu and Kashumura's (1995b) work; high correlations between perceived aesthetics and ease of use of the system were found. A follow-up study by Tractinsky, Shoval-Katz, and Ikar (2000) examined the connection between user perceptions of interface beauty and usability. Results from this study indicated that perceived interface aesthetics were significantly related to perceived usability both prior to product use and also following interaction; the inherent usability of the interface had no effect on user perceptions (Tractinsky, Shoval-Katz, & Ikar, 2000).

Kurosu and Kashimura (1995b) concluded that designers should enhance the apparent usability of a product to increase its appeal to the consumer and the probability of purchase. This recommendation was made based on the assumption that only following an initial positive assessment of apparent usability and product purchase would the user be able to experience the inherent usability present in the interface design through actual use (Kurosu & Kashimura, 1995b). In web site design, however, the user experience of apparent and inherent usability occur almost simultaneously (Fu & Salvendy, 2002). Fu and Salvendy (2002) studied the impact of apparent and inherent usability on user satisfaction in a web site. Apparent usability was varied through background color and interface layout; inherent usability was varied through task path, product classifications, and interface feedback (Fu & Salvendy, 2002). Results indicated that user satisfaction following both searching and browsing tasks was significantly related to perceived inherent usability of the web site (Fu & Salvendy, 2002). Interestingly, however, users were more likely to use and manipulate web sites with high apparent usability, portrayed by the number of items placed into the shopping cart (Fu & Salvendy, 2002). Therefore, aesthetically pleasing web sites with high apparent usability may increase consumer involvement and shopping behavior in ecommerce web sites.

As stated by Tractinsky (2004), "aesthetic evaluations are likely immediate, strong, and stable and may dominate the ensuing interactive experience." Initial and immediate aesthetic evaluations of web site design are critical due to their potential ability to (positively or negatively) bias latter higher-level cognition in the user (Pham et al. 2001). Positive aesthetic impressions of front-end web site design elements may carry over and result in positive impressions of the e-retailer. Furthermore, user perceptions of usability have been shown to be influenced by perceptions of aesthetic design. Although web site design is often assumed to be a purely artistic discipline, a strong foundation of usability, human factors, and human-computer interaction research has provided designers with guidelines to develop more usable, user-friendly, and ergonomic web sites. Implementation of these usability guidelines would subsequently impact the user's perceived aesthetics of the web site design. In the conceptual model developed in this thesis, usability and web design guidelines are included as a key resource of the usability methodology and a precedent to web site design (Figure 1.4.1.).

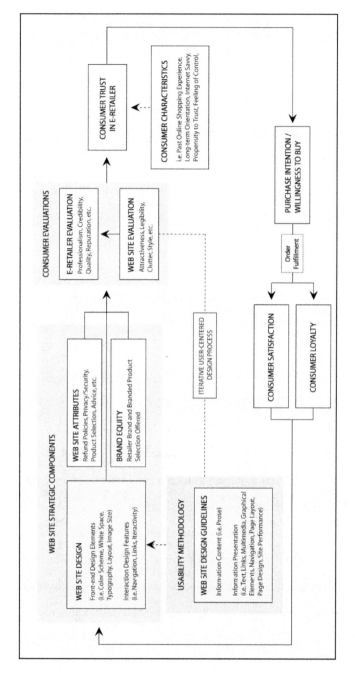

Figure 1.4.1. Conceptual Model: Web Site Design Guidelines

1.4.3. Usability Web Site Design Guidelines

A guideline may be defined as "a design and/or evaluation principle to be observed to get and/or to guarantee a usable user interface" (Mariage, Vanderdonckt, & Chevalier, 2005; Farenc, Palanque, & Vanderdonckt, 1995). They may result from theories on human physiology and biological systems, empirical observations, or from designer judgment (Henneman, 1999). Design guidelines are an especially valuable resource for web site designers regarding a multitude of interface issues such as color usage, screen layout, typography selection, navigation, link organization, etc. Adherence to guidelines may aid designers in the development of more usable, user-friendly, and ergonomic web sites. Web design guidelines developed within a company also aid in ensuring design consistency across various firm offerings, which is crucial in the consistent communication of brand and company values (Henneman, 1999). According to Henneman (1999), design guidelines are divided into two categories: interaction recommendations and style recommendations.

While interaction recommendations target design elements in an effort to improve usability, style recommendations reflect the company brand and aim to achieve a consistent look-and-feel (Henneman, 1999). This thesis focuses on the former category, interaction design guidelines, which aim to improve the usability of web sites and user interfaces.

Interaction design guidelines are abundant in bookstores and on the internet. Despite this, even if a company has the best intention of following prescribed web guidelines, a variety of issues arise. Guidelines are available in various forms that vary in quality, detail, and empirical justification (Mariage, Vanderdonckt, & Chevalier, 2005). Web design guidelines may conflict with each other and are often stated at such a high level that they are difficult to operationalize (Ivory & Hearst, 2002; Ivory,

Hearst, & Sinha, 2001). Common sense heuristics such as "keep it simple" and "remain consistent" are peppered throughout numerous web design and usability sources (for example see: Cooper & Reimann, 2003; Mandel, 1997; Nielsen, 2001; Nielsen, 2000). The benefit of such prescriptive guidelines is that they can be applied throughout the entire web site development process (Ivory & Megraw, 2005). The actual implementation of these heuristics within a design architecture, however, may prove challenging; usage of guidelines may differ based on the type and purpose of the web site and are often "divorced from the context" in which web sites are being developed (Ivory & Megraw, 2005). Furthermore, many web design guidelines are observational and are not validated by empirical evidence (Ivory & Megraw, 2005; Ivory, Sinha, & Hearst, 2001; Evans, 2000). The lack of quantitative dimensions makes proper implementation of these guidelines that much more difficult. The diagram below from Mariage, Vanderdockt, and Chevalier (2005) illustrates a classification system for the wide range of design guidelines available in the literature, organized based upon the guideline's type and source (Figure 1.4.2.). Although identification of individual web site design guidelines based on the classification system below is possible (Mariage, Vanderdockt, and Chevalier, 2005), the level of quality and empirical justification supporting each guideline is often ambiguous and not explicitly stated. Furthermore, web site design guidelines within one source (i.e. an online web guideline source, web site design guideline book) also vary in quality. While some guidelines within a source may be empirically justified, others are often solely based upon observations of the author(s) and lack explicit distinction between the two types.

Research further confirms that web site designers have difficulty applying web site design guidelines. Both novice and professional web site designers struggled to apply web site guidelines effectively (Chevalier & Ivory, 2003). According to a 2002

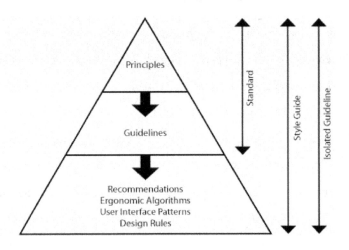

Figure 1.4.2. Types of Guidelines and Sources

survey, only 36 percent of web practitioners (including web designers, usability specialists, information architects, etc.) always used web design guidelines when designing web sites (Ivory, 2003). These percentages may be the basis for the low user success rate of only 56% on e-commerce sites; most e-commerce websites follow only one-third of prescribed usability guidelines (Nielsen, 2001). Design guideline implementation may also be hindered by the lack of a "well-defined, comprehensive set" of usability attributes (Kuan, Bock, & Vathanophas, 2005). Despite the abundance of design guidelines developed by industry experts and researchers, no consensus exists on the variation of design elements that result in a more usable web site.

In order to fully understand the breadth of available web design guidelines, a survey of web design literature was conducted for this thesis. Sources were gathered from the disciplines of design, usability, human-computer interaction, and human factors. Usability web site design guidelines for specific front-end web page design elements were then examined and were utilized as the basis for selection of the four design factors studied in this thesis. A detailed description of the web site design guideline framework formulated for this thesis is provided following the literature review portion. Prior to a detailed discussion of the web site design framework, the remainder of the conceptual model is discussed.

1.4.4. The Three E-Retailer Strategic Components

Usability methodology and an iterative, user-centered design process provide the resources and mindset necessary for the development of good web site design in any organization. These two criterion serve as the foundation for web site design that is usable (efficient, effective, satisfying), ergonomic, and user-friendly. A literature review on the benefits of usability and its impact on the consumer and the success of the e-commerce web site were provided in prior sections of this thesis.

In the conceptual model developed in this thesis, the e-retailer strategically utilizes three components in order to become successful in the online marketplace: (1) web site design, (2) web site attributes, and (3) brand equity. Web site design is comprised of both front-end design elements which are of interest in this thesis, as well as deeper, interaction design features that are integral to successful web site development (i.e. navigation, reactivity, feedback, etc.). Web site attributes is a broad category comprised of the additional features of the web site beyond its design that may provide information to the consumer about the e-retailer (i.e. privacy/security statements, product selection, community chat availability, refund policies, etc.). Finally, brand equity refers to the benefits associated with a recognized brand name (i.e. logo, reputation, awareness, loyalty).

A study on mass communication found that the majority of communication research focused on message content and audience characteristics; the study of how the information content was actually presented was often an afterthought (Wimmer &

31

Dominick, 1997). Similarly, while numerous studies have been conducted to explore the impact of usability on the web site, the user, and e-commerce success, the majority of the literature addresses the e-retailer strategic components of web site attributes (i.e. privacy/security, community chat, search) and brand equity (i.e. name, logo, branded products). Furthermore, studies that have directly addressed the impact of usability on the first strategic component, web site design, often focus on interaction design features such as navigation, interactivity, and reactivity of the web site. Limited research has been conducted to examine how usability and superficial, front-end design elements impact consumer evaluations of a web page. A handful of recent studies, however, have begun to examine the impact of front-end web site design on consumer perceptions of the e-retailer and on consumer trust development.

1.5. Web Site Design as an E-Retailer Strategic Component

With thorough usability testing and a strongly supported user-centered design process, web site design has the ability to become an essential strategic component for the e-retailer. As mentioned earlier in this thesis, low barriers to entry have resulted in a highly competitive online marketplace; consumers who are dissatisfied with an e-retailer can easily switch to a competitive e-retailer with one click of the mouse. Furthermore, human aesthetic responses occur almost immediately and have the ability to bias subsequent cognitive processing (Tractinsky, 2004; Fernandes, Lindgaard, Dillon, & Wood, 2003; Norman, 2000; 2004). Exceptionally usable, ergonomic, and aesthetic web site design therefore provides an e-retailer with significant competitive advantage over alternative e-commerce web sites; positive aesthetic evaluations of the e-retailer web site design may encourage more positive evaluations of the e-retailer itself.

Web site design as an e-retailer strategic component is illustrated in the conceptual model below (Figure 1.5.1.). An introduction to impression formation is provided, followed by an overview of the available research that has explored various aspects of web site design and its relationship to numerous consumer related constructs.

1.5.1. Web Site Design and Impression Formation

Consumers develop their perception of the e-retailer through their first impressions and interactions with the web site (Bart, Shankar, Sultan, & Urban, 2005). The e-commerce web site is a full representation of the store to the consumer; the home page is the new store front (Koufaris, Kambil, & LaBarbera, 2002; McKnight et al., 2002b). Web site design has the ability to influence these initial impressions and interactions; e-retailers must present a positive online image since consumer impressions are grounded on this initial information (Everard & Galletta, 2005). Poor web site usability reflects badly on the company image, decreasing the consumer's intention to return to the e-retailer in the future (Nielsen, 2000). Consumers may see a well-designed, aesthetically pleasing, useful, and easy to use web site as a positive indication of the company's capabilities. Furthermore, research has indicated that consumers use the web site interface as a means to predict their post-consumption satisfaction (Alba, Lynch, Weitz, & Janiszewski, 1997).

Psychological research has shown that a positive image is also important due to the "negativity effect" in impression formation: in the overall impression, negative attributes are given more weight than positive attributes (Anderson, 1965; DeBruin & Van Lange, 2000; Everard & Galletta, 2005; Fiske, 1980; Hamilton & Zanna, 1972; Peeters & Czapinski, 1990). Fiske (1980) found that when shown negative or positive

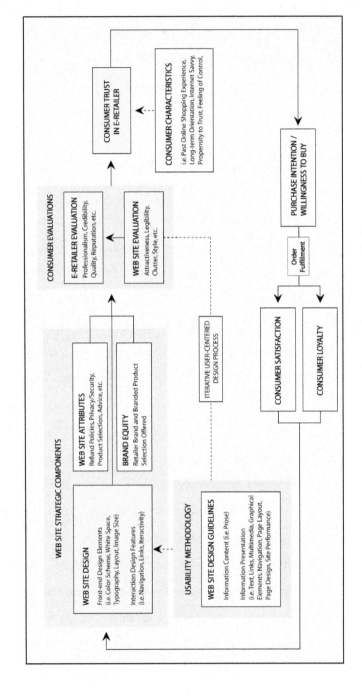

Figure 1.5.1. Conceptual Model: Web Site Design as an E-Retailer Strategic Component

behaviors depicted in photographs, negative behaviors had a larger impact on subject ratings of the target's likeability. In a study by Yzerbyt and Leyens (1991), participants made faster judgments about an actor's suitability for a role when given negative information about their personality. Even at a subliminal level, negative information is more powerful than positive information. Compared to positive words, people have been found to process subliminally presented negative words quicker and more accurately (Dijksterhuis & Aarts, 2003). In an extensive review of "cognitive, affective, and perceptual phenomenon," Baumeister, Bratslavsky, Finkenauer, and Vohs (2001) concluded that "bad" information and events received more attention and cognitive processing than "good" information and events (Bosson, Johnson, Niederhoffer, & Swann, 2006). In the realm of e-commerce, one negative observation about the web site may outweigh the presence of several positive attributes, thus skewing the consumer's overall impression of the e-retailer.

Furthermore, impressions made in the first seven seconds that a visitor views a web site are the most crucial; within this short time period a prospective customer can be "turned off for good" (Cotlier, 2001). As consumer expectations of web sites become more fine-tuned, the initial amount of time during which users evaluate a web site is expected to decrease (Cotlier, 2001). This time crunching trend increases the pressure on e-retailers to immediately present a positive impression and quickly capture a consumer's attention (Cotlier, 2001).

1.5.2. Indirect and Direct Web Site Design Research

Four key studies on web site design are subsequently discussed in detail. The first two, by Fogg et al. (2003) and McKnight et al. (2002b) indirectly explored the impact of front-end web site design on consumer perceptions of e-retailer credibility and consumer trust. The following two studies (Everard & Galletta, 2005; Schlosser et al., 2006) explicitly aimed to assess the role of front-end web site design elements on perceived web site quality, consumer trust, and purchase intention.

A large-scale study conducted by Fogg et al. found that web site design impacted consumer perceptions of web site credibility. Their analysis of 2500 participants indicated that 46.1% of comments cited web site design elements as a basis for web site credibility evaluation (2003). The most frequent participant comments referred to front-end design elements of layout, typography, white space, images, color schemes, etc., and were followed by comments on information structure, information focus, company motive, information usefulness, and accuracy of information (Fogg et al., 2003). The results of Fogg et al. indicated that web site design was utilized as the basis for consumer perceptions of e-retailer credibility.

Fogg et al. argued that the consumer focus on design elements to evaluate credibility could be attributed to the Elaboration Likelihood Model (ELM) (*ibid.*). Introduced in academia approximately twenty-five years ago by Petty and Cocioppo (1981), the ELM may be used to better understand how consumer involvement influences evaluative judgments. The ELM theory was developed from an evolutionary perspective; it is impossible and maladaptive for humans to invest high levels of mental effort to assess everything to which they are exposed (Petty & Wegener, 1999). According to Petty, the most crucial construct of the ELM is the "elaboration continuum", which is defined by "how motivated and able people are to assess the central merits of a person, issue, or position" (Petty & Wegener, 1999). On this continuum, highly motivated, able people take the effort to thoroughly examine all available and relevant information in order to arrive at a "reasoned attitude that is well articulated and well bolstered by supporting information" (Petty & Wegener, 1999). At the low end of the elaboration continuum, minimal effort is invested to examine

36

available information; attitude changes in these people may be based upon heuristics (Petty & Wegener, 1999; Chaiken, 1987), self-perception (Petty & Wegener, 1999), misattribution of affect (Petty & Cacioppo, 1983; Schwartz & Clore, 1983), or classical conditioning (Cacioppo et al., 1992; Petty & Wegener, 1999). The ELM is characterized by dual routes based upon the elaboration continuum: central and peripheral. The central route refers to attitude changes that result from higher effort information processing; the peripheral route refers to attitude changes based on lower effort processes (Petty & Cocioppo, 1981; Petty & Wegener, 1999).

Typical internet behavior today often lacks a high level of motivation characteristic of the central route of the ELM, as is portrayed by the commonly used phrases of "visiting sites" and "surfing the web" (Fogg et al., 2003). With competitive e-retailers available a click away, users make e-retailer assessments at a rapid pace and spend very little time at any one web site. Thus, according to the ELM, consumers with low levels of motivation and involvement will invest less effort into their evaluation strategy and rely on simple, peripheral cues such as attractiveness in their cursory analysis of the target (Petty & Cocioppo, 1981; Fogg et al., 2003). Indeed, peripheral cues such as web site design have been shown to be the basis for the development of low-involvement consumer trust in an unfamiliar e-retailer (Yang, Hung, Sung, & Farn, 2006). A study by Warden, Wu, and Tsai (2006) found that the three characteristics of web site usability, price comparison, and personal information protection served as peripheral cues in consumer evaluations of an e-retailer. Aesthetic design, however, may have a positive impact not only on low effort processing but also in instances of higher effort: "Under even higher elaboration likelihood conditions, attractiveness could serve as an argument if it provided information central to the merits of the attitude object" (Petty & Wegener, 1999). Strategic use of web site design that reflects on aesthetic quality and credibility may help e-retailers effectively

37

capture those consumers whose information processing is characterized by both the peripheral (lower effort) and central route (higher effort) of the ELM.

In the second study by McKnight et al., perceived web site quality strongly predicted trusting beliefs, more so than both retailer reputation and structural assurance (2002b). Consumers inferred e-retailer characteristics from their first impressions of the web site design. Moreover, consumers who perceived the web site as high quality were more likely to trust the e-retailer's competence, integrity, and benevolence and were more willing to enter into a buyer-seller relationship (McKnight et al., 2002b). The authors concluded: "first impressions of the site are a key to trust building" (McKnight et al., 2002b).

The findings from Fogg et al. (2003) and McKnight et al. (2002b) verify the conceptual model developed in this thesis; as the full representation of the store to the consumer, superficial evaluations of the e-commerce web site design become the foundation for higher-level judgments about the e-retailer itself. Consumer evaluations of web site design were related to e-retailer credibility (Fogg et al., 2003) and increased consumer trust (McKnight et al., 2002b).

While the previously discussed studies revealed the impact of web site design on consumer perceptions of credibility and quality, their research objectives did not explicitly aim to assess web site design characteristics. Two recent studies by Everard and Galletta (2005) and Schlosser, White, and Lloyd (2006) directly attempted to better understand the role of web site design as an antecedent of consumer trust and purchase intention.

Everard and Galletta (2005) studied the impact of presentation flaws on perceived site quality, trust, and purchase intention in e-commerce web sites. Three aspects of presentation flaws were specified: poor style, incompleteness, and language errors (Everard & Galletta, 2005). Poor web design style was varied through changes in background (color and pattern), font (size, consistency), and page formatting (table column consistency, word and line spacing). Although the design decisions in the conditions of "good style" versus "poor style" were not varied independent of each other, results showed that subjects rated pages with "good style" higher on perceived quality scores. This suggests that users were able to successfully able to distinguish between, and judge, changes in web site design. Results also supported prior findings and those from McKnight et al. (2002b) that perceived web site quality is an antecedent of consumer trust, and that trust is an antecedent of purchase intention (Everard & Galletta, 2005).

A recent study by Schlosser, White, and Lloyd explored the impact of web site investment on consumer trusting beliefs and online purchase intentions (2006). Web site investment was defined as the amount of time, effort, and money invested into the development of "front-end" design elements of a web site; it was varied through the use of background color, font, and an enhanced zoom feature. The "high investment" web site utilized a white background color, "sophisticated" Garamond font, and an enhanced zoom feature. The "low investment" web site, in contrast, utilized a default gray background color, Times New Roman font, and a limited zoom feature. Web site content and layout were held constant. Results showed that subjects accurately perceived the high investment web site as requiring greater amounts of time, energy, and money to develop (Schlosser et al., 2006). This confirmed that users are able to accurately judge web site design and moreover, that web page design elements of background color, font, and a zoom feature could successfully communicate level of investment to consumers.

Furthermore, Schlosser et al. found evidence that web site investment influenced consumer perceptions of firm ability and online purchase intentions. The high investment web site resulted in higher levels of perceived firm ability, which was significantly correlated with higher online purchase intentions. Perceived firm benevolence and integrity had no impact on purchase intention (Schlosser et al., 2006). The impact of web site investment on purchase intentions, however, was only effective for what Schlosser et al. coined "searchers"; those consumers who browse web sites in order to find, and hopefully buy, a particular product (2006). Searcher behavior was distinct from that of "browsers," who were characterized by more exploratory, recreational, and less "outcome oriented" behavior (Schlosser et al., 2006). While searcher purchase intentions were influenced by ability beliefs, browser purchase intentions were influenced by benevolence beliefs. "Web site design plays such an important role… Instead of serving a purely aesthetic function, it signals that a firm's ability can be trusted, which we found to be the most significant driver of searcher's online purchase intentions" (Schlosser et al., 2006).

As found by Schlosser et al., web site design had the greatest impact on the trust and purchase intention of "searchers," those consumers who had a particular product in mind prior to browsing of e-commerce web sites. A consumer searching for a product or service through an internet search engine may arrive directly at the product description page rather than the home page of an unknown e-retailer; in this scenario, only surface cues are present for the consumer to form judgments about the e-retailer's credibility (Everard & Galletta, 2005). The findings from the latter two studies further strengthen the conceptual model developed in this thesis; results provide empirical evidence that high quality web site design is significantly related to consumer perceptions of e-retailer ability, consumer trust, and purchase intention (Schlosser et al., 2006; Everard & Galletta, 2005).

Cotlier (2001) wrote, "Just as when you meet someone for the first time, it's human nature for customers to visually evaluate a Website the first time they visit it… the Internet is mainly a visual experience." Consumer trust is crucial for the success of e-commerce; without it, consumers would be unwilling to interact or consider purchase from any e-retailer. According to Meyerson et al., initial trust in the e-retailer quickly forms based upon "whatever information is available" (1996). Consumer trust is essentially the key to e-retailer success; successful trust development is related to consumer willingness to buy, purchase intention, satisfaction, and loyalty. A detailed discussion of consumer trust is provided in the following chapter.

1.6. Consumer Trust

This thesis focuses on the impact of usability design guideline implementation on consumer evaluations of e-commerce web pages. While the previous portion of this thesis focused on the importance of usability and web site design, discussion of the remaining two e-retailer strategic components in the conceptual model (web site attributes and brand equity) aims to provide additional context to the secondary research question of this thesis: how may front-end web page design impact consumer trust and product preference?

Prior to discussion of the final two strategic components, a groundwork regarding the dimensions of consumer trust, its role in e-commerce, and the consequences of consumer trust is provided.

1.6.1. Consumer Trust and Its Dimensions

The multidimensional concept of trust has been studied extensively in sociology (i.e. Barber, 1983; Weber & Carter, 1998), psychology (i.e. Couch, Adams, & Jones, 1996; Rotter, 1967; Gabarro, 1978; Johnson-George, & Swap, 1982;), organizational behavior (i.e. Meyerson, Weick, Kramer, 1996; Zaheer, McEvily, &

Perrone, 1998; Zucker, 1986), accounting (i.e. Seal & Vincent-Jones, 1997), management (i.e. Butler, 1991; Driscoll, 1978; Jevons & Gabbott, 2000; Mayer, Davis, & Schoorman, 1995; McKnight, Cummings, & Chervany, 1998; Wicks, Berman, & Jones, 1999), and marketing literature (i.e. Bhattacherjee, 2002; Doney & Cannon, 1997; Ganesan, 1994; Moorman, Deshpande, & Zaltman, 1993; Morgan & Hunt, 1994; Sirdeshmukh, Singh, & Sabol, 2002). Although numerous studies have explored the concept of trust, there is disagreement on its definition, measurement, antecedents, consequences, and role in e-commerce (Lee & Turban, 2001; Grabner-Krauter & Kaluscha, 2003; Everard & Galletta, 2005).

In online buyer-seller relationships, consumers are the trustors and e-retailers are the trustees (Bhattacherjee, 2002). Consumers, unable to effectively monitor or control e-retailer behavior, are vulnerable to its behavior (Bhattacherjee, 2002). As stated by Bart, Shankar, Sultan, and Urban (2005), "trust implies a party's willingness to accept vulnerability," in situations of uncertainty and risk, "with an expectation or confidence that it can rely on the other party" (Doney & Cannon, 1997; Mayer, Davis, & Schoorman, 1995). Trust has also been defined as the extent to which a company is likely to behave in a way that is "benevolent, competent, honest, [and] predictable" (McKnight et al., 2002a).

Consumer e-retailer trusting beliefs have been grouped into three main categories: belief in the retailer's ability, benevolence, and integrity (McKnight, Choudhury, & Kacmar, 2002a; Mayer, Davis, & Schoorman, 1995). According to the literature, benevolence and ability are the two key dimensions of consumer trust (Shankar, Urban, & Sultan, 2002; Doney & Cannon, 1997). The dimension of benevolence in consumer trust is the extent to which a company's motives benefit the consumer and are not opportunistic (Bhattacherjee, 2002; Mayer, Davis, & Schoorman, 1995). The dimension of ability is the consumer's assessment of company

42

competence and its access to the knowledge required to be successful (Bhattacherjee, 2002; Mayer, Davis, & Schoorman, 1995). While perceptions of company benevolence are more relevant for the maintenance of long-term buyer-seller relationships, perceptions of company ability are crucial for initial consumer trust development and consumer conversion. Research conducted by Schlosser et al. (2006) showed that consumers who were targeted in their search for a specific product ("searchers") valued company ability more than benevolence, whereas exploratory and recreational consumers ("browsers") valued company benevolence more than ability.

Customer perceptions and beliefs about company reliability, safety, and honesty are also all important facets of trust (Chaudhuri & Holbrook, 2001). The development of trust, however, is moderated by differences on consumer characteristics. Consumer characteristics that have been shown to drive trust in the literature include: internet savvy (Shankar et al., 2002; Sultan et al., 2002), past web site/shopping experience (Sultan et al., 2002; Jarvenpaa et al., 1999), entertainment/chat use (Sultan et al., 2002; Shankar et al., 2002), predisposition to technology (Shankar et al., 2002), long-term orientation (Shankar et al., 2002; Jarvenpaa et al., 1999), positive trusting stance or trust propensity (Jarvenpaa et al., 1999; Lee & Turban, 2001), consumer collaboration or community (Dayal et al., 1999), and a feeling of control (Dayal et al., 1999; Jarvenpaa et al., 1999). The moderating role of consumer characteristics was thus included in the conceptual model (Figure 1.6.1.).

While the majority of the research has focused on trust development in offline buyer-seller relationships, more recent trust development models have addressed consumer trust in an online context. In online trust, the focus is the web site and includes "consumer perceptions of how the site would deliver on expectations, how believable the site's information is, and how much confidence the site commands"

(Bart et al., 2005). Urban, Sultan, and Qualls developed a cumulative process model of online trust development, in which trust was first developed in the internet and in the web site; second, with the information displayed on the web site; and finally, through delivery fulfillment and service (Urban, Sultan, & Qualls, 2000).

Additional efforts have also broadened the concept of online trust beyond the consumer perspective to include multiple stakeholders such as customers, employees, suppliers, distributors, partners, stockholders, and regulators (Shankar, Urban, & Sultan, 2002; Jones, Wilikens, Morris, & Masera, 2000).

1.6.2. Consumer Trust in E-Commerce

Abundant research has been conducted to understand the antecedents and underlying dimensions of consumer trust in an online context (e.g. Bart, Shankar, Sultan, & Urban, 2005; Bhattacherjee, 2002; Cheung & Lee, 2006; Dayal, Landesberg, & Zeisser, 1999; Hoffman, Novak, & Peralta, 1999; Jarvenpaa, Tractinsky, & Vitale, 2000; Lee & Turban, 2001; Papadopoulou, Kanellis, & Martakos, 2001). The lack of trust characteristic of e commerce may be attributed to the fact that despite its many advantages, internet shopping involves more risk and uncertainty for consumers than traditional shopping contexts (Lee & Turban, 2001). It is much more difficult for consumers to assess the trustworthiness of e-retailers compared to brick and mortar stores (Palmer, Bailey, & Faraj, 2000). Inhibited trust development may be attributed to the lack of physical contact with e-retailers and the 'lack of touch' associated with online shopping (Harris & Goode, 2004; Reichheld & Shefter, 2000). E-commerce transactions involve both a temporal and spatial separation between the consumer and retailer; this lack of "simultaneous exchange" of

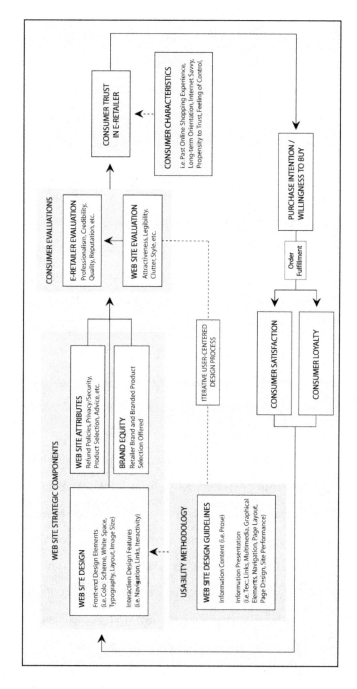

Figure 1.6.1. Conceptual Model: The Moderating Role of Consumer Characteristics

goods, money, and information increases consumer perceived risk (Grabner-Krauter & Kaluscha, 2003).

Furthermore, consumers often avoid safe online activities that are perceived as risky (Dunn, 2004). This behavior has led many researchers to conclude that consumer perceptions and lack of consumer trust are the crucial threats to e-commerce (Schlosser, White, & Lloyd, 2006; Hoffman, Novak, & Peralta, 1999). A study of 1500 online users by the Princeton Survey Research Associates found that trust was the second most important antecedent of consumers visiting a web site (2002). Only 29 percent of users trusted e-commerce web sites (Princeton Survey Research Associates, 2002). Studies have also shown that online shoppers distrusted not only e-retailers and their payment systems, but the nature of online shopping itself (Harris & Goode, 2004; Urban, Sultan, & Qualls, 2000; Hoffman, Novak, & Peralta, 1999). Before they will consider entering into any exchange relationship with an e-retailer, consumers must first develop a sense of trust (Cheung & Lee, 2006).

This thesis focuses on the impact of web page design elements on initial searcher consumer trust development in an unknown e-retailer. Initial trust "implies that trust is placed in an unfamiliar trustee, in the context of a relationship where the parties do not have credible information about each other and where no tie between the parties already exists" (Everard & Galletta, 2005; McKnight, Cummings, & Chervany, 1998). In the interaction between a consumer and potential e-retailer, this initial stage is when subjective judgments are made that will determine whether or not the consumer will enter into a buyer-seller relationship with the company. Consumers will have immediately evaluated the e-retailer based upon aesthetics and front-end web site design; these initial impressions are then strengthened and either supported or refuted following the consumer's first web site experience (Page & White, 2006). Perceptions of uncertainty and risk about the e-retailer are also especially heightened in initial stages. Therefore, it is crucial that e-retailers be able to "engender sufficient trust at this stage in order to overcome consumer's perceptions of risk and to persuade consumers to transact with them" (McKnight et al., 2002b).

Consumer trust has been shown to operate as an "order qualifier" rather than an "order winner" in buyer-seller relationships (Doney & Cannon, 1997). A critical, satisfactory level of trust is thus required in order for a company to be considered as a potential provider of goods and services. In the competitive online environment, only those e-retailers in which the consumer has developed a satisfactory level of trust will product purchase be considered. As substantiated through the discussion of prior research, front-end web page design has the ability to effectively impact consumer evaluations of the e-retailer and their development of trust. According to Urban, Sultan, and Qualls (2000), "Those who wait too long to adopt trust building will be marginalized by existing firms that have learned how to earn consumers' trust as well as by entirely new competitors."

Therefore, as an order qualifier, consumer trust in the conceptual model directly precedes consumer purchase intention and willingness to buy from the e-retailer (Figure 1.6.2.). Following product purchase, order fulfillment encourages varying levels of consumer satisfaction and loyalty to the e-retailer. The valuable consequences of consumer trust are thus contingent upon its successful development based on consumer evaluations of the e-commerce web site.

1.6.3. The Consequences of Consumer Trust

According to the literature, consequences of consumer trust include: long-term exchange relationships (Ganesan, 1994; Morgan & Hunt, 1994; Spekman, 1988), cooperation (Morgan & Hunt, 1994), willingness to buy (Shankar et al., 2002;

47

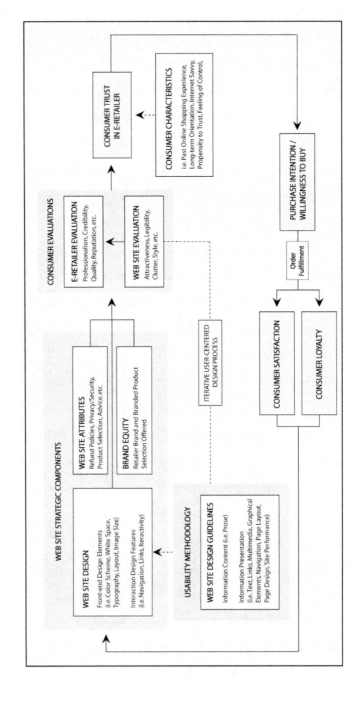

Figure 1.6.2. Conceptual Model: The Consequences of Consumer Trust

48

Jarvenpaa et al., 2000), stakeholder satisfaction (Shankar et al., 2002), higher purchase intention (Yoon, 2002; Stewart, 2003; Sultan et al., 2002), and consumer loyalty (Chaudhuri & Holbrook, 2001; Sirdeshmukh, Singh, & Sabol, 2002; Harris & Goode, 2004; Lynch, Kent, & Srinivasan, 2001). Higher levels of consumer trust have also been shown to be negatively related to early termination of the buyer-seller exchange relationship (Morgan & Hunt, 1994).

Trust development and consumer loyalty may be more crucial online than in traditional offline store environments (Harris & Goode, 2004; Reichheld, Markey, & Holton, 2000). Customers can be more loyal online due to the increasing reliance on the internet for information and products (Shankar, Smith, & Rangaswamy, 2003). According to a study by Chaudhuri and Holbrook (2001), a significant association exists between consumer trust and both purchase and attitudinal loyalty. Sirdeshmukh, Singh, and Sabol (2002) directly related trust to consumer loyalty in relational exchanges. These findings were corroborated by Harris and Goode (2004), whose results indicated a positive and direct relationship between trust and loyalty. A cross-cultural study by Lynch, Kent, and Srinivasan (2001) found that consumer trust was consistently and significantly related to online loyalty in twelve different countries. Establishing online loyalty, however, is dependent first on the building of consumer trust (Harris & Goode, 2004; Reichheld & Schefter, 2000). As Reichheld and Schefter (2000) state: "to gain the loyalty of customers, you must first gain their trust. That's always been the case, but on the Web… it's truer than ever."

Company investment into the development of strong customer relationships provides more than short-term security; research shows that it is the later years of a customer relationship that generate the largest profit returns (Reichheld & Sasser, 1990). The returns from a loyal customer base online provide e-retailers with the steady profit necessary to cover fixed costs and attract new customers through marketing and advertising efforts (Reichheld, Markey, & Holton, 2000). Across various industries, Reichheld and Sasser (1990) found that increasing customer retention by 5% could result in long-run profit increases between 25% and 95%. This phenomenon of increasing profits with increasing length of retailer-customer relationship is also present online (Reichheld, Markey, & Holton, 2000). Interestingly, research has shown that profitable customers prefer to be loyal and "tend to consolidate their purchases in a sector with one online retailer" (Reichheld, Markey, & Holton, 2000). These loyal customers did not value a retailer for providing the lowest price; instead, they valued convenience and considered trust as the key criterion for e-retailer preference (Reichheld, Markey, & Holton, 2000). Consumer trust is crucial in enhancing attitudinal and behavioral loyalty online, and customer loyalty is the key to long-term firm profitability (Gommans, Krishnan, & Scheffold, 2001; Reichheld, Markey, & Hopton, 2000).

Although the presence of customer loyalty implies satisfaction with the e-retailer, Harris and Goode only found partial evidence that trust was positively and directly related to satisfaction (2004). Further studies demonstrated that an asymmetric relationship exists; satisfaction does not directly lead to consumer loyalty (Gommans, Krishnan, & Scheffold, 2001). This finding is particularly pertinent for e-commerce, in which even satisfied consumers may easily switch to a competitor's web site that offers similar goods and services. Therefore, e-retailers must find creative new ways of attracting and retaining a customer base; web site design may fulfill this function.

Trust therefore not only facilitates the acquisition of a strong customer base, it also enables relationship building and customer loyalty (Papadopoulou et al, 2001; Bart, Shankar, Sultan, & Urban, 2005; Doney & Cannon, 1997). A key aspect of 'relationship capital,' trust is a necessity for companies to establish and maintain customer relationships; an increase in relationship capital relates to customer retention and increased sales revenue (Papadopoulou, Kanellis, & Martakos, 2001; Tapscott, Ticoll, & Lowy, 2000). Trust is so essential for success in e-commerce that Urban, Sultan, and Qualls describe it as the 'future currency of the Internet' (2000).

E-retailers have developed numerous additional techniques beyond web site design to help overcome the "trust barrier" in e-commerce. These include (1) providing full safety guarantees and offering to cover any losses due to fraud (e.g. Amazon.com); (2) relying on existing brand reputation if an established brick and mortar business already exists (e.g. BarnesandNoble.com); (3) building brand recognition for web-only businesses (e.g. Travelocity.com, Amazon.com); (4) building transference-based trust (e.g. through third-party trust-certification bodies such as TRUSTe and Verisign); and (5) providing detailed explanations of privacy policies (McKnight, Choudhury, & Kacmar, 2000; Lee & Turban, 2001). The techniques listed above may be placed into the two remaining components of the conceptual model: web site attributes and brand equity. In addition to good web site design, both may be used by the e-retailer as strategic components to engender development of consumer trust in the web site.

1.7. Web Site Attributes as an E-Retailer Strategic Component

The second e-retailer strategic component that may provide competitive advantage to an e-retailer is that of web site attributes (Figure 1.7.1.). The broad category of web site attributes is composed of the additional features of the web site that go beyond its front-end web site design characteristics and provide information to the consumer about the e-retailer (i.e. privacy/security statements, product selection, community chat availability, refund policies).

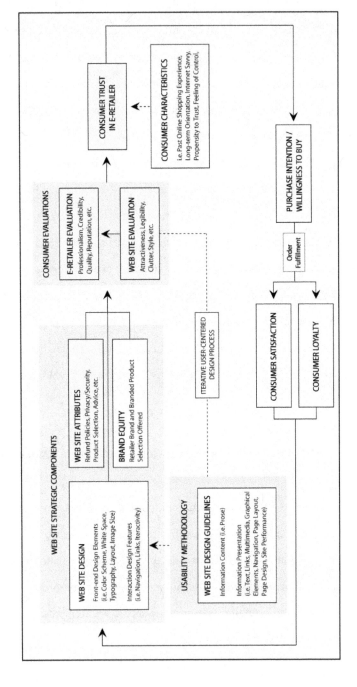

Figure 1.7.1. Conceptual Model: Web Site Attributes as an E-Retailer Strategic Component

The majority of research exploring the impact of web site attributes on the consumer has been conducted in the past decade. As a recent area of research, this e-retailer strategic component has included a variety of web site features and characteristics that may be related to various consumer-related constructs (i.e. trust, purchase intention, loyalty). A consensus on which web site attributes have the most significant impact on consumer web site evaluations and trust development has yet to be achieved. Furthermore, many web site attributes examined in the literature overlap, but are classified differently in each research study.

Web site attributes that have been proven to be drivers of consumer trust include: information quantity, quality, and timeliness, advice availability (Urban, Sultan, and Qualls, 2000), web site longevity, security, product selection, community, order fulfillment, external links, privacy, and search engine presence (Smith et al., 2000; Dayal et al., 1999). Research has also shown that positive consumer perceptions of e-retailer legitimacy, size, and reputation based on the web site were associated with increased consumer trust (Dayal et al., 1999; Jarvenpaa et al., 2000).

Security and privacy control have been especially emphasized in the literature as essential to consumers and as a means of building e-retailer trustworthiness and web equity (Caudill & Murphy, 2000; Hoffman et al, 1999; Page & Lepkowska-White, 2006; Urban, Sultan, & Qualls, 2000; Cheung & Lee, 2006). Privacy and security are often conveyed through the use of explicit statements that "assure customers that personal data will be discreetly used and protected" (Schlosser, White, & Lloyd, 2006). The effectiveness of these statements in promoting trust, however, has not yet been agreed upon in the literature (Schlosser, White, & Lloyd, 2006; Bart, Shankar, Sultan, & Urban, 2005; Palmer, Bailey, & Faraj, 2000). Schlosser et al. found that although consumers read privacy and security statements, they did not influence online purchase intentions unless the statements were noticeably weak or

53

ambiguous (2006). Consumer purchase intention was affected more by web site investment, which varied web site design elements (Schlosser et al., 2006). Furthermore, a large scale study by Fogg et al. found that consumers based perceptions of web site credibility on "surface elements" such as web site design rather than on the presence of privacy policies (Fogg, Soohoo, Danielson, Marable, Stanford, & Tauber, 2002). The unanticipated results of Schlosser et al. (2006) and Fogg et al. (2002) bolster the primary research question of this thesis; front-end web page design elements may significantly impact consumer aesthetic evaluations of e-commerce web page design and higher-level perceptions about the e-retailer.

Comprehensive, large-scale research on the role of web site characteristics as drivers and antecedents of online trust has also recently been conducted. A large-scale analysis of twenty-five web sites and 6700 responses found three underlying dimensions of trust: believability/reliability, visual feel/comfort and quality of the company (Sultan, Urban, Shankar, & Bart, 2002). Nine key web site factors determined consumer perceptions of trust: navigation, advice, no errors, fulfillment, community, privacy/security, trust seals, brand, and presentation (Sultan et al., 2002). A follow-up large-scale study by Bart, Shankar, Sultan, and Urban (2005) then explored the differences in antecedent web site characteristics that drove consumer trust across different web site categories and consumer segments. Their study focused on the web site characteristics of privacy, security, navigation and presentation, brand strength, advice, order fulfillment, community features, and absence of errors (Bart et al., 2005). Results indicated that navigation and presentation, advice, and order fulfillment were especially important for building trust in e-retailer web sites. Furthermore, Bart et al. (2005) found that advice was most important for web site categories with high financial risk (i.e. computers) and that brand strength was most important for high involvement web site categories (i.e. automobiles) (2005). Brand strength also influenced consumer trust more for subjects with higher levels of education (Bart et al., 2005).

Results from Bart, Shankar, Sultan, and Urban (2005) provide evidence that brand has a significant impact on consumer trust development. Brand equity is the final strategic component included in the conceptual model devised in this thesis. A more detailed discussion of brand is provided in the following chapter.

1.8. Brand Equity as an E-Retailer Strategic Component

The final strategic component in the conceptual model, brand equity, has been extensively explored and substantiated as an essential strategic component in the development of consumer trust (Figure 1.8.1.). Indicators of the presence of brand equity include brand-specific trust and loyalty (Aaker, 1996). While consumer trust is generally discussed in terms of the consumer's trust in the e-retailer, in this thesis brand trust is more narrowly defined as the recognizable brand name of the e-retailer or its product offerings.

Recognized and trusted brand names strongly impact consumer evaluations of the web site and e-retailer; presence of a recognized brand name may occur at both the retailer level and at the product manufacturer level. The interaction between the retailer brand and the manufacturer brand in the online context, however, has yet to be extensively studied in the literature (Jevons & Gabbott, 2000). A detailed discussion of the impact of brand is beyond the scope of this thesis; therefore, a more general discussion of its role as an antecedent of consumer trust and loyalty is provided.

Brand trust may be defined as the willingness of a consumer to rely on the ability of a brand to perform its stated function   (Chaudhuri & Holbrook, 2001; Moorman, Deshpande, & Zaltman, 1993; Morgan & Hunt, 1994). The trend of moving

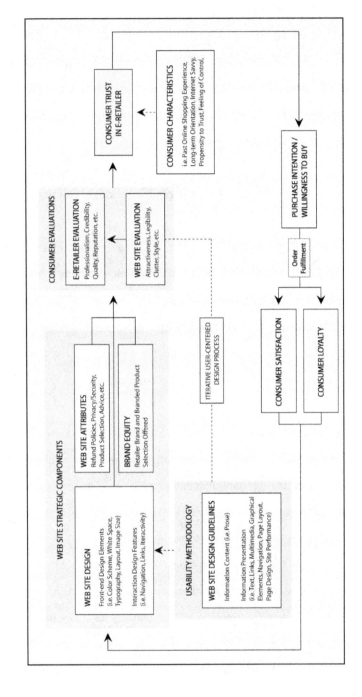

Figure 1.8.1. Conceptual Model: Brand Equity as an E-Retailer Strategic Component

from traditional brick and mortar stores to 'click and mortar' channels has made the creation of strong online brand identity a necessity for any retailer. Strong brand identity, however, is difficult to create in the electronic environment where "physical interaction is reduced and product qualities and benefits must be distilled and captured in a way that can be communicated over the wires" (Rowley, 2004). The limited experience associated with online shopping may lead to decreased consumer enjoyment and reduced sales (Koufaris et al, 2002). Companies are challenged to create a memorable, brand-rich shopping experience using the two-dimensional medium of a website.

Brand equity helps to overcome consumer perceptions of the Internet as "an unsafe, dishonest, and unreliable marketplace" (Gommans, Krishnan, & Scheffold, 2001). Unknown web retailer reliability results in consumer uncertainty online; the presence of a trusted brand reduces the consumer's sense of vulnerability and aids in the development of trust (Chaudhuri & Holbrook, 2001). The product's brand thus serves as a "trust mark" that transfers brand equity to the e-retailer by indicating quality, reliability, and credibility (Shankar, Urban, & Sultan, 2002; Urban, Sultan, & Qualls, 2000). As stated by Berry (2000), "Strong brands increase customers' trust of invisible products while helping them to better understand and visualize what they are buying."

Furthermore, brand loyalty has significant benefits for the e-retailer. Brand loyalty may result in consumers who are willing to pay higher price points, greater market share due to repeat purchases, and increased usage (Chaudhuri & Holbrook, 2001). Amazon.com, a successful brand e-retailer, charges a premium of three to thirteen percentage points on many of their products (Reichheld, Markey, & Holton, 2000). Ease and low advertising costs lower the barriers of entry in the online marketplace; small businesses can effectively compete with large corporations if their web sites and product offerings are comparable (Dholakia & Rego, 1998). A firm must therefore compete with a multitude of competitors offering similar products and services. With the pervasive presence of competitive e-retailers, consumer brand loyalty may also reduce the constant "threat of commoditization" (Urban, Sultan, & Qualls, 2000). The abundant literature on brand equity has solidified and substantiated its place in the conceptual model as a crucial e-retailer strategic component and as an antecedent of consumer trust.

The e-commerce web site is a full representation of the store to the online consumer. Evaluations of its front-end web site design and subsequent perceptions about the e-retailer are thus founded upon the web site itself; visible changes in its design may significantly impact e-commerce success. The conceptual model developed in this thesis posits that web site design should be recognized as a critical and influential strategic component for the e-commerce web site. Although prior models reviewed in the literature frequently incorporated various aspects of web site design, this thesis incorporates web site design as an independent and leading e-retailer strategic component. Furthermore, usability guidelines and the iterative user-centered design process provide the foundation upon which good web site design rests. Although the impact of usability on interactive web site design features and web site attributes have been examined in the literature, examination of inconsistent implementations of usability guidelines regarding front-end web page design has not been conducted. Additionally, there has been no systematic, empirical investigation of the impact of usability-based changes in surface web page design on consumer trust and purchase intention.

The following section describes the web design framework developed for this thesis. Four design factors were selected for study from this framework based upon the usability guidelines literature. A detailed discussion of the framework development process and the hypotheses developed for each of the four design factors selected is then presented.

1.9. Web Site Design Guidelines Framework

In an effort to fully understand the extent of, and potential contradictions within, available web design guidelines, a survey of web design literature was conducted. The creation of a web site design guidelines framework was necessary due to an inherent limitation in the usability literature: no consensus exists (in the dialogue or in the form of a document) regarding the characteristics that make a web site usable. Sources were gathered from the disciplines of design, usability, human-computer interaction, ergonomics, and human factors. Approximately 230 distinct web site design guidelines were compiled from various sources (i.e. Nielsen, 2000; Cooper & Reimann, 2003; U.S. Department of Health and Human Services, 2006; Mandel, 1997; Lynch & Horton, 2002). Following compilation, guidelines were then organized into categories and subcategories based upon the web site design element addressed (i.e. text, links, etc). A full list of the 230 web site design guidelines and the categories may be seen in the appendix (Appendix Table 4.1.).

A visual representation of the web site design guidelines framework is provided below (Figure 1.9.1.; Appendix 1.2.). Preliminary examination of accumulated web design guidelines resulted in the creation of two overarching categories: Information Content and Information Presentation. This important distinction between content and presentation was also present in Bucy and Lang's study of media messages (1999). As can be seen in the image below, web site design guidelines were collected relating to various categories including both front-end web page elements and interactive web site design elements (i.e. navigation and links).

59

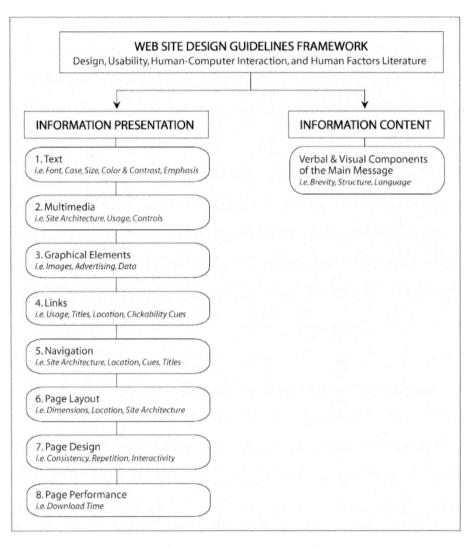

WEB SITE DESIGN GUIDELINES FRAMEWORK
Design, Usability, Human-Computer Interaction, and Human Factors Literature

INFORMATION PRESENTATION

1. Text
   i.e. Font, Case, Size, Color & Contrast, Emphasis

2. Multimedia
   i.e. Site Architecture, Usage, Controls

3. Graphical Elements
   i.e. Images, Advertising, Data

4. Links
   i.e. Usage, Titles, Location, Clickability Cues

5. Navigation
   i.e. Site Architecture, Location, Cues, Titles

6. Page Layout
   i.e. Dimensions, Location, Site Architecture

7. Page Design
   i.e. Consistency, Repetition, Interactivity

8. Page Performance
   i.e. Download Time

INFORMATION CONTENT

Verbal & Visual Components
of the Main Message
i.e. Brevity, Structure, Language

Figure 1.9.1. Web Site Design Guidelines Framework

1.9.1. Information Content

Information Content may be defined as the fundamental main message of the web page. Bucy and Lang defined content as "the verbal and visual information components of a message" (1999). The information on a web site should be relevant, useful, and up to date (Page & White, 2006). A study by Zellweger found a positive relationship between relevance of web site information, consumer likelihood to purchase, and subsequent satisfaction with the e-retailer (1997). The information content, usually consisting of text, may remain constant while its presentation is altered. The majority of recommendations in the category of Information Content relate to prose brevity, structure, and language. A note: visuals may be included in the category of Information Content depending on the type and purpose of a web page. Web sites presenting the work of artists online would deem art images as crucial information content. The majority of web design literature surveyed, however, considered visuals as a complement to main message content and not content within itself.

1.9.2. Information Presentation

Information Presentation refers to the visual presentation or "packaging" of the web page's information content (Bucy & Lang, 1999). The basic elements of text, links, and graphics are the "building blocks of web interfaces" (Ivory & Megraw, 2005). Seven sub-categories under Information Presentation were created in this framework. These include: text, multimedia, graphical elements, links, navigation, page layout, and page design. Breakdown of each of these sub-categories is provided below. Page performance web site design guidelines are included as the eighth category, but these recommendations tend to result from the content and presentation decisions made.

1.9.2.1. Text

Web design guidelines regarding text are abundant. They include recommendations about font, case, size, line length, justification, color & contrast, emphasis, leading, and consistency. Font is made up of four important features: typeface, font size, whether it is bolded, or whether it is italicized (Schriver, 1997). Research suggests that sans serif fonts, especially in small sizes, are more legible than serif fonts (Nielsen, 2000; Schriver, 1997). No clear consensus has been found, however, in the recommended minimum font size to use; guidelines range from nine to fourteen point font size (Ivory & Megraw, 2005).

1.9.2.2. Multimedia

The use of multimedia in web site design has become more popular in recent years and is an integral part of "experiential web site design." Multimedia includes the usage of animation, audio, and video to aid in the presentation of information. Multimedia usage increases web site interactivity and thus the level of involvement and enjoyment experienced by its users. The incorporation of multimedia elements as well as chat rooms and customer service applications aid in making the online shopping experience closer to that of the traditional brick and mortar store (Page & White, 2006; Li et al., 1999). The incorporation of too many multimedia elements into a website, however, can significantly slow the web site; therefore, "less is more" (Page & White, 2006). Guidelines in this sub-category referred to multimedia introductory information, usage, controls, and site architecture.

1.9.2.3. Graphical Elements

According to Ivory and Megraw, the use of graphics in web sites doubled from 2000 to 2003 (2005). Graphical element guidelines aid in the proper inclusion of images, advertising, and data on the web page. Images were usually considered as supplemental to main web page content, as portrayed by the following web guideline: "Use images only when they are critical to the success of a Web site" (U.S. Department of Health and Human Services, 2006). Most research supports the conclusion that the number of images should be minimized on the web site to increase download speed (Ivory & Megraw, 2005). Certain types of images should be avoided: images that contain text, images that are used for navigation, and images that are animated (Ivory & Megraw, 2005; Nielsen, 2000). Despite this, research shows that on commercial web sites a significant relationship existed between graphical elements and site traffic (number of page views) (Bucy & Lang, 1999). On e-commerce web pages, images of products or services offered are central to attracting customers and success.

1.9.2.4. Links

Links are crucial on any well-designed web page to help present and organize information. Design guidelines for links refer to their usage, titles, location, number, color, images, and clickability cues. Image guidelines in this sub-category refer to image link cues and may slightly overlap with guidelines for graphical elements. Contradictory guidelines exist in respect to the ideal link length: some recommend the use of two to four words (Nielsen, 2000), while others recommend the use of seven to twelve "useful" words that provide hints about the content of the destination page (Sawyer & Schroeder, 2000). Additionally, research suggests that the number of links should be minimized, certain link types should be avoided (i.e. graphical, repeated, within-page links), and that multiple links to the same destination should be provided in various locations and forms (Ivory & Megraw, 2005; Nielsen, 2000; Sawyer & Schroeder, 2000).

1.9.2.5. Navigation

Navigation is the method by which users find information within a web site (U.S. Department of Health and Human Services, 2006). According to Taylor and England, the greatest difficulty consumers may face in retailer web sites is locating the information they require or the transaction they wish to complete (2006). They write, "The more difficult this is, the less chance of consumers making a purchase or considering future purchases via the web site" (Taylor & England, 2006). While searching for information, 58% of users were shown to make at least two navigational errors (Forsythe, Ring, Grose, et al., 1996). Studies recommend that web site architecture be organized as broader rather than deeper (Bernhard, 2001) and should utilize a concave architecture that narrows in complexity at intermediate information levels to increase ease of navigation (Norman & Chin, 1998). Navigation web guidelines may be broken down into the following headings: site architecture, location, cues, titles, page design, and screen-based controls.

1.9.2.6. Page Layout

Page layout web design recommendations relate to the overall structure, organization, and dimensions of the web page itself. These web guidelines include page consistency, hierarchy, location, site architecture, frame usage, page dimensions, resolution, and content organization & structure. The heading 'content organization & structure' is an important sub-heading which addresses the presentation and organization of information content. Content organization & structure includes web design guidelines dealing with hierarchy, brevity, chunking, scanning, lists, and headings, titles, & labels.

1.9.2.7. Page Design

Page design refers to the visual presentation of web page content through conscious design decisions. Page Design subcategories included guidelines relating to consistency, repetition, simplicity, interactivity, density, alignment, structure and flow, visual hierarchy, credibility, contrast and layering, icons and symbols, emphasis, and color and contrast.

1.9.2.8. Page Performance

Page performance is a result of design decisions made in the web site. Research has shown that the speed of downloading has a positive impact on the number of web pages accessed, time spent at the web site, and the consumer image of the e-retailer (Dellaert & Kahn, 1999; Dreze & Zufryden, 1997). The maximum time a user will wait for a web page to download before becoming frustrated is approximately four seconds (Nelson, 2000). A delay of 0.1 seconds makes the user feel that the web site is reacting instantaneously; 1.0 seconds is the limit for the user's flow of thought to remain uninterrupted; after 10 seconds, the user loses their focus and no longer pays attention to the download (Nielsen, 1994). This effect can be lessened through incorporation of a "duration time to download" countdown, which lessens consumer uncertainty and frustration (Page & White, 2006; Dellaert & Kahn, 1999; Nielsen, 1994). Page performance guidelines generally recommend the minimization of download times on the web site.

1.10. Selection of Design Factors

The framework developed and described in the previous section placed usability web site design guidelines from the literature into a broader, organized structure. Web site design guidelines vary in their quality, detail, and empirical justification. Each guideline category from the framework was reviewed and examined for quantitative guidelines that could be tested through systemic, empirical research. The web site design guidelines framework was made up of 230 guidelines, which included guidelines that addressed web site issues beyond front-end web page design elements. However, since the focus of this thesis was on front-end design, guideline selection for further research was focused on the category of Page Design. The remaining seven categories of web site design guidelines were excluded from further examination. This research focus narrowed guideline selection from an initial 230 guidelines to approximately 50 guidelines in the category of Page Design.

In addition to empirically validated guidelines that were consistent throughout the majority of web design recommendations, special attention was given to web page design guidelines that appeared conflicting or ambiguous. Design factor selection was based upon consistency (similar guidelines from multiple sources), simplicity, importance (as implied by the number of guidelines found under each category), available literature (or lack thereof), conflicting recommendations, possible interactions with other factors, and most importantly, the design factor's individual visual impact on the overall web page design. Based upon these considerations, the following four design factors were selected from Page Design for further empirical study: background color, white space, thumbnail image size, and thumbnail image location. Detailed descriptions of each of these four design factors are provided below.

1.11. The Four Design Factors

1.11.1. Background Color

Web site visitors respond to visual cues on a psychological level (Holzschlag, 1999). Of all these cues, color is one of the first aspects noticed and has the ability to set the tone for the entire web site experience (Holzschlag, 1999). Web design literature states that designers should avoid using too many colors, complementary colors, and excessive saturation (Cooper & Reimann, 2003; Mandel, 1997; Nielsen, 2000; U.S. Department of Health and Human Services, 2006). Moreover, usability literature recommends the use of one solid background color in web page design (Nielsen, 2000; Schneiderman & Plaisant, 2005). Users have been shown to prefer the use of one dominant color in web page design over the use of many competing colors (Covert, 1987; Schneiderman, 1998). Color use is especially recommended for highlighting important information because brightly colored graphics and text draw the user's attention first (U.S. Department of Health and Human Services, 2006). Although color may be incorporated into web page design in a multitude of ways, alteration of the background color instantly influences the web page's overall 'look and feel'.

Richards and David write, "Color is used on the web to elicit emotional reactions… through color schemes and corporate logos that create in the viewer's mind connections between visual design and the organization" (2005). Color selection is therefore a crucial design decision that can provide cues to the consumer about retailer personality, a key differentiator in a saturated marketplace such as the internet (Aaker, 1996). Consistent color use also helps in the building of brand equity; for example, Tiffany's distinctive green-blue is immediately recognizable by consumers.

67

In a case study of McDonald's online branding, Rowley writes: "Arguably the strongest reminder of the brand is in the color... The McDonald's bright 'fun loving' red acts as a frame for all other images... the web site makes generous use of bright, even garish primary colors" (2004). Red is immediately associated with McDonald's corporate identity and it is undeniably an important component of their online branding.

The case of McDonald's "garish" red, however, is an extreme one; research shows that the majority of web pages utilize a more subtle color scheme. A study by Bucy and Lang found that 65.5% of web site homepages utilized a white background, 12.7% utilized black, 5.1% were multicolored, and 4.1% used blue as their background color (1999). No significant background color tendencies were found to exist in the more specific category of business web sites (Murayama, Saito, & Okumura, 2004). Whereas no clear color trend has been found in business web sites, approximately 70% of corporations in the United States chose blue for their corporate color and logo (Lippincott Mercer, 1997). According to Lippincott Mercer, this phenomenon may be attributed to the fact that blue is liked by both men and women, appears on many national flags, and has long associations with trust and stability (1997). In addition to trust, the color blue has also been shown to be associated with conservativeness, security, technology, cleanliness, and order (Holzschlag, 1999). These associations, however, are culture dependent. In Korea, trust is best represented by pastel colors, especially the color pink (Holzschlag, 1999).

The impact of color on the perceptual system was studied by White (1990). Warm colors (red, yellow, orange) attracted more attention than cool colors and were perceived as being closer to the viewer. Cool colors (blue, green, violet), on the other hand, appeared to be farther away (White, 1990; Richards & David, 2005). Based on these findings, White recommended that warm colors be utilized in the foreground of web page design and that cool colors be used for the background (1990). Furthermore, a study by Pace examined the use of 24 different colors as the background on visual display units (1984). Results of this study found that the use of blue as a background color was associated with reduced error rates in reading (Pace, 1984).

Color was therefore varied in this study through the presence of a plain white background color or a blue background color. Although research discussed above has demonstrated the positive influence of blue, very few studies specified the specific RGB values of the "blue" studied. The lack of inclusion of the color values utilized makes it difficult for researchers to replicate prior studies and to know what "blue" actually means. This thesis utilized a pale blue background color with the following RGB values: Red (199), Green (217), and Blue (217). A pale blue color was selected instead of a deeper blue shade to minimize confounding effects of contrast level with overlaid text on the web page. Furthermore, while many web pages may utilize more dramatic color schemes, it was decided that the use of pale blue and a subtle background color change was more realistic and appropriate for study. Bright, concentrated background colors such as red, yellow, or orange would be expected to have a greater impact on perceived web page quality and overall trust.

As mentioned above, a white background color was utilized in 65.5% of web site homepages (Bucy & Lang, 1999). Increased familiarity with a stimulus results in higher ratings of attractiveness and preference, as seen in abundant psychology research and what has been coined, the "mere exposure effect." Repetitive exposure to a stimuli increases positive affect that may then influence similar stimuli to which the subject has not been previously exposed (Zajonc, 2001). Therefore, since 65.5% of web pages utilized a white background color (Bucy & Lang, 1999), it was hypothesized that increased subject familiarity with white would result in higher web page evaluations. Furthermore, a white background color was hypothesized to increase consumer aesthetic ratings of the web page based upon "classical" aesthetics, which emphasizes simplicity and order (Tractinsky, 2004). White may therefore be perceived as more familiar, simpler, cleaner, and more professional. Although only 4.5% of web pages utilized blue as a background color, it was selected due to its positive associations with trust and stability (Lippincott Mercer, 1997; Holzschlag, 1999), its recommendation as a cool color to be used as the background (White, 1990), and its association with reduced error rates in reading (Pace, 1984). While the pale blue background color may impact consumer perceptions about the e-retailer, the white background color was expected to impact aesthetic evaluations of the web page itself.

Background color may impact webpage aesthetic evaluations, perceptions of professionalism and quality, and consumer trust. While the pale blue background was hypothesized to positively impact consumer perceptions of trust and company quality, the white background color was hypothesized to positively impact ratings of web page aesthetics, professionalism, and high budget.

H1a: The white background color will be positively related to web page aesthetic ratings of color, clutter, and legibility.

H1b: The white background color will be positively related to web page evaluations of the e-retailer as professional and high budget.

H1c: The pale blue background color will be positively related to consumer evaluations of e-retailer trustworthiness and company quality.

1.11.2. White Space

Graphic designers emphasize the importance of white space in numerous web style guides. White space in regards to this thesis may be defined as the negative space present on a web page; use of the phrase "white space" thus refers to the open, negative space on a web page and not the background color.

The balance between the positive and negative space is an essential component of any aesthetic composition (White Space, 2007). In web site design, white space is often at a premium; less white space allows sites to include more information and products in one screenful. Lack of white space, however, may negatively impact perceptions of the web site as difficult to read and cluttered. Abundant white space is often associated with a web site having a "classic, elegant, or rich appearance" (White Space, 2007). Upscale brands often utilize an abundant amount of white space in their advertisements and retail merchandising space.

The amount of white space on a web page may be varied relative to leading in text placement as well as in the distance between lines and paragraphs on the page (Lynch & Horton, 2002). White space may also be increased through the presence of a border around the web page information content.

Literature on white space suggests that the presence of less white space facilitates faster scanning and searching behavior (Bevan, 2004). However, while some research has found that higher density web pages resulted in faster scanning without any impact on accuracy or performance, others have found that the amount of white space had no impact on search performance whatsoever (U.S. Department of Health and Human Services, 2006). Therefore, the relationship between white space, scanning, and searching behavior remains unclear.

Human factors research on the design of warning signs found that the significant effect of white space on urgency ratings was much smaller in comparison to the other factors of text size and border width (Adams & Edworthy, 1995). Due to limited label space, Adams and Edworthy concluded that it would not be worthwhile for designers to vary white space (1995). White space was, however, related to aesthetic appeal ratings of warning label design. Other research showed that users preferred a moderate amount of white space (U.S. Department of Health and Human Services, 2006; Adams & Edworthy, 1995). These research findings are limited and ambiguous. Although a potential contradiction between aesthetic appeal and facilitation of scanning and searching behavior may exist, no clear relationship is supported by the literature.

The factor of white space in e-retail product display web pages may impact aesthetic perceptions. White space in graphic design is emphasized as a means to achieve a more classic, elegant, and rich appearance (White Space, 2007). Although no research has linked white space to e-retailer evaluations, the conceptual model developed in this thesis hypothesizes that aesthetic evaluations form the foundation for higher level e-retailer evaluations. Therefore, higher aesthetic evaluations related to white space are expected to result in higher e-retailer evaluations.

H2a: More white space will be positively related to ratings of web page aesthetics

H2b: White space will have a positive impact on consumer perceptions of the e-retailer as trustworthy, representing a quality company, high budget, or professional.

1.11.3. Thumbnail Image Size

The majority of e-retailer web sites utilize small thumbnail images to provide an initial visual representation of their products. These images are usually paired with brief product descriptions that include the brand name, product name, and price (Lam, Chau, & Wong, 2007). Web site thumbnails function very much like a window display or product shelf in a traditional brick and mortar store. They are used "to attract online shoppers to the inner pages of virtual stores where they are exposed to more detailed product information and store atmospherics (additional graphics, animation, etc.)" (Lam, Chau, & Wong, 2007). The use of small thumbnail images instead of full-sized product images on the internet also effectively reduced the download time of web page visual displays (Nielsen, Molich, Snyder, & Farrell, 2000).

Research shows that thumbnail images required much less cognitive effort than text descriptions and were processed much faster by surfers (Lam, Chau, & Wong, 2007; Woodruff, Rosenholtz, Morrison, Faulring, & Pirolli, 2002). Moreover, searching for a particular product image among other images was faster than searching for the name of the product among other words (Paivio, 1974). Larger images have been shown to draw user attention first and were fixated on for longer periods of time (U.S. Department of Health and Human Services, 2006).

Although thumbnail images are always 'small' in comparison to their full-sized counterparts, no research has been conducted to examine the impact of thumbnail image size on consumer perceptions and product preference. The factor of thumbnail image size has important implications for ecommerce websites. Limited screen real estate places pressure on e-retailers to minimize thumbnails as much as possible to increase the number of products per screen. This minimizing trend may have an impact on consumer perceptions of product quality and purchase intention.

Despite identical product descriptions, differences in thumbnail image size may impact which product consumers would be more likely to purchase.

H3a: The large thumbnail image will be selected for purchase more often than the small thumbnail image.

H3b: The large thumbnail image will be associated with a higher quality product and will receive more positive qualitative feedback than the small thumbnail image.

1.11.4. Thumbnail Image Location

A casual survey of popular ecommerce websites such as Amazon.com, Buy.com, Barnesandnoble.com, etc., illustrates the lack of consistency of thumbnail image location relative to its corresponding product description. While most websites appear to utilize a vertical thumbnail layout, many others use a horizontal layout across the screen. Product descriptions may then be located above, below, to the left, or to the right of the thumbnail image.

As mentioned above, research showed that (1) thumbnail image processing was easier and quicker than text processing (Lam, Chau, & Wong, 2007; Woodruff, Rosenholtz, Morrison, Faulring, & Pirolli, 2002) and that (2) specific image search among other images was faster than searching for a product name among other words (Paivio, 1974). Research on eye-tracking has also shown that users scanned web pages using an "F-shaped" pattern down the left hand side of the page with short, fast scans rightward (Bekman, 2006). Although dominant reading direction impacted scanning behavior and eye movement over thumbnail displays, subjects tended to process the left hand side of the thumbnail display more than the right (Lam, Chau, & Wong, 2007).

Image location in relation to product description may impact on what is scanned first by the user, the image or the text. In this study, thumbnail image location was varied as being either to the left or to the right of the vertical list of product descriptions. It is hypothesized that subjects would prefer to have the thumbnail image to the left of the product description for the following reasons: (1) placement of the image to the left of the description would ensure that it was scanned first according to the "F-shaped" scanning pattern, (2) image processing and search is easier and quicker than text processing and search, and (3) the left hand side of the page is processed more than the right portion of the web page.

H4a: Placement of the thumbnail image array to the left of the product descriptions will be preferred to placement to the right of the product descriptions as seen in higher web page aesthetic ratings.

H4b: Placement of the thumbnail image array to the left of the product descriptions will be positively related to consumer perceptions of the e-retailer as trustworthy, quality, high budget, and professional.

2. METHOD

The following methods chapter discusses the subjects, apparatus, research design, conjoint analysis and experimental design, web page prototype creation, online survey creation and experimental procedure, measures, and data analysis utilized in this thesis research.

2.1. Subjects

Subjects (N=229) were recruited from two moderately sized, northeastern American universities. Four total versions of the online survey were created; two survey versions for each university. Prior to participation, subjects were randomly assigned to one of the two versions designated to their university. In the first university, participants were recruited from a marketing course providing extra credit to its students. Out of a total of 142 students, 91 students, or 65% of the class, signed up to participate in the online survey. All 91 students successfully completed and submitted their survey responses, indicating a 100% response rate within those who desired extra credit. Subjects from the second university were recruited using a recruitment web site provided by the psychology department. 163 students signed up to participate in the online survey for either extra credit or monetary compensation ($10.00). Of the 163 students who signed up, 138 successfully completed the survey, resulting in an 85% response rate.

In the sample of 150 females and 79 males, ages ranged from 18 to 35 with a mean age of 20.2 years. The median value for the number of hours spent on the internet on an average weekday was 4 hours. The mean value of 6.76 hours spent on the internet on an average weekday was not an accurate representation of the data;

some participants responded to the question in terms of number of hours spent on the internet per week, thus skewing the results. The median number of hours spent by participants on the internet on an average weekend day was 4 hours. Additionally, the mean number of products purchased online by participants in the last four weeks was 2.77. Further analysis of the subject responses to the initial questionnaire are provided in the results section of this paper.

This research project protocol was reviewed and approved by the Cornell University Committee on Human Subjects (UCHS).

2.2. Apparatus

Comparison was made between sixteen distinct web page prototype designs (Appendix Figures 1.3 – 1.18). Each of the sixteen designs incorporated a "high" or "low" level of the four design factors as determined by experimental design (Table 2.4.2.). Data was collected through use of an online questionnaire created in Websurveyor. Both prototype and Likert question order were randomized, and all phrasing and formatting were held constant throughout the survey's four versions. Due to online data collection, the computer monitor utilized to view each web page image and to complete the survey varied by participant and could not be controlled.

2.3. Research Design

A repeated-measures research design was used for this study because of its advantages in sample size and statistical power. Four randomized versions of the online survey were created to mitigate any carry-over effects and to control for confounding factors related to prototype order, subject attention, and fatigue. Subjects were randomly assigned to one of two versions depending on the university and were emailed the appropriate survey link.

2.4. Conjoint Analysis and Experimental Design

Conjoint analysis has been utilized in the literature as a means to "derive an estimate of the best combination of product attributes" (Kirvesoja & Vayrynen, 2000; Green & Srinivasan, 1990; Green & Rao, 1971). Use of conjoint allows developers to estimate the consumer value of each product attribute and then make design tradeoffs among product features (Moore, Louviere, & Verma, 1999). In market research, representative consumers rate various products against each other to find the best levels of the key attributes being studied (Kirvesoja & Vayrynen, 2000). Conjoint analysis is a methodology to measure (1) the consumer's weighting of the relative importance of various product attributes, and (2) consumer preferences for each level of those attributes deemed important (Green & Srinivasan, 1990; Green & Rao, 1971). Conjoint analysis has also been used in product development to provide insight into product design concepts and prototype designs (Green and Krieger, 1989; Roozenburg and Eekels 1995). Selection of product attributes for study and the levels for each are selected prior to analysis; as the number of attributes and levels increase so do the number of product prototypes (Kirvesoja & Vayrynen, 2000). Prototype number may then be reduced utilizing conjoint analysis design methods in SAS (Kuhfeld, 2005).

A full-profile conjoint analysis was utilized, in which participants holistically rated web page prototypes on various dependent measures; each of the four design factors were not assessed independently (Kirvesoja & Vayrynen, 2000). By assessing the impact of usability guideline implementation on front-end web page design elements, the conjoint analysis in this thesis assesses both usability and marketing goals. The utility associated with each independent design factor may then be assessed through regression analysis (Scholl, Manthey, Helm, & Steiner, 2005).

Four design factors were selected in this thesis based upon the usability web site design guidelines: background color, white space, thumbnail image size, and thumbnail image location. Each of the four design factors were then varied at two levels based upon the literature. The justification and evidence for each factor level was discussed in the previous section. While background color, white space, and thumbnail image location were varied between prototypes, thumbnail image size was varied within each prototype design. A fifth additional factor of Thumbnail Order was also added into the experimental design, which referred to the placement of the large or small thumbnail image as first or second in the list of five product images. Its inclusion in the experimental design was solely to aid in the prototype development process; its presence ensured that thumbnail image size was equally counterbalanced as the first or second image within the array in all sixteen web page prototypes. A summary of the five factors and each factor level is provided in Table 2.4.1.

Table 2.4.1. The Five Design Factors and Levels

	Factor	Level 1	Level 2
1	Background Color	Pale blue background color	White background color
2	White Space	More white space: no gray border present	Less white space: gray border present
3	Thumbnail Image Location	To the left of the product description	To the right of the product description
4	Thumbnail Image Size	Large thumbnail image	Small thumbnail image
5	Thumbnail Order	First thumbnail image in the list of products	Second thumbnail image in the list of products

The full factorial experimental design utilizing all five factors at two levels would result in thirty-two distinct web page prototypes. However, given the number of questions assessing each web page prototype in the survey, complete assessment of thirty-two prototypes by each participant would not be feasible due to survey length. Therefore, instead of a full factorial experimental design, a fractional design was utilized in this thesis. Conjoint analysis design methods in SAS were used (Kuhfeld, 2005) to reduce the number of prototypes necessary to examine the most essential attributes of the web page. The design also needed to test for possible interactions between color and white space, white space and image size, and color and image size. Use of optimal design methods in SAS (Kuhfeld, 2005) resulted in a combination of each of the five design factors into sixteen distinct web page prototypes. The breakdown of each of the five factors and levels for the sixteen prototypes is provided in Table 2.4.2.

As shown in the table of the experimental design (Table 2.4.2.), eight blocks were created within the sixteen web page prototypes. Each block represented one distinct product; each product was shown to participants twice during the survey. Research has shown that web site design had the most influence on consumer trust and purchase intention in purchases that involved higher economic (i.e. increased price) or social risk (i.e. buying for a significant other) (Schlosser et al., 2006).

Furthermore, the mediating role of trust was stronger for infrequently purchased, high-involvement items such as electronic products (Bart et al., 2005). Therefore, two product categories were selected for the web page prototypes: (1) ergonomic office products and (2) electronic products. Product categories were selected due to perceived differences in price, purchase frequency, and consumer involvement. In general, electronics products were perceived to be higher priced, purchased less often, and higher-involvement than ergonomic office products.

Table 2.4.2. Experimental Design

Prototype	Block	Back-ground Color	White Space (WS)	Thumbnail Image Location	Thumbnail Image Size	Thumbnail Order
1	1	White	More WS	Right	Small	Second
2	1	Pale Blue	More WS	Left	Large	First
3	2	White	More WS	Left	Small	First
4	2	Pale Blue	Less WS	Left	Large	Second
5	3	White	More WS	Right	Large	First
6	3	Pale Blue	Less WS	Right	Small	Second
7	4	White	Less WS	Left	Small	Second
8	4	Pale Blue	Less WS	Right	Large	First
9	5	Pale Blue	More WS	Right	Large	Second
10	5	Pale Blue	Less WS	Left	Small	First
11	6	Pale Blue	More WS	Left	Small	Second
12	6	White	Less WS	Right	Large	Second
13	7	White	More WS	Left	Large	Second
14	7	White	Less WS	Right	Small	First
15	8	White	Less WS	Left	Large	First
16	8	Pale Blue	More WS	Right	Small	First

Within each product category, four products were selected for display. Eight web page prototypes (four blocks) displayed the following ergonomic office products: monitor arms, footrests, lighting, and keyboard trays. The remaining eight prototypes (four blocks) displayed the following electronics products: digital cameras, web cameras, GPS navigators, and PDA handhelds.

2.5. Web Page Prototype Creation

A generic e-commerce web page design was created based upon model websites such as Amazon.com, Buy.com, and BarnesandNobles.com. Responses to an initial survey indicated that the prototype design had no apparent similarities to any

81

recognizable e-retailer. Logo and company name information were excluded in the prototype to remove the influence of a known or unknown e-retailer brand name.

The sixteen distinct web page prototypes were created in Adobe Illustrator according to factor combinations outlined in the experimental design (Table 2.4.2.). Once complete, the sixteen prototype files were saved as jpeg images and placed into individual web pages on the CUErgo web server. Images of the sixteen web page prototypes and each prototype's corresponding factor levels may be seen in the appendix (Appendix Figures 1.3 – 1.18).

Detailed descriptions of the web page prototype creation process for each of the four design elements are provided below.

2.5.1. Background Color

Background color was varied through the presence of a plain white background or a solid pale blue background. Background color impacts contrast levels with overlaid text; a shade of pale blue was selected to provide color without significantly reducing contrast with page content. The RGB values of the pale blue were Red (199), Blue (217), and Green (217). An identical shade of pale blue was utilized for eight web page prototypes, while the remaining eight had a white background color. Luminance values were also measured using a luminance contrast meter[1]; the pale blue background had a luminance of 123 cd/m^2 and the white background color had a luminance value of 172 cd/m^2. Based upon the luminance values measured, the white background color was thus approximately 28.5% brighter than the pale blue background color. These luminance values were obtained in a room with dim lighting; although absolute light levels in a room may change based upon the environment, the

---

[1] Brüel and Kjær Luminance Contrast Meter Type 1100

relative differences in brightness between the two background colors would not change. The variation of background color was through the entire area of the web page, as shown in Figure 2.5.1 and Figure 2.5.2.

2.5.2. White Space

White space was varied in the web page prototypes in a bilateral, symmetrical fashion through the presence of a gray border surrounding main web page information content. Web page prototypes without the gray border (more white space) had approximately 22% more white space than those with the surrounding gray border. The dimensions and location of the gray border were held constant for each of the eight web page prototypes that were characterized by less white space. The presence of the gray border (less white space) occupied areas of potential white space in the web page prototype (Figure 2.5.3.). The lack of presence of the gray border (more white space) visually extended the main web page content area further to the left and right hand side of the page (Figure 2.5.4.).

The variation of white space, however, did not influence the layout of the main page content; line lengths were held constant despite increased room for product descriptions. In a real, active website, the area occupied by this gray border would be filled with advertisements, logos, and additional internal and external links. The usage of a plain gray border allowed for the study of white space without the confounding factor of advertisements and additional brand presence. White space was not varied using the distance between web page content due to the possible confounding factor of page length. Increased white space within page content would have increased overall web page length, impacting the amount of scrolling performed by participants.

Figure 2.5.1. White Background Color Variation

Figure 2.5.2. Pale Blue Background Color Variation

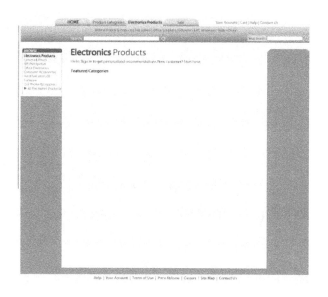

Figure 2.5.3. Less White Space Variation

Figure 2.5.4. More White Space Variation

Symmetrical white space variation was also utilized rather than an asymmetrical variation (i.e. more white space present on the right side of the web page).

2.5.3. Thumbnail Image Size

A total of five product images with matching product descriptions were displayed on each web page prototype. Product images for each category (office products or electronics) were found online from popular e-commerce websites. Product descriptions were created based on those found accompanying the images. Price information was excluded from the product descriptions to prevent price-based product choice. All identifiable manufacturer brand information (name and/or logo) was also removed from product descriptions and the images of the products themselves to prevent brand-based product choice. Products were then ambiguously renamed in the accompanying description with names that could not be associated with a brand or identifiable product category.

The first two images present in the thumbnail array displayed identical products; minor differences in product orientation or color were permitted to further participant perceptions of two distinct but very similar products. Accompanying product descriptions and specifications (i.e. height, width, and weight) were held constant for the first two products to ensure that subject selection would be based solely upon the thumbnail image. Thumbnail image size was then varied within these first two product images; the 'large' image was consistently made 75% larger in size than the 'small' image (Figure 2.5.5.). Which of the two product images was 'large' and which was 'small' was counterbalanced between the two prototypes in each block. Therefore, the same product image was never large or small in both web page prototypes. Additionally, the factor of Thumbnail Order in the experimental design ensured that the order of the large and small image was evenly distributed throughout the sixteen prototypes. Eight of the prototypes had the large thumbnail image as first in the array and the small image as second, while the remaining eight had the large thumbnail image as second and the small image as first. The remaining three images and product descriptions in the thumbnail array of five products were held constant between the two prototypes of each block (Figure 2.5.5.).

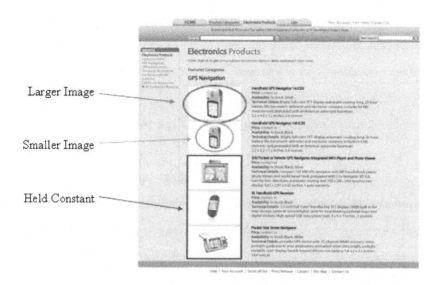

Figure 2.5.5. Thumbnail Image Size Variation

Although subjects were asked to choose between only the first two products for purchase, the array of five thumbnail images with matching product descriptions emphasized the impact of image location on scanning behavior. The greater number of products displayed also emphasized the variation of white space in the prototype. Inclusion of only two items in the thumbnail array may have negatively influenced consumer e-retailer evaluations due to a lack of product selection. Consumers have

87

been shown to expect a greater selection of products in online environments compared to those in traditional brick and mortar stores (Lohse & Spiller, 1998).

2.5.4. Thumbnail Image Location

Thumbnail image location was varied by moving the thumbnail array of five products to the left or to the right of the product descriptions (Figure 2.5.6.; Figure 2.5.7.). Variation of thumbnail location did not impact product description line length. The web page area taken up by the product image and description was held constant regardless of thumbnail array location.

2.6. Online Survey Creation and Experimental Procedure

Following prototype creation, an online survey was constructed using Websurveyor. Given that this study examined the impact of very subtle changes in front-end web page design, an online data collection method was selected in order to maximize sample size and statistical power. Use of traditional data collection methods would have limited sample size according to experimenter time and availability.

Four versions of the online survey were created and utilized for data collection. Each of the four versions included the sixteen prototypes in a different random order to control for confounding factors related to differences in survey placement, participant attention, and fatigue. Because every block of two prototypes displayed identical products (i.e. prototypes 1 and 2 were both in block 1), the sixteen prototypes were first divided into groups of 'odd' and 'even'. This ensured that in any given group (odd or even), a product category appeared only once. The groups of odd or even were then counterbalanced in each of the four versions and prototype order

88

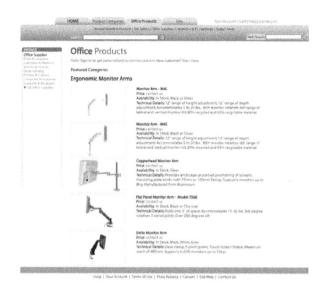

Figure 2.5.6. Left Thumbnail Image Location Variation

Figure 2.5.7. Right Thumbnail Image Location Variation

within each group was randomized. Participants were thus shown eight randomized, distinct product categories from the first group followed by the repeated eight product categories in randomized order from the second group. Randomization of all Likert questionnaire items was also achieved using Websurveyor.

Once subjects were recruited, they were randomly assigned to one of two versions of the online survey created for their university. Their full names and email addresses were entered into the survey list in order to allow them access. Participants were then sent an email with the survey link and the deadline by which it should be completed to receive compensation. Reminder emails were also sent to those participants who had not yet completed the survey two days before the deadline date.

Participants entered the link of the web address provided by the experimenter in their web browser and were immediately asked to enter in their email for survey authentication. This authentication step allowed participants to stop and resume the survey from any location and IP address. The first page of the online survey requested verification of basic information such as name, email, mailing address, and type of compensation requested (extra credit or monetary) (Appendix Figure 1.19). Participants were then required to answer all items in the initial questionnaire prior to continuing onto the survey instructions.

An image of the complete set of survey instructions as provided in the online survey may be seen in the appendix (Appendix Figure 1.20). Participants were informed of the basic purpose of the study: that they would be rating a series of sixteen web page images. Participants were also alerted that the company name, company logo, product brand names, and product prices were intentionally removed from all of the web page images. This statement was necessary to prevent any impact of recognized brand name or price on web page prototype ratings. By removing brand

and price information, participants were forced to make peripheral judgments based upon design differences between each prototype.

A scenario was also included in the instructions to provide subjects with a context for their participation in the study. It began: "You are in need of certain products for your personal use." By including the phrase "personal use", participants could infer that they would be purchasing products for their own use with their own resources. As opposed to a hypothetical situation or an unlimited budget, a personal shopping experience was selected to increase subject perceived risk. The scenario continued with, "Instead of going to a store, you decide to search for the products online. In the midst of your Internet search you arrive at a product display web page from a web site offering the item you are shopping for." Since each web page image was of a product display page, this statement provided participants with additional context as to exactly how and why they arrived at the web page shown.

Due to the length of the survey, participants were finally informed that they would be given the option of completing the second half of the survey at a later time. Because web page ratings were independent of each other and comparisons were not made across prototypes, this option was provided in order to minimize abandonment rates and maximize sample size.

Prototype images were provided in a link at the top of each consecutive survey page (Appendix Figure 1.21). Links were indicated with the phrase: "Click this link to view the [first] web page image." Order terms (first, second, etc) provided additional feedback to the participant about their progress through the survey. Once clicked, this external link opened a new browser window with the prototype image. Browser window size was standardized to be 1000 pixels in width and 700 pixels in height. Additional JavaScript and HTML code was also entered into Websurveyor to 'pop up' the new browser window on the computer screen. This provided feedback that participants had (1) clicked on the prototype link, (2) could find the image browser window, and (3) ensured that they were looking at the correct image while answering survey questions. Without the pop up code, pilot participants became confused as to whether or not they had clicked on the link and had difficulty locating the newly opened browser on a busy desktop.

Participants then completed the first half of the survey until the halfway point, at which they made a decision to either take a break or continue. Following completion of the second half, participants clicked on "submit survey" to successfully submit their responses.

Following submission, complete responses were verified through Websurveyor by the experimenter. An email was then sent to participants thanking them for their participation and informing them that they had either (1) been given extra credit in the course specified, or (2) that their information had been submitted for monetary compensation and a check would arrive in the mail. Extra credit points were awarded through the psychology department recruiting website or through generated extra credit lists sent to the course professor. Participants who requested monetary compensation were recorded in an excel spreadsheet with their mailing information; a spreadsheet was submitted weekly to department accounting for processing.

2.7. Measures

2.7.1. Initial Questionnaire

Subjects first completed questions in an initial questionnaire regarding basic demographic information, internet usage, and online shopping experience. Participants also responded to a question assessing online shopping experience in specific product categories. Then, subjects responded to final set of various Likert statements, which assessed three distinct scales: the Online Shopping Attitude Index, Internet Savvy Index, and Design Sensitivity Index. Initial questionnaire items are discussed and provided below in more detail.

2.7.1.1. Demographic Information, Internet Usage, and Online Shopping Experience

Subjects were asked the following five open-ended questions to assess demographics, internet usage, and online shopping experience as shown in the table (Table 2.7.1.).

Table 2.7.1. Initial Questionnaire, Demographics, Internet Usage, and Online Shopping Experience

Construct	Question
Subject Demographics	What is your gender?
Subject Demographics	What is your age?
Internet Usage	Approximately how many hours on an average weekday do you spend on the Internet?
Internet Usage	Approximately how many hours on an average weekend day (Saturday or Sunday) do you spend on the Internet?
Online Shopping Experience	Approximately how many products have you purchased online in the past 4 weeks?

In addition, subjects were asked an additional question regarding online shopping experience in specific product categories (Table 2.7.2.). Participants were to rate each category on a six point scale in which 1 was Never, 2 was Daily, 3 was Weekly, 4 was Monthly, 5 was Every Few Months, and 6 was Yearly. Participant responses to the categories of Office Supplies and Electronics were noteworthy due to the display of products from these categories in the web page prototypes created in this thesis.

93

Table 2.7.2. Initial Questionnaire, Online Shopping Experience by Product Category

Construct	Question
Online Shopping Experience	How often have you purchased products online from the following categories in the past 6 months? If you frequently purchase a type of product not listed below, please enter it into the comments field.
Product Category	Music (songs, CDs, etc.)
	Software
	Books
	Office Supplies
	Computers & PC Hardware
	Kitchen & Housewares
	Electronics
	DVDs
	Apparel or Accessories
	Other

2.7.1.2. Online Shopping Attitudes, Internet Savvy, and Design Sensitivity

Subjects were then asked to rate a series of Likert statements on a seven-point Likert scale, in which 1 was Strongly Disagree, 2 was Moderately Disagree, 3 was Slightly Disagree, 4 was Neither Agree nor Disagree, 5 was Slightly Agree, 6 was Moderately Agree, and 7 was Strongly Agree. Statements assessed participant attitudes towards online shopping, internet savvy and expertise, and their design sensitivity. The phrase "Design Sensitivity" referred to how important web page design was to participants and how much they believed it consciously influenced their internet behavior. While some users may be minimally impacted by the visual appearance of a web site, others may be more "sensitive" to changes in web page design. Four of the Likert statements were phrased negatively and question order was randomized using Websurveyor. Responses to Likert statements in each group were then combined to create an overall index value. A table of statements and the construct it measures may be seen in Table 2.7.3. Questions adapted from prior research have been indicated. The table below indicates each construct and the Likert items utilized for assessment.

Table 2.7.3. Initial Questionnaire, Online Shopping Attitudes, Internet Savvy, and Design Sensitivity

Construct	Likert Statement
Online Shopping Attitudes	I use the internet for shopping (Bart et al., 2005).
	I do not like to shop online.
	I prefer shopping online to shopping in an actual store.
	Shopping on the internet is more risky compared to other ways of shopping (Schlosser et al, 2006).
Internet Savvy	I make extensive use of the internet.
	I consider myself to be a novice internet user.
	I am confident in my ability to assess the quality of the design of a web site (Bart et al., 2005).
	I am confident in my ability to assess trustworthiness of web sites (Bart et al., 2005).
Design Sensitivity	I pay close attention to how a web site looks.
	My feelings about a company are impacted by the visual appearance of their web site.
	If I dislike the visual appearance of a web page, I will not remain on the web site for very long.

Following data collection, the mean response to each group of Likert statements was calculated and utilized as a scale for each construct. These variables were then named the Online Shopping Attitude Index, Internet Savvy Index, and Design Sensitivity Index. Reliability analysis prior to index creation indicated that some Likert statements did not correlate as well with the remaining group and were thus excluded to increase individual scale reliability. Further discussion of index creation is provided in the results section of this paper.

2.7.2. Web Page Prototype Questionnaire

Subjective evaluation of each of the sixteen distinct web page prototypes was assessed through the use of a questionnaire. After viewing each web page image by clicking on the link, participants rated the prototype on a series of statements using a seven point Likert scale from strongly disagree to strongly agree. The scale was as follows: 1 was Strongly Disagree, 2 was Moderately Disagree, 3 was Slightly Disagree, 4 was Neither Agree nor Disagree, 5 was Slightly Agree, 6 was Moderately Agree, and 7 was Strongly Agree. Six of the twelve statements were negative in phrasing while the remaining six reflected positive statements. Likert statement order was automatically randomized for each participant through Websurveyor.

A table of each Likert statement and the construct it measured is provided below (Table 2.7.4.). While eight of the twelve statements evaluated front-end web page aesthetics, the remaining four statements aimed to measure how web design affected consumer perceptions of the e-retailer. These web page prototype evaluations were of primary interest; as discussed earlier in this thesis, aesthetic evaluations of the web page were expected to form the foundation for higher level e-retailer evaluations.

Color is a critical design factor that has a significant impact on the overall look and feel of the web page. Two Likert statements were included in the web page prototype questionnaire to evaluate color: (1) I dislike the color scheme of this web page, and (2) I like how color is used on this web page. Although participants may like the colors chosen in the prototype, they may not like how the colors were used in the web page design. A distinction was therefore made between color scheme and color use for assessment of the design factor background color.

Table 2.7.4. Web Page Prototype Questionnaire, Aesthetic and E-Retailer Evaluations

Construct	Likert Statement
Aesthetic Evaluation	I dislike the color scheme of this web page.
	I like how color is used on this web page.
	It would be difficult for me to quickly find the product I wanted on this web page.
	I dislike the location of the product images.
	It is easy for me to see which product description goes with which image.
	The web page is easy to read.
	The web page looks cluttered.
	I dislike how the web page looks (Bart et al., 2005).
E-Retailer Evaluation	The web page looks professional (Bart et al., 2005; Fogg et al., 2001).
	This looks like a web page for a quality company (Bart et al., 2005).
	This looks like a low-budget web page.
	I would trust buying products from this web page.

While some Likert statements were intended to target a specific factor, other statements were hypothesized to be impacted by multiple design factors. None of the Likert statements assessed thumbnail image size, which unlike the other three design factors, was varied within-prototype. A table of each prototype Likert statement and the design factor(s) it was expected to be impacted by is provided below (Table 2.7.5.).

The following measures relating to behavior intention and product preference were of secondary interest in this research. Participants were asked two questions related to behavior intention: purchase intention and search behavior. Behavioral intent is the "intermediary between attitude and behavior" (Gommans, Krishnan, Scheffold, 2001). Research has indicated a strong correlation between behavioral intent and actual behavior exists (McKnight *et al.*, 2002b).

Table 2.7.5. Web Page Prototype Questionnaire, Design Factor Assessment by Likert Statement

Likert Statement	Design Factor			
	Back-ground Color	White Space	Thumbnail Image Location	Thumbnail Image Size
I dislike the color scheme of this web page.	x			
I like how color is used on this web page.	x			
It would be difficult for me to quickly find the product I wanted on this web page.	x		x	
I dislike the location of the product images.			x	
It is easy for me to see which product description goes with which image.	x		x	
The web page is easy to read.	x	x	x	
The web page looks cluttered.	x	x	x	
I dislike how the web page looks.	x	x	x	
The web page looks professional.	x	x	x	
This looks like a web page for a quality company.	x	x	x	
This looks like a low-budget web page.	x	x	x	
I would trust buying products from this web page.	x	x	x	

Both purchase intention and search behavior would be impacted by a cumulative effect of all four design factors. Participants responded to these questions on a seven point Likert scale, where 1 was Highly Unlikely, 2 was Moderately Unlikely, 3 was Slightly Unlikely, 4 was Neither Likely nor Unlikely, 5 was Slightly Likely, 6 was Moderately Likely, and 7 was Highly Likely.

While behavioral intention related to product purchase is crucial for the e-retailer bottom line, search behavior is an important issue in building a strong customer base. E-retailers must be able to immediately attract consumers and retain their interest in order to prevent their potential consumers from searching for an alternate e-retailer. These two behavioral intention questions are provided in Table 2.7.6.

Table 2.7.6. Web Page Prototype Questionnaire, Behavior Intention Items

Construct	Question
Behavior Intention: Purchase	If this web page offered the product you wanted, how likely would you be to purchase a product from this web page?
Behavior Intention: Search for Alternatives	If you saw this web page, how likely would you be to continue searching for other web pages that have the same products?

Next, a purchase intention question was asked to test the impact of the design factor thumbnail image size. Up to this point, thumbnail image size had not been assessed by any items in the web page questionnaire. As previously mentioned, thumbnail image size was varied within each prototype; therefore, each web page prototype had both a large image and small image. In order to assess the impact of thumbnail image size on purchase intention, participants were asked to select which of the first two products in the thumbnail array they would be more likely purchase. Response options were tailored to the product names displayed in each prototype. An optional follow-up question probed for further qualitative information on the reason behind their product choice (Table 2.7.7).

Table 2.7.7. Web Page Prototype Questionnaire, Purchase Intention Items

Construct	Question
Behavior Intention: Purchase	Assuming the products on this web page suit your needs, which of these two products displayed would you be more likely to purchase: the First or the Second product shown on the above web page?
Qualitative Feedback	Why? Briefly explain why you'd be more likely to purchase the product you selected in the previous question.

An optional open-ended question was also included as the last question for each web page prototype (Table 2.7.8.). Participants could provide any additional feedback that they felt had not been addressed through the series of Likert statements.

Table 2.7.8. Web Page Prototype Questionnaire, Qualitative Feedback

Construct	Question
Qualitative Feedback	Is there anything you would change with the design of this web page?

2.8. Data Analysis

All data was exported from the online assessment in WebSurveyor into an Excel document. Data analysis was performed using SPSS 15. Initial questionnaire data were analyzed using descriptive statistics.

Web page prototype questionnaire data was edited prior to analysis to aid in proper interpretation of the results. Subjective ratings of each of the sixteen distinct web page prototypes were obtained through responses to a series of twelve Likert statements on a seven point scale from strongly disagree to strongly agree. While six of these statements reflected positive assessments of the web page prototype, agreement with the remaining six statements was a negative assessment. Prior to data analysis, negatively phrased statements were reversed and renamed to reflect positive assessments of the web page prototypes. For all statements, higher scores reflected increasingly positive assessments of the web page prototype design.

With 229 subjects each rating sixteen web page prototypes, a total of 3664 data points were analyzed using mixed model analysis. The independent design variables (background color, white space, thumbnail image location, thumbnail image size) were included in the model using effects coding.

A two-level linear mixed model analysis was then utilized to analyze web page prototype questionnaire data, which effectively controlled for the subject-to-subject variability in responses as well as the repeated measure nature of the data. Analysis was conducted for each of the Likert statements as separate dependent variables in the mixed model. Subject ID was entered as a random effect in the mixed model, with the between-prototype design factors of thumbnail image location, background color, and white space entered as fixed effects. Initial questionnaire items or their respective indices (reflecting observable individual differences) were also entered as fixed effects in the model. Finally, the interaction between white space and background color and interactions of the design factors with gender were also included as fixed effects.

The mixed model for the dependent variable Image Size Picked also included the independent variable thumbnail image size, which was varied within prototype. Results are provided in the following section.

3. RESULTS

The results of this thesis are divided into two key sections: initial questionnaire results and web page prototype questionnaire results.

3.1. Initial Questionnaire

3.1.1. Internet Usage

The median value for the number of hours spent on the internet on an average weekday was 4 hours. The mean value of 6.76 hours was not an accurate representation of the data; some participants responded to the question in terms of number of hours spent on the internet per week, thus skewing the results (Appendix Figure 2.1). The median number of hours spent on the internet on an average weekend day was 4 hours. Similar to the previous question, the mean value of 5.04 hours was not an accurate representation of the data regarding hours spent on the internet on an average weekend day (Appendix Figure 2.2).

3.1.2. Online Shopping Experience

The mean number of products purchased online by subjects in the last four weeks was 2.77 with a range from 1 to 50; the median number of products purchased online was equal to 2 (Appendix Figure 2.3). These results may also be skewed to the right; unfortunately, data collection for this question in the online survey precluded respondents from entering the value of zero. Therefore, responses of 1 product may also have included some subjects who purchased 0 to 1 products online in the last four weeks.

Subjects were also asked to indicate how often they had purchased nine distinct product categories online in their past shopping experience. They rated each product category on a six-point scale, in which 1 was Never, 2 was Daily, 3 was Weekly, 4 was Monthly, 5 was Once Every Few Months, and 6 was Yearly. A table of descriptive statistics with the mean, median, and mode values for all of the nine product categories may be seen in the appendix (Appendix Table 2.4).

49.8% (N = 116) of the respondents never purchased music online, with 21.9% (N = 51) purchasing music online once every few months (Appendix Figure 2.5). This result was surprising since youth are often the key audience for many artists and music distribution programs (i.e. iTunes, Napster). While 67% (N = 156) of subjects never purchased DVD movies online, 18.9% (N = 44) purchased them online once every few months (Appendix Figure 2.6). 50.2% (N = 117) of subjects purchased books online once every few months, with 20.2% (N = 47) never purchasing books online and 21.9% (N = 51) purchasing them online yearly (Appendix Figure 2.7). These values are likely strongly influenced by the university semester system when new books are purchased for student classes. For the product category of electronics, 39.5% (N = 92) of respondents never bought them online, 27.5% (N = 64) bought them online once every few months, and 27% (N = 63) bought electronics online yearly (Figure 3.1.1; Appendix Figure 2.8). As a high involvement, high cost product category, lower purchase frequencies of yearly or once every few months align with current literature (i.e. Aaker, 1996). The category of electronics products was shown in half of the web page prototypes; electronics purchase frequency in the sample is therefore of special interest.

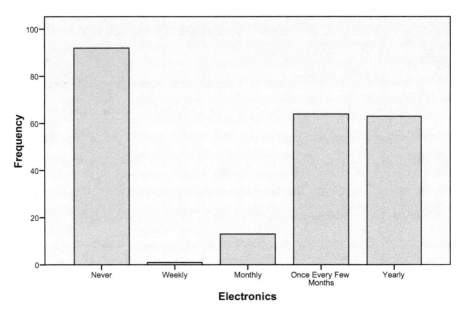

Figure 3.1.1. Frequency of Online Electronics Purchase

Computers and PC hardware may also be identified as high involvement, high cost products; while 56.2% (N = 131) never purchased computers and PC hardware online, 30% (N = 70) purchased them online yearly (Appendix Figure 2.9). Interestingly, 33.9% (N = 79) of subjects purchased apparel or accessories products online once every few months, with 21% (N = 49) purchasing them online monthly and 27% (N = 63) never purchasing apparel or accessories online (Appendix Figure 2.10). These results indicate that online shopping for apparel and accessories products is quite common in the students sampled. Finally, 71.2% (N = 166) of respondents had never purchased software online (Appendix Figure 2.11); 78.5% (N = 183) had never purchased office supplies online (Appendix Figure 2.12); and 88.8% (N = 207) of subjects had never bought kitchen or housewares products online (Appendix Figure 2.13).

An optional category of 'Other' was also included to account for product categories overlooked but frequently purchased by the sample. Participants indicated the following categories: beauty and personal hygiene products, tickets (airplane, movie, and concert tickets), sporting goods and exercise equipment, food and grocery items (coffee, wine, power bars), pharmacy products (protein supplements), plants/flowers, and entertainment (TV series on iTunes, video games). Additional responses that were entered as 'Other' were general gift items and products purchased through eBay.

The two product categories of electronics and office products were selected for display in the web page prototypes. Online shopping experience results indicated that respondents more often purchased high involvement electronics products online compared to the lower involvement product category of office supplies. Differences in past shopping history may be attributed to the product category and not necessarily to involvement level; the majority of office supplies are readily available at any local store, while electronics may be more difficult to locate. Additionally, as a high involvement product, shopping online for electronics provides greater selection and easier comparison of products, features, and prices.

3.1.3. Online Shopping Attitudes, Internet Savvy, and Design Sensitivity

The initial questionnaire also included a series of statements which subjects rated using a seven-point Strongly Disagree – Strongly Agree Likert scale.

3.1.3.1. Online Shopping Attitudes

Four statements were used to assess subject online shopping attitudes: (1) I use the internet for shopping, (2) I do not like to shop online, (3) I prefer shopping online to shopping in an actual store, and (4) Shopping on the internet is more risky compared to other ways of shopping. Two of these statements were phrased negatively while the remaining two were positive.

31% (N = 71) of subjects slightly agreed and 24% (N = 55) moderately agreed with the statement "I use the internet for shopping" (Figure 3.1.2; Appendix Figure 2.14). As portrayed by responses regarding online shopping experience, many subjects had previously bought apparel or accessories, books, electronics, and computers online. Due to the young, college-aged sample, this was not surprising.

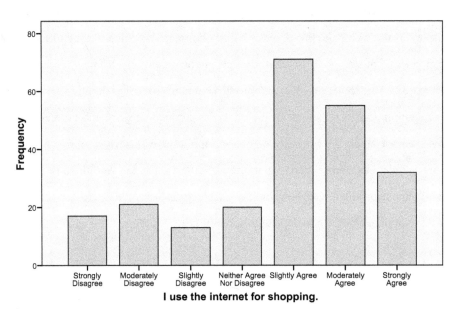

Figure 3.1.2. Frequencies, Use the Internet for Shopping

For the statement, "I do not like to shop online," 24% (N = 55) selected moderately disagree, 20.1% (N = 46) selected strongly disagree, 17.9% (N = 41) selected slightly disagree, and 17.5% (N = 40) selected neither agree nor disagree (Figure 3.1.3; Appendix Figure 2.15). The majority of responses were on the disagree side of the scale, indicating an overwhelmingly positive attitude toward online shopping in the sample.

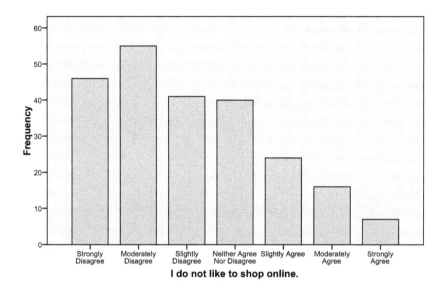

Figure 3.1.3. Frequencies, Do Not Like to Shop Online

25.8% (N = 59) of the sample moderately disagreed, 21.4% slightly disagreed, and 15.3% strongly disagreed with the statement "I prefer shopping online to shopping in an actual store" (Figure 3.1.4.; Appendix Figure 2.16). Despite a positive attitude towards shopping online as shown above, the majority of respondents disagreed that they preferred shopping online to more traditional shopping contexts.

Furthermore, 35.4% (N = 81) slightly agreed and 26.6% (N = 61) moderately agreed with the statement, "Shopping on the internet is more risky compared to other ways of shopping" (Appendix Figure 2.17). Aligning with past research, participants believed there was increased risk associated with online shopping. These results verify the fundamental disconnect present in e-commerce; the presence of a temporal and spatial separation between the consumer, product, and retailer remains a considerable obstacle to its adoption by consumers.

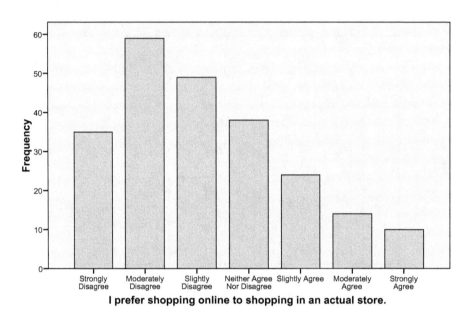

Figure 3.1.4. Frequencies, Prefer Shopping Online to Shopping in an Actual Store

3.1.3.2. Online Shopping Attitude Index (OSAI)

A reliability analysis of the previously discussed four Likert Statements indicated a Cronbach's Alpha value of .700 (Appendix Table 2.18). The item-total statistics table indicated a significant increase in reliability if the following item was excluded: "Shopping on the internet is less risky compared to other ways of shopping." The concept of risk assessed in this Likert statement was thus deleted from the potential scale because it did not correlate as well with the other three measures of the overall construct. The Online Shopping Attitude Index was then created by finding the average response of subjects across the three remaining items. This scale had a Cronbach's Alpha value of .759, which indicated good reliability.

108

3.1.3.3. Internet Savvy

The following four statements assessed subject internet savvy and expertise: (1) I make extensive use of the internet, (2) I consider myself to be a novice internet user, (3) I am confident in my ability to assess the quality of the design of a web site, and (4) I am confident in my ability to assess trustworthiness of web sites.

36.7% (N = 84) strongly agreed and 30.6% (N = 70) moderately agreed with the statement, "I make extensive use of the internet" (Appendix Figure 2.19). Correspondingly, 28.8% (N = 66) strongly disagreed and 28.4% (N = 65) moderately disagreed with the statement, "I consider myself to be a novice internet user" (Appendix Figure 2.20). These results were expected since subjects were sampled from universities and had a mean age of 20.2 years; computer technology and the internet are utilized daily for a variety of educational and recreational purposes by students.

30.1% (N = 69) moderately agreed and an equal percentage, 30.1% (N = 69), slightly agreed with the statement, "I am confident in my ability to assess trustworthiness of web sites" (Figure 3.1.5; Appendix Figure 2.21). 29.3% (N = 67) slightly agreed and 26.6% (N = 61) moderately agreed with the statement, "I am confident in my ability to assess the quality of the design of a web site" (Appendix Figure 2.22). These results indicate a general confidence in subject ability to assess trustworthiness and design quality of web sites. Subjects were slightly more confident with their ability to assess the trustworthiness of the web site than its design quality.

3.1.3.4. Internet Savvy Index (ISI)

Reliability analysis of the prior four Internet Savvy Likert statements indicated a Cronbach's Alpha value of .596 (Appendix Table 2.23). According to the possible Cronbach's Alpha values, exclusion of any of the four items would only reduce the scale's reliability. Therefore, the mean value was calculated from all four items in the creation of the Internet Savvy Index despite a generally low reliability value.

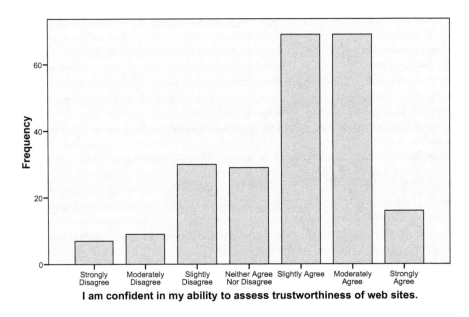

Figure 3.1.5. Confidence in Ability to Assess Trustworthiness of Web Sites

3.1.3.5. Design Sensitivity

Finally, participant design sensitivity was assessed by the following three statements: (1) I pay close attention to how a web site looks, (2) My feelings about a company are impacted by the visual appearance of their web site, and (3) If I dislike the visual appearance of a web page, I will not remain on the web site for very long.

Similar patterns were observed in subject responses to these three statements. 31.9% (N = 73) slightly agreed and 25.8% (N = 59) moderately agreed with the statement, "I pay close attention to how a web site looks" (Appendix Figure 2.24). For the statement, "My feelings about a company are impacted by the visual appearance of their web site," 35.4% (N = 81) slightly agreed and 27.5% (N = 63) moderately agreed with this statement (Appendix Figure 2.25). 31.9% (N = 73) slightly agreed and 27.5% (N = 63) moderately agreed with the statement, "If I dislike the visual appearance of a web page, I will not remain on the web site for very long" (Appendix Figure 2.26). The majority of participants therefore slightly or moderately agreed with the statements assessing design sensitivity. While these statements determined subject's conscious responses and behaviors to web site design, the impact of design on users is often an unconscious process that is not accurately portrayed through self report techniques.

3.1.3.6. Design Sensitivity Index (DSI)

Reliability analysis of the prior three Design Sensitivity Likert statements indicated a low, negative Cronbach's Alpha value of -.415 (Appendix Table 2.27). According to the possible Cronbach's Alpha values, exclusion of the item "If I like the visual appearance of a web site, I will remain on the web site for a longer period of time" would increase the reliability of the scale to a positive number. This item was thus deleted from the scale, resulting in a higher Design Sensitivity Index reliability value of .774.

3.2. Web Page Prototype Evaluations

Evaluations of the web page prototypes were divided into two categories: aesthetic evaluations and e-retailer evaluations. As discussed earlier, a two-level linear mixed model analysis was conducted to analyze the impact of design factors on the aesthetic and e-retailer evaluations. Results are provided below; summary tables of the

F-values and significance levels for aesthetic and e-retailer evaluations are also provided.

3.2.1. Aesthetic Evaluations

Eight Likert statements assessed the aesthetics and overall design quality of the web page. The eight aesthetic evaluations of the web page prototypes were: (1) The web page is easy to read, (2) I like how the web page looks, (3) The web page does not look cluttered, (4) I like the location of the product images, (5) It would be easy for me to quickly find the product I wanted on this web page, (6) I like the color scheme of this web page, (7) I like how color is used on this web page, and (8) It is easy for me to see which product description goes with which image. A table indicating which design factor(s) each Likert statement was expected to be influenced by was provided in the methods portion of this paper.

Detailed results for each of the eight aesthetic evaluation dependent variables are subsequently provided.

3.2.1.1. Easy to Read: "The web page is easy to read"

Mixed model analysis indicated that Easy to Read ratings were significantly affected by the design factors of thumbnail image location ($F_{1, 3428}$ = 43.142, p = .000) and background color ($F_{1, 3428}$ = 8.886, p = .003). The interaction between white space and background color was also found to be significant ($F_{1, 3428}$ = 9.925, p = .002) (Appendix Table 3.1). The three initial questionnaire indices were all insignificant; however, the individual initial questionnaire items of "I like to shop online" ($F_{1, 212}$ = 3.855, p = .051) and the number of hours spent on the internet on an average weekday

($F_{1,\ 212} = 3.672$, $p = .057$) were also marginally significant and positively related to Easy to Read ratings (Appendix Table 3.1).

Image location to the left of the product description consistently resulted in higher mean easy to read ratings of the web page prototype than when images were on the right (mean left = 5.19; mean right = 4.96). Prototypes with a white background color also received more positive ratings than those with a pale blue background color (mean white background = 5.12; mean pale blue background = 5.03). Furthermore, the effect of thumbnail image location was greater than the effect of background color on easy to read ratings (Appendix Table 3.2; Appendix Figure 3.3).

There was also an interaction of background color with white space (Figure 3.2.1.). Interestingly, background color had minimal impact on Easy to Read ratings for prototypes with less white space; the mean rating for web pages with the pale blue background (mean pale blue background = 5.06) was identical to those with the white background color (mean white background = 5.06). However, background color significantly impacted easy to read ratings in prototypes with more white space. Mean ratings of prototypes with a white background and more white space (mean white background = 5.18) were higher than easy to read ratings of prototypes with a pale blue background and an identical amount of increased white space (mean pale blue background = 4.99) (Appendix Table 3.2). Despite being statistically significant, the practical difference between 4.99 and 5.18 is slight; both values remained close to the "slightly agree" rating on the seven point Likert scale.

3.2.1.2. Like Look: "I like how the web page looks"

The original dependent variable, Dislike Look, was reversed and renamed to reflect a positive web page assessment. Web page prototype ratings of Like Look were significantly associated with the design factors of thumbnail image location ($F_{1, 3428}$ = 34.400, p = .000) and background color ($F_{1, 3428}$ = 25.030, p = .000).

The interaction effect between gender and color was also significant ($F_{1, 3428}$ = 5.531, p = .019). The mixed model analysis also showed a significant positive relationship of Like Look with initial questionnaire items of "hours spent on the internet on a weekday" ($F_{1, 212}$ = 7.046, p = .009) and "I like shopping online" (Like Shop) ($F_{1, 212}$ = 5.859, p = .016); a significant negative relationship was present between Like Look and subject "hours spent on the internet on a weekend day" ($F_{1, 212}$ = 4.482, p = .035), and (Appendix Table 3.4).

Mean Values of Easy to Read

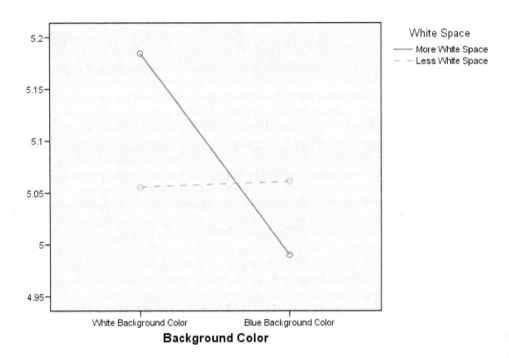

Figure 3.2.1. Easy to Read Interaction Effect, Background Color with White Space

Regardless of background color, participants aesthetically preferred web page prototypes with the thumbnail image located to the left of the product description (mean left = 4.39; mean right = 4.12) (Appendix Table 3.5; Appendix Figure 3.6). As was seen with easy to read ratings, web page prototypes with a white background received higher aesthetic ratings on overall look than web page with a pale blue background (mean white background = 4.35; mean pale blue background = 4.16). The interaction between gender and color showed that the highest ratings of Like Look were made by males rating prototypes with a white background color (mean white background = 4.56); males rated prototypes with a pale blue background color as less visually appealing (mean pale blue background = 4.23) (Appendix Table 3.7). Females also preferred web page prototypes with a white background color (mean white background = 4.24) over those with a blue background (mean pale blue background = 4.12). The profile plot provided portrays the interaction effect between gender and color for Like Look (Figure 3.2.2). Males rated web page prototypes higher along Like Look for both background colors compared to women. More importantly, as can be seen from the slope of the two lines in the plot, changes in background color had a higher impact on male ratings of visual appeal than on those of women.

3.2.1.3. Not Cluttered: "The web page does not look cluttered"

The original dependent variable, Cluttered was reversed and renamed Not Cluttered. Web page evaluations of Not Cluttered were significantly associated with thumbnail image location (F1, 3428 = 48.322, p = .000) and background color (F1, 3428 = 9.962, p = .002). The mixed model analysis also showed a positive, significant relationship of ratings of Not Cluttered with the subjects' number of hours spent on the internet on a weekday (F1, 212 = 5.468, p = .020) (Appendix Table 3.8).

Thumbnail image location to the left of the product description (mean left = 4.91) resulted in lower clutter ratings compared to when thumbnail image location was to the right (mean right = 4.65) (Appendix Table 3.9; Appendix Figure 3.10). Additionally, prototypes with a white background received slightly higher mean ratings (mean white background = 4.84) and were considered less cluttered than prototypes with a pale blue background (mean pale blue background = 4.72). Web page prototypes with a white background color and the thumbnail image location to the left of the product images received the highest overall mean score (mean = 4.99).

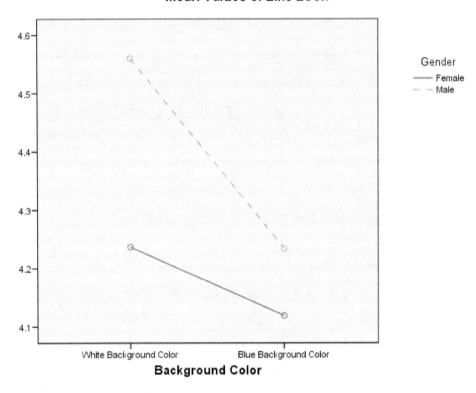

Mean Values of Like Look

Figure 3.2.2. Like Look Interaction Effect, Background Color with Gender

116

3.2.1.4. Like Image Location: "I like the location of the product images"

Dislike Image Location was also flipped and renamed. The mixed model analysis for Like Image Location indicated that evaluations were significantly related to thumbnail image location ($F_{1, 3428}$ = 219.335, p = .000) and background color ($F_{1, 3428}$ = 4.416, p = .036) (Appendix Table 3.11). The Likert statement Like Image Location directly assessed the design factor thumbnail image location; the high F-value ($F_{1, 3428}$ = 219.335, p = .000) of this dependent variable provided some face validity that Like Image Location accurately assessed thumbnail image location in each web page prototype.

Ratings of Like Image Location were also significantly associated with gender ($F_{1, 212}$ = 7.694, p = .006), "I like to shop online" (Like Shop) ($F_{1, 212}$ = 7.104, p = .008), "I am confident in my ability to assess the design quality of a web site" (Assess Design Quality) ($F_{1, 212}$ = 4.477, p = .036), and the number of hours spent on the internet on a weekday ($F_{1, 212}$ = 9.116, p = .003). As self reported ratings of Like Shop, Assess Design Quality, and hours spent on the internet increased, so did ratings of Like Image Location. Additionally, the interaction between gender and image location was also highly significant ($F_{1, 3428}$ = 16.801, p = .000) (Appendix Table 3.11).

A white background color (mean white background = 4.64) was slightly preferred over a pale blue background color (mean pale blue background = 4.56); thumbnail image location to the left (mean left = 4.96) was preferred to its location on the right (mean right = 4.24) ((Appendix Figure 3.13; Appendix Table 3.12). Although background color was significant, it had less of an impact on web page prototype ratings compared to thumbnail image location, as seen in both the plot and the differences in mean rating values (Appendix Table 3.12; Appendix Figure 3.13). A main effect relationship was also present for gender; males on average rated the web page prototypes higher than females for Like Image Location (Figure 3.2.3).

Mean Values of Like Image Location

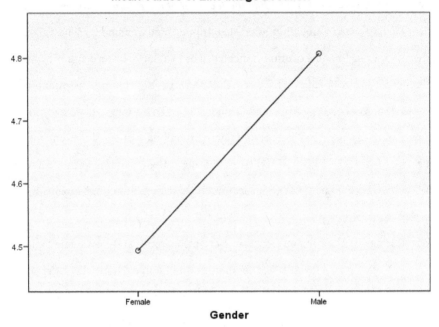

Figure 3.2.3. Like Image Location, Main Effect of Gender

On average, males rated web page prototypes higher than females for image location. The mean values of the interaction between gender and thumbnail image location indicated that males highly preferred the left image location (mean left males = 5.05) compared to thumbnail image location on the right (mean right males = 4.57) and females preferred thumbnail image location to the left slightly less than males (mean left females = 4.92). Thumbnail image location to the right yielded the lowest ratings of Like Image Location for females (mean right females = 4.07). This relationship between gender and thumbnail image location may also be seen in Figure 3.2.4.

Mean Values of Like Image Location

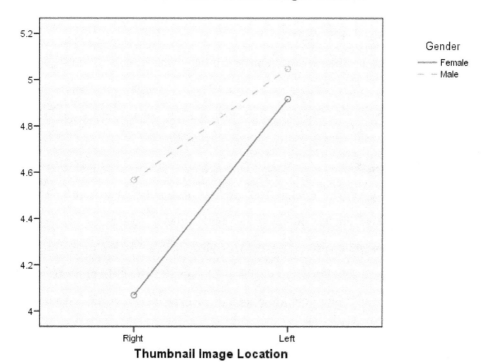

Figure 3.2.4. Like Image Location Interaction Effect, Background Color with Gender

3.2.1.5. Easy to Find Product: "It would be easy for me to quickly find the product I wanted on this web page"

Difficult to Find Product was flipped and renamed. The mixed model analysis of Easy to Find Product showed that ratings of the web page prototypes were significantly related to the only one design factor: thumbnail image location ($F_{1, 3428}$ = 22.891, p = .000). Two interaction effects were also found to be significant: (1) background color and white space ($F_{1, 3428}$ = 4.460, p = .035) and (2) gender and thumbnail image location ($F_{1, 3428}$ = 13.640, p = .000). Easy to Find Product was also significantly and positively related to number of hours spent on the internet on a

119

weekday ($F_{1, 212}$ = 4.235, p = .041) and marginally significant with "I like to shop online" ($F_{1, 212}$ = 3.507, p = .062) (Appendix Table 3.14). Finally, the Internet Savvy Index was also marginally significant with subject responses ($F_{1, 223}$ = 3.449, p = .065).

There was a main effect of thumbnail image ; when thumbnail image appeared to the left of the product descriptions (mean left = 5.11) it was consistently preferred in ratings of Easy to Find Product compared to when thumbnail image was located to the right (mean right = 4.90) (Appendix Figure 3.16).

The interaction between background color and white space indicated that for web page prototypes with a white background color, more white space resulted in higher Easy to Find Product ratings (mean more white space = 5.08) than less white space (mean less white space = 4.98) (Appendix Table 3.15). Web page prototypes with a pale blue background color displayed an opposite effect. In prototypes with a pale blue background color, less white space (mean pale blue-less white space = 5.00) resulted in higher ratings than when there was more white space (mean pale blue-more white space = 4.96). As can be seen in the differences between the mean values and in the profile plot, the impact of white space on mean ratings of Easy to Find Product was much more considerable in web page prototypes with a white background color (Figure 3.2.5.).

The interaction between gender and thumbnail image location was also highly significant. A plot of this relationship may be seen in the plot provided (Figure 3.2.6.). Females rated web page prototypes with thumbnail image location to the left the highest (mean left females = 5.15); males also preferred left thumbnail image location (mean left males = 5.03). Males rated thumbnail image location to the right (mean right males = 4.99) slightly higher than the ratings of females (mean right females = 4.85).

Mean Values of Easy to Find Product

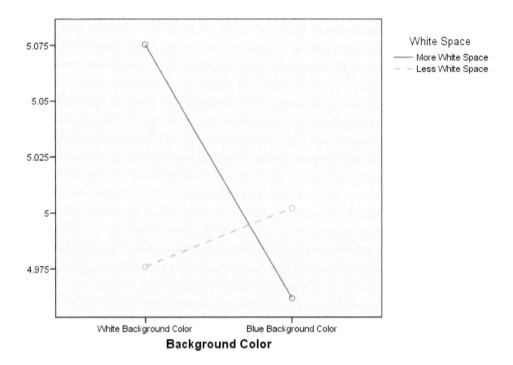

Figure 3.2.5. Easy to Find Product Interaction Effect, Background Color with White Space

3.2.1.6. Like Color Scheme: "I like the color scheme of this web page"

Like Color Scheme was significantly related to thumbnail image location ($F_{1, 3428}$ = 7.063, p = .008) and background color ($F_{1, 3428}$ = 36.949, p = .000). Initial questionnaire items of "I like to shop online" ($F_{1, 212}$ = 6.261, p = .013) and "I shop online" ($F_{1, 212}$ = 6.769, p = .010) were also significant (Appendix Table 3.17). No interactions were significant with Like Color Scheme.

A main effect existed in the relationship between background color and thumbnail image location (Appendix Figure 3.19). A white background color (mean white background = 4.27) was preferred over a pale blue background color (mean pale blue background = 4.00), and thumbnail image location to the left of the product description (mean left = 4.19) was preferred over its location to the right (mean right = 4.07) (Appendix Table 3.18).

Mean Values of Easy to Find Product

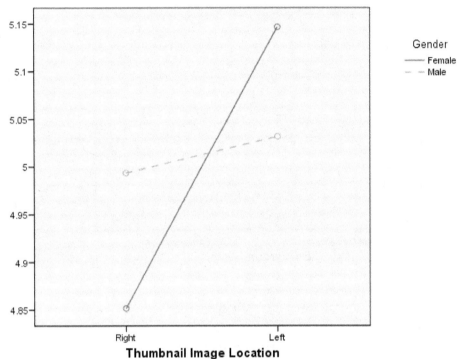

Figure 3.2.6. Easy to Find Product Interaction Effect, Thumbnail Image Location with Gender

3.2.1.7. Like Color Use: "I like how color is used on this web page"

Like Color Use was significantly associated with both thumbnail image location ($F_{1, 3428}$ = 4.705, p = .030) and background color ($F_{1, 3428}$ = 36.810, p = .000). Similar to Like Color Scheme, no interaction effects were significant for Like Color Use. Ratings of color usage were also significantly related to the initial questionnaire item of "shopping on the internet is less risky compared to other ways of shopping" (Less Risky) ($F_{1, 212}$ = 4.657, p = .032) (Appendix Table 3.20). More interestingly, Like Color Use was significantly associated with the initial questionnaire index of Design Sensitivity ($F_{1, 223}$ = 5.708, p = .018) (Appendix Table 3.21).

A profile plot revealed that prototypes with a white background color and left thumbnail image location were preferred by participants (Appendix Figure 3.23). A white background color resulted in higher mean ratings of color use (mean white background = 4.24) compared to prototypes with a pale blue background color (mean pale blue background = 3.98). Background color had greater impact on Like Color Use mean ratings than thumbnail image location (Appendix Table 3.22).

3.2.1.8. Easy to See Product with Description: "It is easy for me to see which product description goes with which image"

Mixed model analysis of subject responses to Easy to See Product with Description indicated that ratings were significantly related to the design factor of thumbnail image location ($F_{1, 3428}$ = 97.853, p = .000). The interactions between background color and white space ($F_{1, 3428}$ = 9.241, p = .002) and between gender and thumbnail image location ($F_{1, 3428}$ = 17.492, p = .000) were also significant. Easy to See Product with Description was also related to the following initial questionnaire items: (1) number of hours spent on the internet on a weekday ($F_{1, 212}$ = 4.967, p = .027), (2) "I like to shop online" ($F_{1, 212}$ = 5.643, p = .018), (3) "I prefer shopping online to shopping in an actual store" ($F_{1, 212}$ = 4.581, p = .033), and (4) "I make extensive use of the internet" ($F_{1, 212}$ = 3.334, p = .069) (Appendix Table 3.24).

Mean ratings of web page prototypes with thumbnail image location to the left (mean left = 5.53) were higher than when thumbnail image was located to the right of the product description (mean right = 5.15) (Appendix Table 3.25). Participants therefore found that it was easier to match product descriptions with their appropriate images in those web page prototypes with the thumbnail image location to the left of the product description (Appendix Figure 3.26).

The relationship between background color and white space illustrated an interaction effect between the two variables (Figure 3.2.7).

Mean Values of Easy to See Product w Description

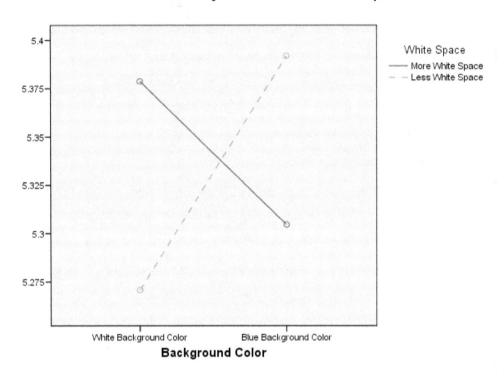

Figure 3.2.7. Easy to See Product with Description Interaction Effect, Background Color with White Space

In web page prototypes with more white space, participants rated it easier to see which product description went with its corresponding image when there was a white background color (mean white background-more white space = 5.38). The white background color was preferred over a pale blue background color in web page prototypes with the same amount of more white space (mean pale blue background-more white space = 5.27) (Appendix Figure 3.25). Alternatively, web page prototypes with a pale blue background color were rated higher on this variable when there was less white space in the design (mean pale blue background-less white space = 5.39) compared to when there was more white space (mean pale blue background-more white space = 5.30). This interaction effect indicates that ratings for Easy to See Product with Description were almost identical for web pages with more white space and a white background color and web pages with less white space and a pale blue background color.

The interaction effect between gender and thumbnail image location was also significant. Females rated web page prototypes with thumbnail image location to the left (mean left females = 5.63) much higher than when thumbnail image location was to the right (mean right females = 5.16). Similarly, males also preferred left hand location (mean left males = 5.33) to that of the right (mean right males = 5.13). The effect of thumbnail image location, as can be seen from the mean values, was much more pronounced for females than for males. This relationship may also be seen in plot (Figure 3.2.8.).

3.2.1.9. Summary of Aesthetic Evaluation Results

A summary table for the web page aesthetic evaluations is provided below with the F-value for each significant relationship (Table 3.2.1.). The number of stars indicate significance; one star (*) represents a p-value less than .05, two stars (**) represents a p-value less than .01, and three stars (***) represents a p-value less than .001. An (a) represents a marginally significant p-value less than .07.

125

Mean Values of Easy to See Product with Description

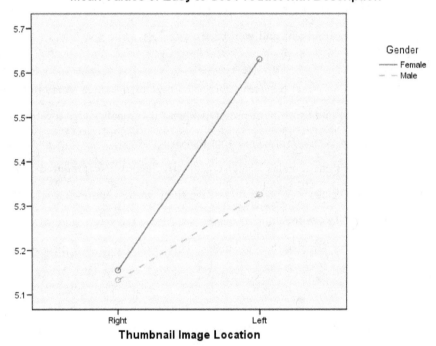

Figure 3.2.8. Easy to See Product with Description Interaction Effect, Thumbnail Image Location with Gender

Table 3.2.1. Summary of Results, Aesthetic Evaluations of the Web Page Prototypes

Aesthetic Evaluation	Design Factors			Interactions			Online Shopping Attitude Index (OSAI)				Internet Savvy Index (ISI)			Design Sensitivity Index (DSI)		
Dependent Variable	Thumbnail Image Location	Background Color	Gender	White Space x Color	Gender x Image Location	Gender x Color	Like to Shop Online	Prefer to Shop Online	Internet Shopping Less Risky	Shop Online	ISI	Extensive Use of Internet	Assess Design Quality	DSI	Internet Hours Weekday	Internet Hours Weekend
Easy to Read	43.1***	8.9**		9.9**			3.9a								3.7a	
Like Look	34.4***	25.0***				5.5*	5.9*								7.0**	4.5*
Not Cluttered	48.3***	10.0**													5.5*	
Like Image Location	219.3***	4.4*	7.7**		16.8***		7.1**						4.5*		9.1**	
Easy to Find Product	22.9***			4.5*	13.6***		3.5a				3.5a				4.2*	
Like Color Scheme	7.1**	36.9***					6.3*			6.8**						
Like Color Use	4.7a	36.8***							4.7*					5.7*		
Easy to See Product Description with Image	97.9***			9.2**	17.5***		5.6*	4.6*				3.3a			5.0*	

127

With a few exceptions, aesthetic evaluations of the sixteen distinct web page prototypes revealed three consistent trends: (1) white background color was preferred over the pale blue background color, (2) thumbnail image location to the left of the product description resulted in higher mean ratings compared to when thumbnail images were located to the right of product descriptions, and (3) white space as an independent variable was not significantly associated with ratings of web page prototypes along any of the dependent variables.

Significant interaction effects between the design factors of background color and white space were evident for the aesthetic evaluations Easy to Read, Easy to Find Product, and Easy to See Product Description with Image. While the interaction between gender and background color was significant for only Like Look, the interaction between gender and thumbnail image location was significant for Like Image Location, Easy to Find Product, and Easy to See Product Description with Image. Gender as an independent fixed effect was significant for only one aesthetic evaluation: Like Image Location.

The Internet Savvy Index was significant for ratings of Easy to Find Product; its individual items were also significant for some aesthetic evaluations of the web page prototypes. The Design Sensitivity Index (DSI) was significant for Like Color Use, but surprisingly, none of the DSI items were significant for any dependent variables. Although the Online Shopping Attitudes Index (OSAI) itself was not significant, many of its items were significant for multiple aesthetic evaluations. The OSAI item "I like to shop online" was significant for six out of eight total aesthetic evaluations.

3.2.2. E-Retailer Evaluations

Although the remaining four Likert statements were assessments of the web page prototype, they served as a basis for inference about characteristics of the e-retailer. Negatively phrased Likert statements were reversed to reflect positive assessments of each web page prototype. The four e-retailer evaluations were as follows: (1) The web page looks professional, (2) This looks like a web page for a quality company, (3) This looks like a high budget web page, and (4) I would trust buying products from this web page.

3.2.2.1. Professional: "The web page looks professional"

Responses to "the web page looks professional" were significantly explained by the design factors thumbnail image location ($F_{1, 3428} = 24.138$, p = .000) and background color ($F_{1, 3428} = 30.796$, p = .000). The interactions between white space and color ($F_{1, 3428} = 7.882$, p = .005) and gender and color ($F_{1, 3428} = 7.197$, p = .007) were also significant (Appendix Table 3.27). Mixed model analysis also showed that ratings of web page prototype professionalism were significantly associated with the initial questionnaire Internet Savvy Index (ISI) ($F_{1, 223} = 4.015$, p = .046) (Appendix Table 3.28).

The presence of a white background color and thumbnail image location to the left of the product description resulted in the highest ratings of web page professionalism (Appendix Figure 3.30). The mean value for prototypes with a white background color was 4.74, compared to the mean value of 4.57 when there was a pale blue background color (Appendix Table 3.29). Similarly, the mean value for thumbnail image location on the left (mean left = 4.74) was higher than when it was

129

located to the right of the product descriptions (mean right = 4.57) (Appendix Table 3.29).

The plot provided portrays the interaction effect present between background color and white space in ratings of web page professionalism (Figure 3.2.9.). Web page prototypes with a white background color and more white space (mean white background-more white space = 4.76) were rated as much more professional by participants than prototypes with more white space but a pale blue background (mean pale blue background-more white space = 4.50). Presence of less white space in prototypes with a pale blue background (mean pale blue background-less white space = 4.64) resulted in lower ratings of professionalism compared to prototypes with more white space (mean white background-less white space = 4.74). As seen in the plot, white space had a greater impact on ratings of professionalism for prototypes with a pale blue background. Additionally, background color had a significant impact on web page professionalism ratings when there was more white space included in the design.

The interaction effect between gender and background color in ratings of web page professionalism indicated that a white background color was perceived to be more professional by both males (mean white background males = 4.83) and females (mean white background females = 4.69) (Appendix Table 3.31). As seen in the plot provided, while males rated web page prototypes with a white background color as more professional compared to females, females rated the pale blue background color as more professional compared to males (Figure 3.2.10.). The mean female Professional rating for prototypes with a pale blue background was 4.59; the mean male rating for the pale blue background was 4.54.

Mean Values of Professional

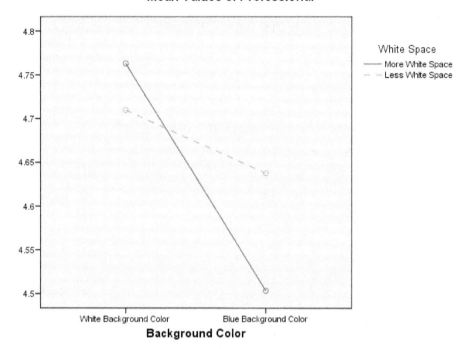

Figure 3.2.9. Professional Interaction Effect, Background Color witn White Space

3.2.2.2. Quality Company: "This looks like a web page for a quality company"

Responses to "this looks like a web page for a quality company" were significantly related to thumbnail image location ($F_{1, 3428}$ = 12.993, p = .000) and background color ($F_{1, 3428}$ = 30.998, p = .000). There was a significant interaction between background color and gender ($F_{1, 3428}$ = 4.876, p = .027) (Appendix Table 3.32). The individual initial questionnaire item of "I am confident in my ability to assess the trustworthiness of web sites" was also significant ($F_{1, 212}$ = 3.987, p = .047). Other items were marginally significant: "If I like the visual appearance of a web page, I will remain on the web site for longer" ($F_{1, 212}$ = 3.694, p = .056), and the number of hours spent on the internet on a weekday ($F_{1, 212}$ = 3.713, p = .055)

(Appendix Table 3.32). Although only one of these individual initial questionnaire items was included in the index, the Internet Savvy Index was significantly related to ratings of the web page as representing a quality company ($F_{1, 223}$ = 4.285, p = .040) (Appendix Table 3.33).

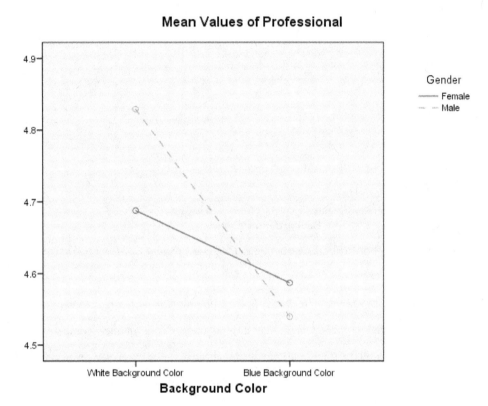

Figure 3.2.10. Professional Interaction Effect, Background Color with Gender

A plot of background color versus thumbnail image location depicted the main effect relationship (Appendix Figure 3.35). A white background color (mean white background = 4.65) received higher ratings than prototypes with a pale blue background color (mean pale blue background = 4.48). Similarly, thumbnail image location to the left of the product description (mean left = 4.63) resulted in higher ratings of the web page representing a quality company compared to when thumbnail image location was to the right (mean right = 4.51) (Appendix Table 3.34).

The interaction effect between gender and background color in ratings of web page quality may be seen in the plot provided (Figure 3.2.11). A white background color received higher Quality Company ratings for both males (mean white background males = 4.76) and females (mean white background females = 4.59). In prototypes with a pale blue background, males (mean pale blue background males = 4.50) reported slightly higher mean Quality Company ratings than females (mean pale blue background females = 4.48).

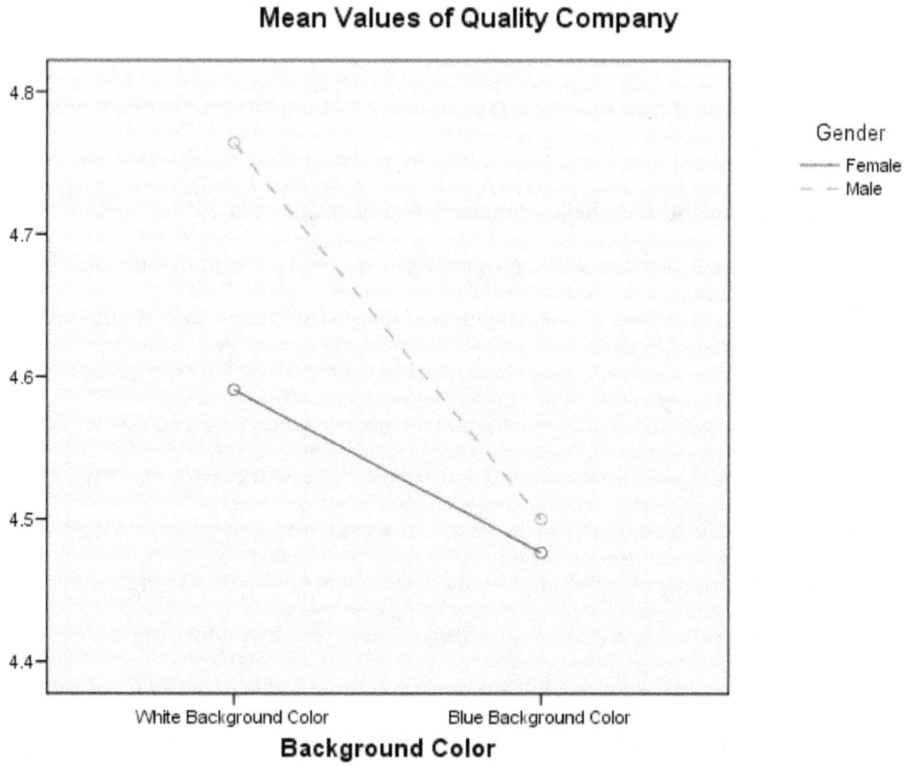

Mean Values of Quality Company

Figure 3.2.11. Quality Company Interaction Effect, Background Color with Gender

3.2.2.3. High Budget: "This looks like a high budget web page"

The dependent variable Low Budget was flipped to portray a positive web page assessment. Mixed model analysis of subject responses to High Budget showed that they were significantly associated with the design factors of thumbnail image location ($F_{1, 3428}$ = 5.118, p = .024) and background color ($F_{1, 3428}$ = 29.829, p = .000). The interaction between white space and color was also significant ($F_{1, 3428}$ = 4.828, p = .028). The only initial questionnaire item that related to High Budget ratings was the number of hours spent online on a weekend day ($F_{1, 212}$ = 5.841,p = .017) (Appendix Table 3.38).

A plot of background color versus thumbnail image location portrayed a main effect relationship in participant ratings of the web page as high budget (Appendix Figure 3.40). A white background color (mean white background = 4.44) resulted in higher ratings than a pale blue background color (mean pale blue background color = 4.24). Thumbnail image location to the left (mean left = 4.39) resulted in higher budget ratings of the web page compared to image location to the right of product descriptions (mean right = 4.30) (Appendix Table 3.39). Additionally, background color had a greater impact on consumer perceptions of budget than thumbnail image location.

There was a significant interaction of background color and white space ($F_{1, 3428}$ = 4.828, p = .028) (Figure 3.2.12). Overall, a white background color was preferred to a pale blue background color. However, for web page prototypes with a white background, presence of more white space (mean white background-more white space = 4.49) resulted in higher ratings than if there was less white space (mean white background-less white space = 4.40) (Appendix Table 3.39). However, for prototypes with a pale blue background color, utilization of less white space (mean pale blue background-less white space = 4.28) resulted in higher ratings of the prototype than if there was more white space (mean pale blue background-more white space = 4.21).

Mean Values of High Budget

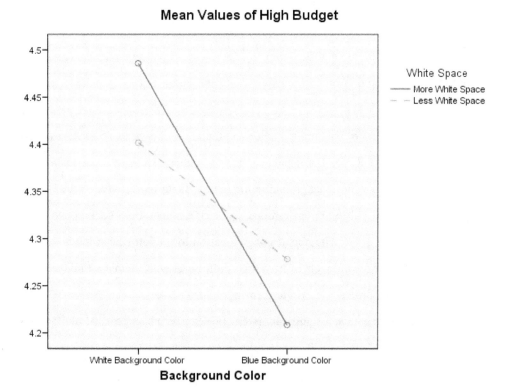

Figure 3.2.12. High Budget Interaction Effect, Background Color with White Space

3.2.2.4. Trust Buying Product: "I would trust buying products from this web page"

This Likert statement directly addressed the conscious impact of front-end design elements on consumer trust. Trust Buying Product was significantly related to thumbnail image location ($F_{1, 3428}$ = 12.333, p = .000) and background color ($F_{1, 3428}$ = 13.740, p = .000). The interaction between gender and white space was highly significant ($F_{1, 3428}$ = 9.149, p = .003); the interaction between background color and white space was almost significant at the .07 level ($F_{1, 3428}$ =3.212, p = .073)

(Appendix Table 3.41). Trust Buying Product was also very significantly related to the Internet Savvy Index ($F_{1, 223}$ = 5.625, p = .019) (Appendix Table 3.42). One individual item from the initial questionnaire was significant: "if I like the visual appearance of a web site I will stay for a longer period of time" ($F_{1, 212}$ = 3.928, p = .049). Other items were marginally significant: the number of hours spent online on a weekday ($F_{1, 212}$ = 3.767, p = .054) and "I make extensive use of the internet" ($F_{1, 212}$ = 3.835, p = .052) (Appendix Table 3.41).

Main effects of background color and thumbnail image location were observed (Appendix Figure 3.44). Participants reported higher levels of trust in web page prototypes with a white background color (mean white background = 4.65) than in prototypes with a pale blue background color (mean pale blue background = 4.55) (Appendix Table 3.43). Thumbnail image location to the left (mean left = 4.66) also resulted in higher mean levels of trust than prototypes with thumbnail image location to the right of the product descriptions (mean right = 4.54).

There was almost a significant interaction between background color and white space ($F_{1, 3428}$ =3.212, p = .073) (Figure 3.2.13.). Overall, trends showed that web page prototypes with a white background color were trusted more by participants. Within those prototypes with a white background color, however, higher mean ratings of trust existed for web pages with more white space (mean white background-more white space = 4.68) than if there was less white space (mean white background-less white space = 4.63). Alternatively, web page prototypes with a pale blue background color received higher ratings of perceived trust with the presence of less white space (mean pale blue background-less white space = 4.58) compared to more white space (mean pale blue background-more white space = 4.52).

Mean Values of Trust Buying Product

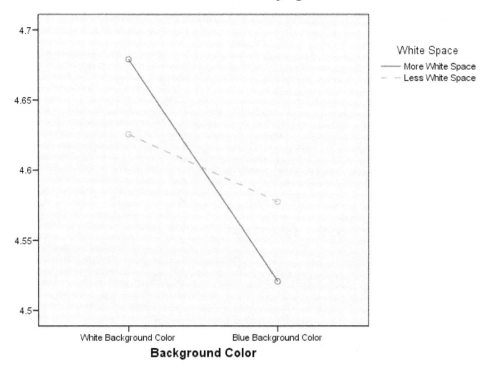

Figure 3.2.13. Trust Buying Product Interaction Effect, Background Color with White Space

The interaction between gender and white space in ratings of Trust Buying Product illustrated an interesting trend (Figure 3.2.14.). Males trusted web page prototypes with more white space (mean more white space males = 4.71) to a greater extent than females (mean more white space females = 4.54). Females, however, trusted web page prototypes with a pale blue background color (mean pale blue background females = 4.61) more than males (mean pale blue background males = 4.59) (Appendix Table 3.45). Most importantly, while females trusted buying products more from web page with less white space, males placed more trust in web pages with more white space (Figure 3.2.14.).

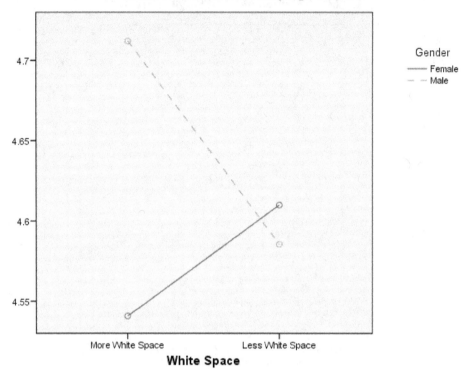

Figure 3.2.14. Trust Buying Product Interaction Effect, Background Color with Gender

3.2.2.5. Summary of E-Retailer Evaluation Results

As was provided for the aesthetic evaluations of the web page prototypes, a summary table of the F-values for each e-retailer evaluation is provided below (Table 3.2.2.). The number of stars indicate significance; one star (*) represents a p-value less than .05, two stars (**) represents a p-value less than .01, and three stars (***) represents a p-value less than .001. An (a) represents a marginally significant p-value less than .07.

Table 3.2.2. Summary of Results, E-Retailer Evaluations of the Web Page Prototypes

Dependent Variable	Design Factors		Interactions			Internet Savvy Index (ISI)			Design Sensitivity Index (DSI)	
	Thumbnail Image Location	Background Color	WS x Color	Gender x WS	Gender x Color	ISI	Extensive Use of Internet	Assess Trust-worthiness	If Like Design Stay Longer	Internet Hours per Weekday
Professional	24.1***	30.8***	7.9**		7.2**	4.0*				
Quality Company	13.0***	31.0***			4.9*	4.3*		4.0*	3.7a	3.7a
High Budget	5.1*	29.8***	4.8*							5.8*
Trust Buying Product	12.3***	13.7***		9.1**			3.8a		3.9*	3.8a

E-retailer evaluations based on the web page prototype designs followed many similar patterns evident in the aesthetic evaluations. Thumbnail image location and background color were significant predictors of all four e-retailer evaluations. Three out of the four e-retailer evaluations revealed a significant interaction effect between the design factors of background color and white space. Despite evident interaction effects, profile plots of mean values portrayed that consumer perceptions of the web page as professional, high budget, and trustworthy were highest for those web page prototypes with a white background color and more white space. Thumbnail image location to the left of the product description also consistently resulted in more positive e-retailer evaluations.

Gender effects were also evident; the interaction between gender and color was significant for two e-retailer evaluations (Professional and Quality Company) and the interaction between gender and white space was significant for Trust Buying Product. For the majority of gender interactions, males tended to rate the web page prototypes higher than females along the relevant dependent variables.

The Internet Savvy Index was significant for Professional and Quality Company; although items from the Design Sensitivity Index were significant, the index itself was not. Neither the Online Shopping Attitudes Index nor its items were significant for any e-retailer evaluations.

3.2.3. Behavior Intention

Two additional questions assessed behavior intention on a seven point scale from highly unlikely to highly likely: (1) If you saw this web page, how likely would you be to continue searching for other web pages that have the same products, and (2) If this web page offered the product you wanted, how likely would you be to purchase a product from this web page? These two questions were expected to be impacted by all three design factors of background color, white space, and thumbnail image location.

3.2.3.1. Won't Continue Search: "If you saw this web page, how likely would you be to not continue searching for other web pages that have the same products?"

Responses of 'highly likely' to the original dependent variable, Continue Search, would have negative implications for building a loyal consumer base since e-retailers want to attract and retain new customers. Responses were thus flipped to represent a positive assessment of the web page and it was renamed Won't Continue Search. Mixed model analysis of subject responses indicated that no design factors were significant for Won't Continue Search. Only two items were significant; the initial questionnaire items of "I am confident in my ability to assess the trustworthiness of a web site" ($F_{1,\ 212}$ = 4.424, p = .037), and "I consider myself an expert internet user" ($F_{1,\ 212}$ = 4.490, p = .035) (Appendix Table 3.46). Comparison of the mean values may be seen in the Appendix (Appendix Table 3.47); a white background color and thumbnail image location to the left of the product description resulted in slightly higher ratings by participants.

3.2.3.2. Purchase Likely: "If this web page offered the product you wanted, how likely would you be to purchase a product from this web page?"

Purchase Likely was significantly associated with the design factors thumbnail image location ($F_{1,\ 3428}$ = 9.443, p = .002) and background color ($F_{1,\ 3428}$ = 8.215, p = .004). Age was also significant as an independent fixed effect ($F_{1,\ 223}$ = 5.420, p = .021) (Appendix Table 3.48). The interaction between gender and white space was also significant ($F_{1,\ 3428}$ = 3.871, p = .049), along with the Internet Savvy Index (ISI)

$(F_{1, 223} = 6.617, p = .011)$ (Appendix Table 3.49). Initial questionnaire items of "internet shopping is less risky compared to other ways of shopping" $(F_{1, 212} = 3.424, p = .066)$ and "I feel confident assessing the trustworthiness of a web site" $(F_{1, 212} = 4.189, p = .042)$ were also related to subject purchase intention (Appendix Table 3.48).

A profile plot of background color versus thumbnail image location shows the main effects (Appendix Figure 3.51). A white background color (mean white background = 4.42) received higher ratings of purchase intention than a pale blue background color (mean pale blue background = 4.31) (Appendix Table 3.50). Furthermore, thumbnail image location to the left of the product description (mean left = 4.42) also resulted in higher likeliness of purchase from the web page compared to thumbnail image location to the right of the product descriptions (mean right = 4.31).

The interaction between gender and white space may be seen in the plot provided (Figure 3.2.15). Males were more likely to purchase from a web page with more white space (mean more white space males = 4.51) than less white space (mean less white space males = 4.43). Females, on the other hand, had higher purchase intention from web pages with less white space (mean less white space females = 4.34) than those with more (mean more white space females = 4.27).

3.2.4. Purchase Intention and Product Preference

A third, final Likert statement directly assessed the impact of the fourth design factor, thumbnail image size, on purchase intention and product preference. Participants responded to the following question utilizing a seven point Likert scale where 1 was Highly Unlikely and 7 was Highly Likely: Assuming the products on this web page suit your needs, which of these two products displayed would you be more likely to purchase: the First or the Second product shown on the above web page?

Thumbnail image size was varied within each prototype; subjects selected which product they would be more likely to purchase from two options tailored to the names of specific products shown on each web page prototype.

An additional, optional qualitative question was also included in the survey to receive information on the reasoning underlying participant product choice: Why? Briefly explain why you'd be more likely to purchase the product you selected in the previous question.

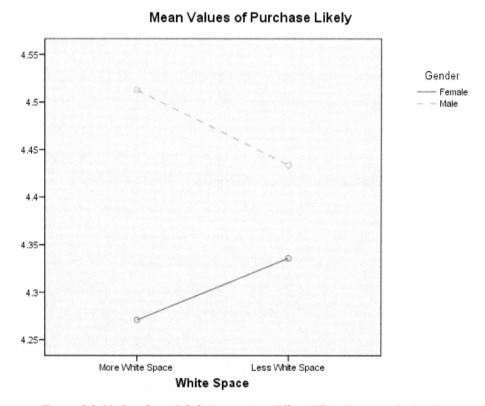

Figure 3.2.15. Purchase Likely Interaction Effect, White Space with Gender

143

3.2.4.1. Image Size Picked: Assuming the products on this web page suit your needs, which of these two products displayed would you be more likely to purchase: the First or the Second product shown on the above web page?

Image Size Picked was significantly associated with the design factors thumbnail image location ($F_{1, 3426}$ = 112.110, p = .000), background color ($F_{1, 3426}$ = 15.786, p = .000), and as expected, thumbnail image size ($F_{1, 3426}$ = 29.953, p = .000). As observed with all of the previous dependent variables, the independent design factor of white space was not significant ($F_{1, 3426}$ = .670, p = .413). The interaction between background color and white space, however, was significant ($F_{1, 3426}$ = 39.992, p = .000). Surprisingly, age ($F_{1, 212}$ = 4.833, p = .029) was also significantly associated with subject image size choice (Appendix Table 3.52).

An examination of the frequencies of responses to Image Size Picked may be seen in the Appendix (Appendix Table 3.53). When given an option of which product they would be more likely to purchase, 73.4% of participants chose the large product image for purchase while only 26.6% of participants selected the small product image (Appendix Figure 3.54). Therefore, thumbnail image size clearly had a significant impact on which product was chosen for purchase by participants.

Responses to the optional qualitative question were then reviewed to better understand the reasons behind the image chosen for purchase. Responses indicated that many times the product was chosen solely based on the presence of the larger image ("The picture is larger and more visually satisfying than the second item's picture," "bigger image," "The second picture was larger and took up more of the space available so it appears to give the consumer more information"). The larger image was also associated with being higher quality ("The first looks more durable and like it would produce better quality," "Bigger picture = better product"), more attractive ("looks cooler," "Bigger image, it seems more appealing"), and more

144

professional ("more professional looking"). Additionally, numerous participants mentioned that it was easier to see product details and features in the larger image ("I guess the capacity of two products are the same, but second one's picture is bigger so I can see the detail").

Interestingly, some participants also inferred about the intentions of the e-retailer based on the image size, as seen in the following two sample comments: (1) "The picture is larger, which seems to indicate pride in the product. The second product, though identically described, seems to be receiving a poor recommendation from the site since its picture is smaller than those of the other products on the page," and (2) "The first and second are exactly the same, but the second provides a larger picture which makes me feel like I am able to see more of the product itself and assess it, while the first feels as though the sellers do not want me to get a close look at the product."

Participants often selected the smaller image due to size value in the specific product category. For example, one participant, in selecting a digital camera, wrote: "The two products are the same, however in the second picture, the angle of the picture of the camera makes it look smaller and more compact, which is what I would be looking for in a camera." Similar responses about the small size and the desirable compactness of a product were also found in other product categories.

3.2.4.2. Summary of Behavior and Purchase Intention Results

A summary table for the two behavioral intention items and the last purchase intention item is provided (Table 3.2.3.). The number of stars indicate significance; one star (*) represents a p-value less than .05, two stars (**) represents a p-value less than .01, and three stars (***) represents a p-value less than .001. An (a) represents a marginally significant p-value less than .07.

145

The additional independent variable of thumbnail image size was incorporated into the mixed model for the dependent variable Image Size Picked. Thumbnail image size was not included in the regression models for Won't Continue Search or Purchase Likely since it was varied within prototype, hence the 'N/A' shown in the table.

Thumbnail image location and background color were significant for Purchase Likely and Image Size Picked. Although no design factors were significant for Won't Continue Search, mean values portrayed results similar to those found in the significant Purchase Likely regression model; white background color and thumbnail image location to the left of product descriptions resulted in more positive ratings of the web page and thus, measures of behavior intention. Age was significant as an independent fixed effect for Purchase Likely and Image Size Picked. The interaction between gender and white space and the Internet Savvy Index were also significant for Purchase Likely.

3.2.5. Hypotheses and Results Summary

A summary of the hypotheses of this thesis and the support or lack of support for each based upon the mixed model analysis is provided in Table 3.2.4. Further discussion of the hypotheses and this research is provided in the discussion section.

3.2.6. Individual-Level Analysis

The results prior to this section were from a mixed model analysis of the data, which controlled for the subject to subject variability. In order to further investigate the amount of individual heterogeneity in the data, conjoint methodology was pursued for additional post-hoc analysis.

146

Table 3.2.3. Summary of Results, Behavior Intention and Purchase Intention

Behavior Intention	Design Factors				Interactions		Online Shopping Attitude Index (OSAI)	Internet Savvy Index (ISI)		
Dependent Variable	Thumbnail Image Location	Background Color	Thumbnail Image Size	Age	White Space x Color	Gender x White Space	Internet Shopping Less Risky	ISI	Expert Internet User	Assess Trustworthiness
Won't Continue Search									4.5*	4.4*
Purchase Likely	9.4**	8.2**		5.4*		3.9*	3.4a	6.6*		4.2*
Image Size Picked	112.1***	15.8***	30.0***	4.8*	40.0***					

Table 3.2.4. Summary, Support of Thesis Hypotheses

Design Factor		Hypothesis	Supported	Not Supported
Background Color	H1a:	The white background color will be positively related to web page aesthetic ratings of color, clutter, and legibility.	X	
	H1b:	The white background color will be positively related to web page evaluations of the e-retailer as professional and high budget.	X	
	H1c:	The blue background color will be positively related to consumer evaluations of e-retailer trustworthiness and company quality.		X
White Space	H2a:	More white space will be positively related to ratings of web page aesthetics.		X
	H2b:	White space will have a positive impact on consumer perceptions of the e-retailer as trustworthy, representing a quality company, high budget, or professional.		
Thumbnail Image Size	H3a:	The large thumbnail image will be selected for purchase more often than the small thumbnail image.	X	
	H3b:	The large thumbnail image will be associated with a higher quality product and will receive more positive qualitative feedback than the small thumbnail image.	X	
Thumbnail Image Location	H4a:	Placement of the thumbnail image array to the left of the product descriptions will be preferred to placement to the right of the product descriptions as seen in higher web page aesthetic ratings.	X	
	H4b:	Placement of the thumbnail image array to the left of the product descriptions will be positively related to consumer perceptions of the e-retailer as trustworthy, quality, high budget, and professional.	X	

Creation of the sixteen distinct web page prototypes was based upon an experimental design that allowed for individual level regressions. For each of the 229 participants, fifteen regression analysis were run (one for each of the fifteen dependent variables), with the appropriate design factors as the independent variables. Each regression had sixteen observations, representing the sixteen web page prototypes. Conjoint analysis utilizes the regression coefficients from the individual regression models to estimate the part-worths for each level of the independent design factors and their relative importance. These part-worths allow one to determine which levels of each independent attribute are preferred by the respondents.

The model fit for each individual regression can be judged by the R squared value. Some subjects showed no variation in their responses across the sixteen web page prototypes; these regressions could not be performed. The respective N values are also provided below, which represent the number of individual regressions summarized in the table. A table of the minimum, maximum, and median R square values as well as the mean importance values obtained through conjoint analysis is provided (Table 3.2.5.).

The individual R square values range from 0.015 to 1.000, with the median value varying around 0.300. This indicates that for some individuals the design factors were good predictors of their assessment of the web page prototype, while for others they were not. These individual R square values are much higher than the very low values seen in the pooled analysis, as they allow the individual beta coefficients to be different across respondents.

Furthermore, the mean importance values portray the individual variation in the importance of each design factor in web page prototype evaluations. The mean importance values also depict a similar trend to the pooled analysis findings; for the majority of the dependent variables, background color was the most important

149

Table 3.2.5. Individual-Level Analysis, Results

Dependent Variable	R Square			Mean Importance Value			
	Minimum	Maximum	Median	White Space	Image Location	Back-ground Color	Image Size
Easy to Read (N=208)	0.020	0.869	0.323	0.3049	0.3312	0.3639	-
Like Look (N=222)	0.051	0.955	0.387	0.2967	0.3020	0.4013	-
Not Cluttered (N=215)	0.043	0.870	0.318	0.3251	0.3253	0.3496	-
Like Image Location (N=220)	0.015	1.000	0.397	0.2422	0.4631	0.2947	-
Easy to Find Product (N=213)	0.017	0.934	0.277	0.3078	0.3413	0.3509	-
Like Color Scheme (N=223)	0.051	1.000	0.441	0.2744	0.2517	0.4738	-
Like Color Use (N=223)	0.047	1.000	0.472	0.2901	0.2265	0.4834	-
East to See Product with Description (N=209)	0.026	0.962	0.333	0.3130	0.3698	0.3172	-
Professional (N=215)	0.033	0.868	0.394	0.3064	0.2934	0.4002	-
Quality Company (N=215)	0.026	0.942	0.326	0.3227	0.2658	0.4115	-
High Budget (N=218)	0.026	0.942	0.356	0.3115	0.2973	0.3912	-
Trust Buying Product (N=210)	0.025	0.927	0.318	0.3127	0.2713	0.4159	-
Won't Continue Search (N=192)	0.049	0.895	0.376	0.2528	0.2345	0.3072	-
Purchase Likely (N=207)	0.080	0.877	0.378	0.2538	0.2219	0.3175	-
Image Size Picked (N=209)	0.079	0.750	0.333	0.2216	0.2901	0.2499	0.2383

150

determinant of prototype ratings. Thumbnail image location was most important for the dependent variables of Like Image Location, Easy to See Product with Description, and Image Size Picked.

The individual attribute part worths allow one to determine which particular attribute levels are preferred by the respondents. The four design factors in this thesis were each varied at two levels. Therefore, the preferred level of each design factor had the higher part worth value. The table below shows the percentage of respondents who preferred each level of the three design factors (background color, thumbnail image location, white space) (Table 3.2.6.). The fourth design factor, thumbnail image size, was varied within-prototype and was thus not included. For some respondents, the part worths for the two attribute levels were zero, indicating that the design factor was not important in their web page prototype evaluation for that dependent variable. In other words, these respondents were indifferent (IND) to changes in the specific design factor.

As seen in the table, a clear difference exists in the percentages of respondents who preferred each attribute level. While some of the attribute levels were preferred by two-thirds of the respondents, other attribute levels were split evenly across the two levels. A white background color was preferred for the majority of the dependent variables, with the exception of Easy to See Product with Description and Trust Buying Product. For Easy to See Product with Description, a pale blue background color (50%) was preferred over a white background color (40%). For Trust Buying Product, preference was equally divided between the white (46%) and pale blue (46%) background colors. Thumbnail image location to the left was highly preferred by respondents over thumbnail image location to the right of the product descriptions; preference percentages were often higher than 50%. Thumbnail image location to the left was most preferred for the dependent variable of Image Size Picked, with a

151

Table 3.2.6. Individual Preference Percentages for Design Factor Levels

Dependent Variable	Background Color Preference			Thumbnail Image Location Preference			White Space Preference		
	Pale blue	IND[z]	White	Right	IND[a]	Left	Less	IND[a]	More
Easy to Read (N=208)	40%	13%	47%	28%	11%	61%	46%	10%	44%
Like Look (N=222)	47%	9%	54%	30%	8%	62%	53%	7%	40%
Not Cluttered (N=215)	41%	11%	48%	27%	10%	63%	44%	6%	50%
Like Image Location (N=220)	42%	11%	47%	32%	8%	60%	46%	12%	42%
Easy to Find Product (N=213)	43%	6%	51%	35%	9%	56%	42%	9%	49%
Like Color Scheme (N=223)	43%	4%	53%	37%	10%	53%	47%	9%	44%
Like Color Use (N=223)	45%	4%	51%	40%	9%	51%	49%	8%	43%
East to See Product with Description (N=209)	50%	10%	40%	25%	9%	66%	48%	9%	43%
Professional (N=215)	43%	9%	48%	32%	10%	58%	53%	8%	39%
Quality Company (N=215)	44%	6%	50%	35%	10%	55%	52%	8%	40%
High Budget (N=218)	39%	11%	50%	39%	11%	50%	49%	11%	40%
Trust Buying Product (N=210)	46%	8%	46%	33%	15%	52%	49%	9%	42%
Won't Continue Search (N=192)	40%	10%	50%	42%	14%	44%	41%	13%	46%
Purchase Likely (N=207)	44%	6%	50%	37%	9%	54%	52%	8%	40%
Image Size Picked (N=209)	29%	16%	55%	14%	14%	72%	45%	21%	34%

a. IND = Indifferent

preference percentage of 72%. Finally, less white space was preferred for the majority of the dependent variables. More white space was preferred for the dependent variables of Not Cluttered (50%), Easy to Find Product (49%), and Won't Continue Search (46%). Increased white space in relation to Not Cluttered and Easy to Find Product may relate to perceptions of web page legibility. The pooled regression model for Won't Continue Search was not significant and is therefore not discussed here. Furthermore, the interaction between white space and color was not included in the table of preference percentages above. On the individual level, this interaction effect was only significant for approximately 10% of the sample for the dependent variables, with the exception of Professional (25%).

3.2.5.1. Sample of Detailed Individual Results

Detailed results reporting for each of the fifteen dependent variables are not presented; instead, the dependent variable Professional is used as a model for the patterns present in the remaining variables seen in Table 3.2.4.

The pooled regression model for Professional had an R square value of 0.17 and was significant ($F_{4, 3659}$ = 15.673, p = .000). An individual analysis of the data portrayed a mean R square value of 0.394, with a minimum value of 0.033 and a maximum value of 0.868. The histogram below shows the high level of heterogeneity in the sample for the Professional model fits (Figure 3.2.16.).

Additionally, the individual analysis showed that background color had the highest mean importance value for ratings of web page professionalism. These findings aligned with the group analysis; responses to "the web page looks professional" were significantly explained in the pooled model by thumbnail image location, background color, and the interaction between background color and white space.

153

Histogram

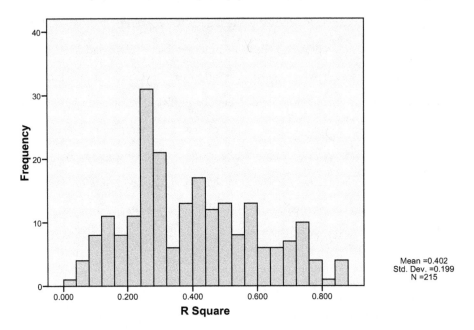

Figure 3.2.16. Individual-Level Analysis, Professional R Square Variability

Variability, however, also existed in the importance level of background color (Figure 3.2.17.). Therefore, while background color was an important indicator of e-commerce web site professionalism for some participants, it was not a factor for others. Similar histograms with a large range between importance values were also present for thumbnail image location and white space (Figure 3.2.18.; Figure 3.2.19.). The interaction between white space and background color on an individual level, however, was only significant for approximately 25% of the sample, compared to approximately 10% for the remaining dependent variables. Thus, while the interaction effect was somewhat important in ratings of web page professionalism, it had minimal impact on other web page prototype ratings.

Histogram

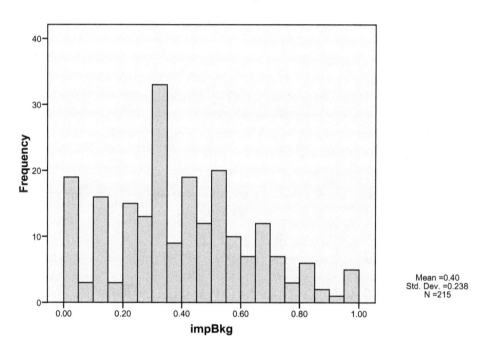

Figure 3.2.17. Individual-Level Analysis, Professional, Importance Values of
Background Color

Histogram

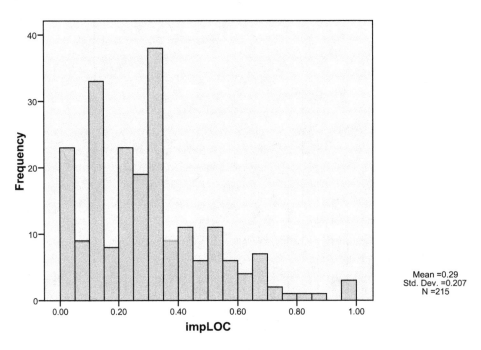

Figure 3.2.18. Individual-Level Analysis, Professional, Importance Values of Thumbnail Image Location

Histogram

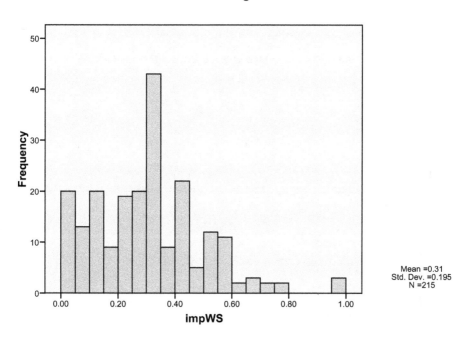

Figure 3.2.19. Individual-Level Analysis, Professional, Importance Values of White Space

The variable Professional serves as a model for the variation evident in the remaining dependent variables. A high level of individual heterogeneity is present in the sample, as can be seen through the histogram plots of the individual R square values and the mean importance values for background color, white space, and thumbnail image location. At the individual level, however, the R square values are much higher and vary around the 0.30 range. The heterogeneity of the data is lost when analyzed at a group level; individual differences counteract each other and result in very low R square values in all of the pooled regression models. Significance at the pooled level of analysis, together with the individual level of analysis, indicates a strong effect of front-end design elements on consumer evaluations of e-commerce web pages.

4. DISCUSSION

This thesis aimed to explore two key research questions. The primary research goal of this study was to examine how front-end web page design variation of four design factors, selected and varied based upon the usability guideline literature, impacted consumer aesthetic and e-retailer evaluations of e-commerce web pages. The secondary research question was to explore how changes in these front-end web page design elements impacted consumer trust, product preference, and purchase intention. Based upon a literature review, a conceptual model was also developed in which web site design was incorporated as an e-retailer strategic component; usability and the iterative user-centered design process provided the foundation in this model for effective, efficient, and satisfying web site design.

4.1. Aesthetic and E-Retailer Evaluations of the Web Page Prototypes

Results indicated that variation of front-end web page design elements impacted aesthetic evaluations of the simulated e-commerce web pages as well as higher-level evaluations of the e-retailer. Main effects indicated that the majority of web page prototypes with thumbnail image location located to the left and with a white background color were rated higher on both aesthetic and e-retailer evaluations by participants.

Additional exploratory individual-level conjoint analysis of the data revealed a high level of heterogeneity in the sample. Therefore, while certain design factors were crucial for some participants in their web page prototype evaluations, for others they may have been less important. This variation was evident in the frequency plots of the

159

individual R square values and mean importance values for each of the design factors. Mean R square values at the individual level varied around 0.30.

Based upon the usability, human-computer interaction, and ergonomics literature it was hypothesized that subjects would prefer the thumbnail image location to the left of the product descriptions because of the natural "F-shaped" scanning pattern (Bekman, 2006), faster image processing and search compared to that of text (Lam, Chau, & Wong, 2007; Woodruff, Rosenholtz, Morrison, Faulring, & Pirolli, 2002; Paivio, 1974), and increased processing and attention to the left-hand side of the web page (Lam, Chau, & Wong, 2007). The results showed that thumbnail image location was highly significant (p<.01) for all aesthetic evaluations of the prototypes, except for Like Color Use, which was significant (p<.05). Moreover, left thumbnail image location resulted in higher subject ratings of Like Look, which was an indication of overall web page aesthetics. Subject aesthetic evaluations of the sixteen web page prototypes showed that left thumbnail location was consistently preferred and perceived as more aesthetically pleasing. Hypothesis 4a of this thesis, "Placement of the thumbnail image array to the left of the product descriptions will be preferred to placement to the right of the product descriptions as seen in higher web page aesthetic ratings" was therefore supported.

Hypothesis 4b regarding thumbnail image location and e-retailer evaluations stated, "Placement of the thumbnail image array to the left of the product descriptions will be positively related to consumer perceptions of the e-retailer as trustworthy, quality, high budget, and professional." Although no literature was found directly connecting thumbnail image location to e-retailer evaluations of Professional, High Budget, Quality Company, or Trust Buying Product, the conceptual model developed in this thesis proposed that aesthetic evaluations of the web page would become the foundation for higher-level evaluations of the e-retailer itself. Therefore, since hypothesis 4a was supported and left thumbnail location was preferred, it was hypothesized that left thumbnail location would also be related to more positive ratings of an e-retailer. Results showed that this was in fact true and hypothesis 4b was supported; left thumbnail image location was highly significant (p<.01) in subject evaluations of the e-retailer as professional, representative of a quality company, and trustworthy for product purchase. Thumbnail image location was moderately significant (p<.05) for the e-retailer evaluation of high budget.

The literature review on background color led to the development of the following hypothesis (H1a): "The white background color will be positively related to web page aesthetic ratings of color, clutter, and legibility." This was hypothesized due to the increased familiarity of consumers to a white web page background color (Bucy & Lang, 1999), the mere exposure effect (Zajonc, 2001), and the association of white with classical web site aesthetics (Tractinsky, 2004). Results indicated that background color was highly significant (p<.01) for evaluations of Easy to Read, Like Look, Not Cluttered, Like Color Scheme, and Like Color Use. It was also moderately significant (p<.05) for the dependent variable of Like Image Location. These results support hypothesis H1a; a white background color was related to higher aesthetic evaluations of the web page on dimensions of color and clutter. The association of a white background color with aesthetic web page evaluations of legibility, however, is less apparent. Although background color was related to Easy to Read, it was not significant for the remaining two dependent variables assessing overall legibility (Easy to See Product with Description, Easy to Find Product). Background color was, however, significant for these legibility assessments in its interaction with white space. Discussion of these interaction effects are provided later in the discussion. Background color was also highly significant for Like Look (p<.01), indicating higher

161

overall aesthetic evaluations for web pages with a white background compared to those with pale blue.

Background color was highly significant for all four e-retailer evaluations (p<.01). Hypothesis H1c was as follows: "The blue background color will be positively related to consumer evaluations of e-retailer trustworthiness and company quality." Based upon the literature, it was hypothesized (H1c) that a blue background color would be associated with higher e-retailer evaluations of trustworthiness and company quality due to its recommendation as a cool color to be used in the background (White, 1990), its association with reduced reading error rates (Pace, 1984), and most importantly, the positive associations of blue with trust and stability in the United States (Lippincott Mercer, 1997; Holzschlag, 1999). Results from this thesis, however, found the opposite effect and hypothesis H1c was not supported. A white background color was related to higher e-retailer ratings along all four dependent variables of Professional, High Budget, Quality Company, and Trust Buying Product. Therefore, hypothesis H1b was supported, which stated: "The white background color will be positively related to web page evaluations of the e-retailer as professional and high budget." The significant association of a white background color with higher e-retailer ratings for all items may have arisen because the study also found that a white background color was be positively associated with web page aesthetic evaluations. White was expected to be related to higher aesthetic ratings due to increased familiarity, the mere exposure effect, and its association with classical aesthetics. Similar to the argument made above for thumbnail image location, the conceptual model developed in this thesis posits that aesthetic evaluations of web pages will influence higher-level consumer evaluations of the e-retailer. Since white background color resulted in more positive aesthetic ratings, it may also have had a positive influence on evaluations of the e-retailer.

Furthermore, many prior studies examining the impact of a blue background color neglected to provide the RGB values of the specific shade of blue studied. This study used a pale blue background color in the web page prototypes to minimize the confounding factor of contrast with overlaid text. The RGB values of this pale blue were provided to ensure that it could be replicated and implemented if desired. Future researchers should ensure that detailed RGB values of background color are provided. Additional issues that may have attributed to the lack of support for hypothesis H1c include the type of display screen utilized (i.e. CRT) and the sample studied. Adults and the elderly may perceive pale blue differently than young adults due to developmental changes in the perceptual system over the lifetime.

Background color had significant effects on both aesthetic and e-retailer evaluations of the web page prototypes. Although this may provide further evidence for the conceptual model, luminance levels were not made equivalent prior to testing. Differences in luminance values between the white (172 cd/m^2) and pale blue (123 cd/m^2) background colors may be the basis for differences in participant evaluations of the web page prototypes. Thus, it is difficult to separate the effects of "color" from those of "brightness". Future research should ensure that luminance values are equivalent in simulated web site designs to test the true impact of background color on consumer evaluations.

The design factor of white space was not significantly associated with consumer aesthetic evaluations for any of the eight Likert statements or significant in any of the four e-retailer evaluations. Therefore, hypothesis H2a was not supported by the results of this thesis: "More white space will be positively related to ratings of web page aesthetics." The literature on white space was limited; although no research was found linking white space to e-retailer evaluations, based upon the conceptual model it was hypothesized that positive aesthetic evaluations would result in positive e-retailer evaluations. Hypothesis H2b, "White space will have a positive impact on consumer perceptions of the e-retailer as trustworthy, representing a quality company, high budget, or professional," was not supported by the results. White space had neither an impact on aesthetic evaluations nor any significant impact on e-retailer evaluations of the web page prototypes.

Although white space as an independent design factor was not significant, its interaction with background color was a significant factor for some aesthetic and e-retailer evaluations of the web page prototypes. In aesthetic evaluations, interaction effects between white space and background color was highly significant ($p<.01$) for the dependent variables of Easy to Read and Easy to See Product with Description, and significant ($p<.05$) for Easy to Find Product. These three dependent variables may be grouped together as assessing overall web page legibility. Web page prototypes with a white background color and more white space resulted in higher subject ratings of legibility than those with less white space; alternatively, web pages with a pale blue background and less white space were rated higher along the legibility dimensions than prototypes with more white space. This interaction effect was especially strong for Easy to See Product with Description, in which a plot of the mean values revealed an interaction effect between the two variables. These aesthetic evaluations portray a complex relationship between consumer aesthetic evaluations of web page legibility; further examination of the basis of the interaction effects observed in this thesis should be conducted.

The interaction between white space and color was also found to be highly significant for e-retailer evaluations Professional ($p<.01$), moderately significant for evaluations of high budget ($p<.05$), and marginally significant for ratings of Trust Buying Product ($p<.07$). These three interaction effects all showed a similar pattern; while web page prototypes with a white background color received higher e-retailer

164

evaluations when there was more white space, prototypes with a pale blue background color received higher ratings when there was less white space. The relationship between subject evaluations of the e-retailer and the independent variables of this study is therefore also complex; three out of the four e-retailer evaluations portrayed an interaction effect between variables.

4.2. The Impact of Gender on Aesthetic and E-Retailer Evaluations

Gender as an independent variable and as a fixed effect in the mixed model was significant for only one dependent variable: Like Image Location. Males rated web page prototypes much higher along the dimension of Like Image Location regardless of thumbnail image location to the left or to the right of the product descriptions. Although gender as an independent variable was only significant for Like Image Location, it was significant for many other aesthetic and e-retailer evaluations through its interactions with color, thumbnail image location, and white space.

The interaction between gender and background color was significant for the aesthetic variable Like Look, which assessed the overall visual appeal of the web page prototypes. Although both males and females preferred the white background color to pale blue, males preferred the white background significantly more than females. Furthermore, male ratings of the visual appeal of the web page were more drastically impacted by a change in background color than those of females. The gender and background color interaction effect was also significant for the e-retailer evaluations of Professional and Quality Company. A similar pattern to Like Look was evident for these variables; males rated the white background color higher than females and their evaluations of the web page changed more significantly with changes in background color. Female responses to Like Look, Professional, and Quality Company followed male preference trends, but rating values were less influenced by background color (evident in the slope of the line).

The interaction between gender and thumbnail image location was also significant for three aesthetic web page evaluations. This interaction effect was significantly related to subject responses for Like Image Location, Easy to Find Product, and Easy to See Product with Description. Males rated web page prototypes with left thumbnail image location higher than females, although the change in image location on ratings of Like Image Location was more pronounced in females. In Easy to Find Product, females rated prototypes with left thumbnail image location as much higher than males; changes in thumbnail image location had a more significant effect on females than males. Finally, although both genders rated prototypes with left thumbnail location higher for Easy to See Product with Description than location to the right, ratings of prototypes with right thumbnail location were similar for both genders. The gender and thumbnail image location interaction was not significant for any e-retailer evaluations.

The final interaction between gender and white space was significant for only two dependent variables: Trust Buying Product and Purchase Likely. Results indicated that males placed higher trust in prototypes with more white space compared to females, while females trusted purchase from prototypes with less white space more than males. A similar, but less exaggerated, effect was also observed in Purchase Likely; males were more likely to purchase from a prototype with more white space and females were more likely to purchase from one with less white space.

The interactions between gender and the design factors showed variation in subject responses and provided additional insight into the heterogeneity present in the sample. The trends in the results discussed above indicate that while male web page evaluations may respond more to changes in background color, female perceptions may be more sensitive to changes in thumbnail image location. Additionally, some sex-based differences may exist in white space preferences of web pages. Results from this study showed that males preferred web page prototypes with more white space while females preferred those with less white space for Trust Buying Product and Purchase Likely. Further research is necessary to understand the relationship between gender, front-end design, and consumer aesthetic and e-retailer evaluations of the web page.

4.3. Consumer Trust, Purchase Intention, and Product Preference

The secondary research question of this thesis asked how front-end web page design elements may impact consumer trust, purchase intention, and product preference, but no explicit hypotheses were advanced.

Consumer trust was only partially evaluated utilizing the dependent variable Trust Buying Product. The front-end web page design elements of thumbnail image location ($p<.01$) and background color ($p<.01$) were significantly associated with Trust Buying Product. The interaction between white space and background color ($p<.07$) was marginally significant. Results provide initial evidence that web page design may influence consumer trust development and further substantiate the conceptual model developed in this thesis. The results showed that front-end web page evaluations impact consumer aesthetic evaluations of a web page and form the basis for higher-level evaluations of the e-retailer, which may impact consumer trust development. Examination of the role of front-end web page design in consumer trust should be conducted with more in-depth measures.

Results indicated that subject responses for Purchase Likely were associated with the design factors of thumbnail image location ($p<.01$) and background color

167

(p<.01). These findings also provide initial evidence that front-end web page design may impact consumer purchase intention from the web page.

The final variable of Image Size Picked included the fourth design factor of Thumbnail Image Size as a fixed effect in the mixed model. Image Size Picked was significant with the design factors of thumbnail image location (p<.01), background color (p<.01), thumbnail image size (p<.01), and the interaction between white space and background color (p<.01). These results indicate that although qualitative responses seemed to point to thumbnail image size as the main driver of product preference, the process may be more involved than being simply based upon thumbnail image size.

Limited research has been conducted in the literature regarding the impact of thumbnail image size on consumer product preference. Hypothesis H3a regarding thumbnail image location was as follows: "The large thumbnail image will be selected for purchase more often than the small thumbnail image." Frequency analysis showed that 73.4% of participants chose the large product image for purchase while only 26.6% of participants selected the small product image. Hypothesis H3a was thus supported by the results. Hypothesis H3b related to the qualitative responses gathered from subjects regarding the reason behind their product selection: "The large thumbnail image will be associated with a higher quality product and will receive more positive qualitative feedback than the small thumbnail image." This hypothesis was also supported by the results; the larger image was commented as being of higher quality, more attractive, and more professional. An especially intriguing finding regarding subject comments and image size were that some participants inferred e-retailer intentions based upon the image size (i.e. "The picture is larger, which seems to indicate pride in the product. The second product, though identically described, seems to be receiving a poor recommendation from the site since its picture is smaller than those of the other products on the page").

The quality and size of the product images on the web page therefore have vast potential implications for the e-retailer. Limited screen real estate places pressure on e-retailers to minimize thumbnail size and white space as much as possible to increase the number of products per screen. Results from this thesis, however, indicate that consumers greatly prefer larger images and that image size influences not only their perceptions about the product, but also the e-retailer's motivations in product promotion. This study examined the first thumbnail image provided by an e-retailer on a product display web page. Future research should explore more interactive thumbnail images that may be zoomed into, rotated, have multiple views, etc. The availability of in-depth images of the product may mitigate the impact of thumbnail image size on consumer evaluations of the web page.

4.4. Individual Differences in E-Commerce Web Page Evaluations

An exploratory analysis of respondent web page prototype evaluations at the individual level showed a high level of heterogeneity in the sample. Mixed model analysis does not report any R square value to indicate the overall 'fit' of the model. Individual level analysis of the same data resulted in R square values that varied around 0.30, which indicated that the models accounted for approximately 30% of the variation in subject responses.

Preference percentages were calculated for each of the two levels of the three between-prototype design factors (background color, thumbnail image location, thumbnail image size) using conjoint analysis methodology. Although one of the two attribute levels was usually more preferred by respondents, preference percentages

169

were rarely one-sided. For Trust Buying Product, percentages of white versus pale blue background color were even. These individual level findings, and often slight differences in preference percentages across the two attribute levels, suggest that the development of high-level, universal usability recommendations should be implemented with caution. This insight was also supported by the differences in subject responses based upon gender, which were discussed in the earlier section. Significant preference differences may exist among individual perceptions of e-commerce web pages. Practitioners should aim to understand their consumers in order to successfully segment the target groups and the respective web site designs.

Web site usability is design in the context of its users; individual differences in an e-retailer's target consumer group must thus be thoroughly understood prior to web site design to ensure that e-retailer perceptions are positive. Given a lack of any universal standards or consensus in the literature, this thesis developed a comprehensive web site design guidelines framework. However, upon closer analysis, the individual differences in web page design preferences observed in this research may provide a basis for the disjointed usability literature: a lack of consensus in the field reflects the inherent heterogeneity in individual evaluations of web page design. Therefore, a more in-depth examination of the factors underlying consumer aesthetic and e-retailer evaluations based upon usability guideline implementation must be studied in the future. Furthermore, the impact of usability guidelines must also be examined on consequent constructs of consumer trust, product preference, purchase intention, and loyalty.

4.5. Contributions of this Research

This thesis developed a web site design guidelines framework based on an analysis of approximately 230 guidelines from the usability, human-computer interaction, human factors, and design literature. The creation of a web site design guidelines framework was necessary due to an inherent limitation in the usability literature: no consensus exists (in the dialogue or in the form of a document) regarding the characteristics that make a web site usable. Web site usability guidelines significantly vary in quality, depth, and empirical support. The development of a web site design guidelines framework therefore compiled various design recommendations from the disjointed literature present in academic journals, expert books, and web guides on the internet. Following selection of the four design factors (background color, thumbnail image location, thumbnail image size, and white space), they were each varied in two levels based upon recommendations in the literature.

Usability measures focus on three key constructs in relation to the user's interaction with a web site: efficiency, effectiveness, and satisfaction. While these three aspects are crucial for user satisfaction with a web site, the ultimate goal of the e-retailer is to engender consumer trust and increase purchase intention. Very little research has assessed the impact of front-end usability web page guideline implementation on consumer evaluations of the e-retailer. The variation of four design elements were thus studied in their impact not only on consumer evaluations of web page aesthetics, but of the e-retailer itself. Furthermore, constructs of consumer trust, product preference, and purchase intention, widely used in the marketing literature, were also explored as a secondary focus.

The present results show that subtle design changes can have a strong influence on evaluations of web page design. Background color (white vs. pale blue), thumbnail image location (left vs. right), white space (less vs. more) and thumbnail image size (large vs. small) each impacted consumer evaluations of web page aesthetics and higher-level evaluations of the e-retailer itself. Between the four factors, thumbnail image location and background color were the most crucial aspects of the web page prototype influencing aesthetic and e-retailer evaluations. The interaction between white space and background color was also important. Gender interactions with background color, thumbnail image size, and white space were significant for numerous web page evaluations, providing initial evidence for the role of consumer characteristics in web page evaluations. These results provide support for the conceptual model developed in this thesis. Although the design changes made across the sixteen web page prototypes were slight, aesthetics and design have been shown in prior research to strongly impact the individual on a very basic, primitive level (Tractinsky, 2004; Fernandes, Lindgaard, Dillon, & Wood, 2003; Norman, 2004; Pham et al. 2001; Zajonc and Markus 1982). These lower-level responses may then sway higher-level cognitions and consumer perceptions of the e-retailer. Therefore, changes in the front-end web page design elements of an e-retailer web site may have crucial implications for the consumer's conscious and unconscious e-retailer web site evaluations. Gender differences in lower-level responses necessitate an in-depth understanding of one's target consumers.

The conceptual model developed here integrated usability and web site design as strategic components of an internet web site. Although prior models have been developed, very few have included the role of front-end design in consumer evaluations of a web page (Fogg et al., 2002; Sultan, Urban, Shankar, & Bart, 2002). As a window to the consumer, aesthetic evaluations of a web site may be the foundation for higher-level evaluations of the e-retailer. The present conceptual model integrates usability and web site design into a process between a consumer's first interaction with the e-retailer and successful development of consumer trust, loyalty, and satisfaction. In this model, web site design becomes not only an aesthetic issue, but one essential to the e-retailer's survival and success in a competitive online marketplace. Although this thesis focused on the e-retailer, the conceptual model may also be broadened and applied to any web site sponsor, including non-profit organizations, government organizations, hospitals, etc. The three strategic components of web site design, web site attributes, and brand equity work together to aid in the development of user trust and to encourage further exploration for any web site sponsor.

Finally, the initial results of this thesis indicate possible conflicts between more usable front-end web page design decisions and positive consumer evaluations. Although a blue background color was considered more usable and ergonomic according to the literature, results indicated that the pale blue studied in this research was associated with lower consumer evaluations of web page aesthetics and e-retailer evaluations. Further research is necessary to explore the impact of prescribed usability guidelines on consumer evaluations of aesthetics and of the e-retailer. Joint research between usability and HCI and marketing is an area of future research with enormous potential.

4.6. Limitations and Future Research

This thesis provides a starting point for the exploration of how front-end web page design elements, varied according the web page design guidelines literature, impact consumer aesthetic evaluations, e-retailer evaluations, consumer trust, purchase intention, and product preference. Results provide initial evidence that front-end design element have the power to significantly influence consumer perceptions of an e-commerce web site. Despite this, numerous limitations of this study provide abundant avenues for future research in the realm of web site design and marketing.

First, this research used university students, which may not be representative of the actual population and may affect the generalizability of the results. Despite this limitation, it maybe argued that comfort and experience with e-commerce websites and use of the internet is much more evident in younger populations. Increased adoption of e-commerce in the future will likely be due to younger, not older, members of society. Second, this research depended on self-report measures of consumer evaluations of aesthetics, the e-retailer, trust, purchase intention, and product preference. Self-report measures are inherently biased by the subject, and are not as strong as objective data techniques.

Next, are limitations associated with the experimental procedure and design of the study. The web page prototypes developed in this thesis displayed eight different products from the categories of electronics or ergonomics products. A broader array of various product categories should be investigated; research has shown that the product category has a significant influence on the prioritization of usability attributes (Venkatesh & Agarwal, 2006). Subjects in this study were also given a scenario in which they were asked to pretend they were considering purchase from the e-commerce web page prototype. This hypothesized scenario resulted in lower involvement with the products shown in the prototypes than if they were actual consumers searching the web with high purchase intention. Research utilizing fully interactive, working web page prototypes may thus be able to counteract this hypothesized effect by asking subjects to complete the entire product search and selection process directly prior to purchase. Despite this limitation, previous research on impression formation and aesthetics have found that initial impressions are rapid, stable, and may influence subsequent cognitive processes. Consumer evaluations of two-dimensional web page prototypes, used in this study, assess this initial and immediate reaction to a stimulus. Research that utilizes fully interactive web sites may not only increase participant involvement, but would also have the ability to test interactive web site design guidelines (i.e. navigation, links) beyond those of only the web page.

More apparent changes in the design factors would also be expected to result in stronger effect sizes. Future research should examine the impact of more exaggerated changes in front-end web page design. In regards to the four design factors selected for study in this thesis, variation of each may have been more exaggerated in the following ways. Background color may be varied not between white and pale blue, but between more vibrant (and less ergonomic) warm colors (i.e. red, orange, yellow) and deeper cool colors (i.e. purple, green, and blue). Use of more vibrant colors would significantly impact not only the overall look-and-feel of the web page, but the amount of contrast with overlaid text. Second, this thesis focused on right versus left thumbnail image location; future research may also study the impact of thumbnail arrays being located both above and below their respective product descriptions. To current knowledge, no studies have been conducted to examine these thumbnail array location differences on the consumer. White space surprisingly had no impact on any aesthetic or e-retailer evaluations in this study. White space was bilaterally and symmetrically varied through the border surrounding the main web page content. Alternative variation of white space may be made more apparent through its variation asymmetrically, within page content (not only in surrounding areas), and in the creation of more congested web page images in which white space significantly impacts legibility. Finally, future research should aim to study the impact of thumbnail image size between web page prototypes as opposed to its implementation as a within-prototype factor. Thumbnail image size may be varied for all thumbnail images in the

175

array as small or large. With screen retail becoming increasingly expensive, e-commerce web sites must balance the demands between small thumbnail images and increased product displays per screen and that of its impact on consumer perceptions of product quality. Future research may provide additional levels in the conjoint analysis that represent subtle as well as more obvious design changes for each design factor.

Furthermore, although this thesis focused on the impact of front-end design elements, interaction design features such as navigation, reactivity, and interactivity are also included as part of the e-retailer strategic component of web site design. Interaction design features were not feasible for study in this thesis due to a lack of time, resources, and knowledge required in web page prototype creation. Future research should aim to assess the impact of these deeper aspects of web site design on consumer evaluations of the web site.

Empirical support for, or improvements upon, the conceptual model developed in this thesis is also an avenue of future research which would encourage further examination of the relationship between usability, web site design, and consumer evaluations of the e-commerce web site. The relative importance between the three strategic components of web site design, web site attributes, and brand equity in the conceptual model requires additional research. Prior research has already demonstrated the importance of security and privacy, FAQ availability, multimedia presence, price, brand, shipping cost, etc. in consumer decision-making and e-commerce sales. Future research may also examine a broader set of front-end design elements beyond the four elements of background color, white space, thumbnail image location, and thumbnail image size selected for this study.

This thesis focused on the e-commerce e-retailer; the conceptual model was therefore examined in this context. As mentioned earlier, the model may be broadened to include any web site presence on the internet, not just that of an e-retailer. Future studies may examine the conceptual model not only in the realm of e-commerce, but in that of non-profit web sites, government organization sites, etc. Front-end web site design elements for those internet sites that have limited brick-and-mortar presence may become increasingly important as consumers become more demanding of usability and visual appeal. The conceptual model may also have important implications for usability practitioners and managers. Many usability proponents must argue for time and additional resources in the product development cycle; empirical research that supports the crucial role of front-end design, usability guidelines, and the iterative design process in consumer evaluations is essential in encouraging increased investment in usability methodology.

APPENDIX 1

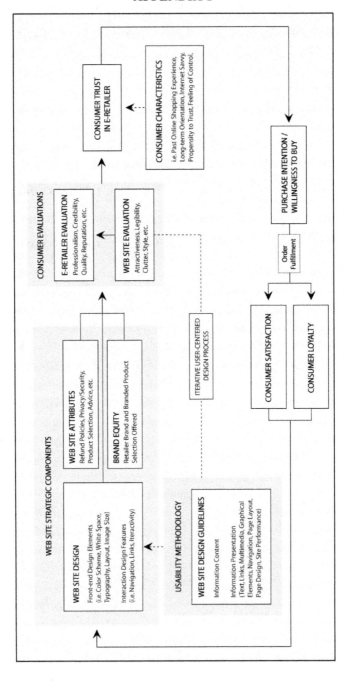

Figure 1.1. Conceptual Model

178

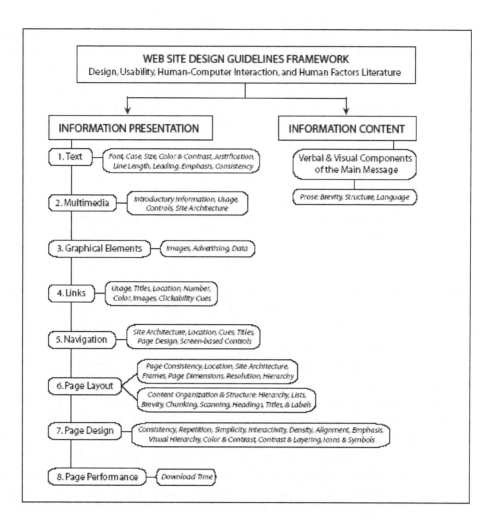

WEB SITE DESIGN GUIDELINES FRAMEWORK
Design, Usability, Human-Computer Interaction, and Human Factors Literature

INFORMATION PRESENTATION

1. Text — Font, Case, Size, Color & Contrast, Justification, Line Length, Leading, Emphasis, Consistency

2. Multimedia — Introductory Information, Usage, Controls, Site Architecture

3. Graphical Elements — Images, Advertising, Data

4. Links — Usage, Titles, Location, Number, Color, Images, Clickability Cues

5. Navigation — Site Architecture, Location, Cues, Titles, Page Design, Screen-based Controls

6. Page Layout — Page Consistency, Location, Site Architecture, Frames, Page Dimensions, Resolution, Hierarchy
— Content Organization & Structure: Hierarchy, Lists, Brevity, Chunking, Scanning, Headings, Titles, & Labels

7. Page Design — Consistency, Repetition, Simplicity, Interactivity, Density, Alignment, Emphasis, Visual Hierarchy, Color & Contrast, Contrast & Layering, Icons & Symbols

8. Page Performance — Download Time

INFORMATION CONTENT

Verbal & Visual Components of the Main Message

Prose: Brevity, Structure, Language

Figure 1.2. Web Design Guidelines Framework

Prototype	Block	Back-ground Color	White Space (WS)	Thumbnail Image Location	Thumbnail Image Size	Layout
1	1	White	More WS	Right	Small	Second

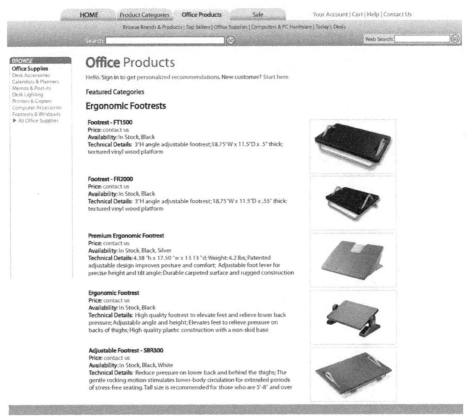

Figure 1.3. Ergonomic Office Products, Ergonomic Footrests

Prototype	Block	Back-ground Color	White Space (WS)	Thumbnail Image Location	Thumbnail Image Size	Layout
2	1	Blue	More WS	Left	Large	First

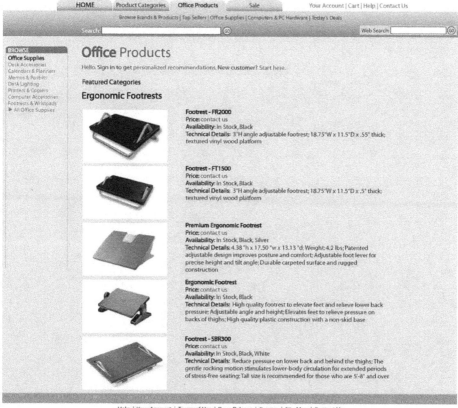

Figure 1.4. Ergonomic Office Products, Ergonomic Footrests

Prototype	Block	Background Color	White Space (WS)	Thumbnail Image Location	Thumbnail Image Size	Layout
3	2	White	More WS	Left	Small	First

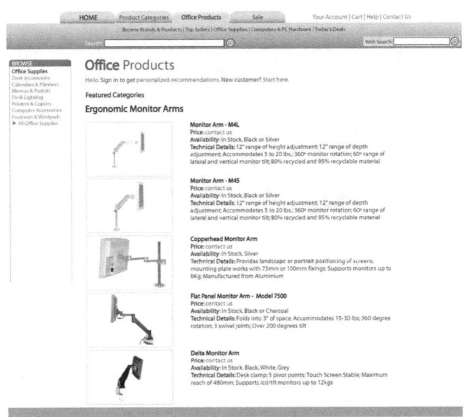

Figure 1.5. Ergonomic Office Products, Ergonomic Monitor Arms

Prototype	Block	Back-ground Color	White Space (WS)	Thumbnail Image Location	Thumbnail Image Size	Layout
4	2	Blue	Less WS	Left	Large	Second

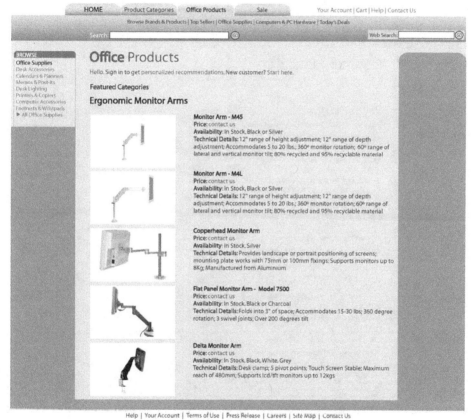

Figure 1.6. Ergonomic Office Products, Ergonomic Monitor Arms

Prototype	Block	Back-ground Color	White Space (WS)	Thumbnail Image Location	Thumbnail Image Size	Layout
5	3	White	More WS	Right	Large	First

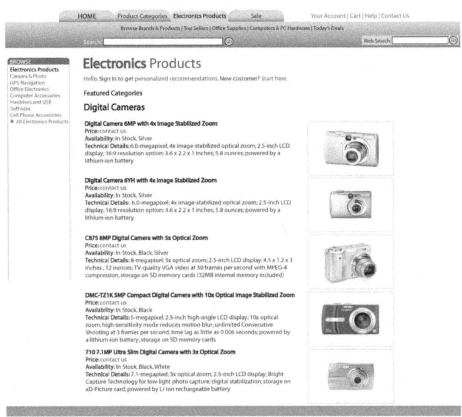

Figure 1.7. Electronics Products, Digital Cameras

Prototype	Block	Back-ground Color	White Space (WS)	Thumbnail Image Location	Thumbnail Image Size	Layout
6	3	Blue	Less WS	Right	Small	Second

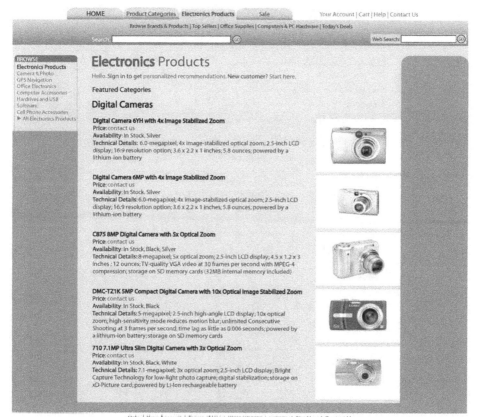

Figure 1.8. Electronics Products, Digital Cameras

Prototype	Block	Background Color	White Space (WS)	Thumbnail Image Location	Thumbnail Image Size	Layout
7	4	White	Less WS	Left	Small	Second

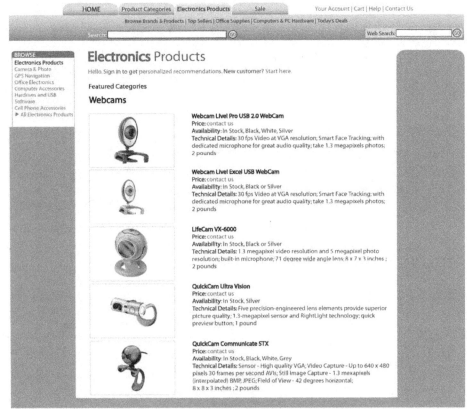

Figure 1.9. Electronics Products, Webcams

Prototype	Block	Back-ground Color	White Space (WS)	Thumbnail Image Location	Thumbnail Image Size	Layout
8	4	Blue	Less WS	Right	Large	First

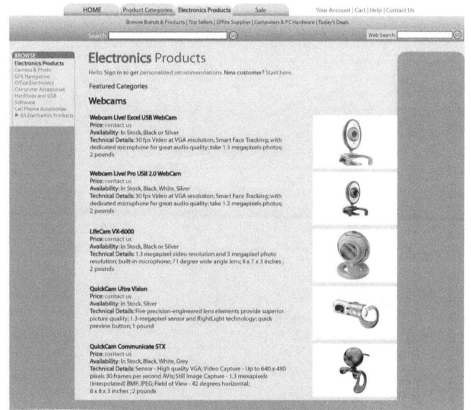

Figure 1.10. Electronics Products, Webcams

187

Prototype	Block	Back-ground Color	White Space (WS)	Thumbnail Image Location	Thumbnail Image Size	Layout
9	5	Blue	More WS	Right	Large	Second

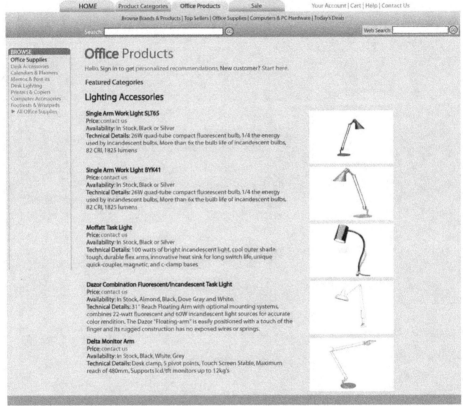

Figure 1.11. Ergonomic Office Products, Lighting Accessories

Prototype	Block	Back-ground Color	White Space (WS)	Thumbnail Image Location	Thumbnail Image Size	Layout
10	5	Blue	Less WS	Left	Small	First

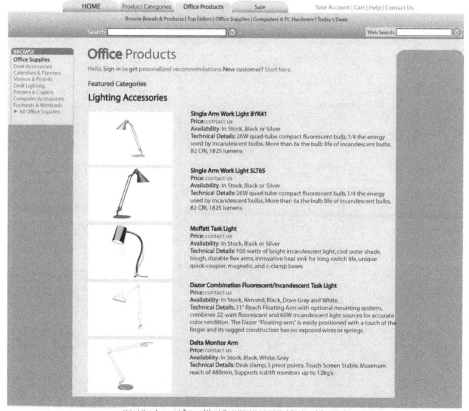

Figure 1.12. Ergonomic Office Products, Lighting Accessories

189

Prototype	Block	Back-ground Color	White Space (WS)	Thumbnail Image Location	Thumbnail Image Size	Layout
11	6	Blue	More WS	Left	Small	Second

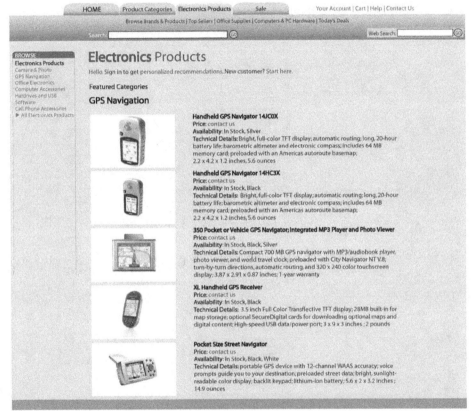

Figure 1.13. Electronics Products, GPS Navigation

Prototype	Block	Background Color	White Space (WS)	Thumbnail Image Location	Thumbnail Image Size	Layout
12	6	White	Less WS	Right	Large	Second

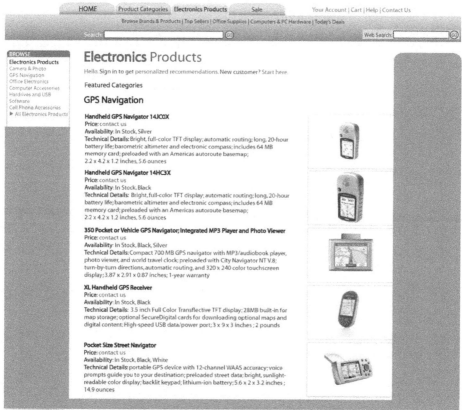

Figure 1.14. Electronics Products, GPS Navigation

Prototype	Block	Back-ground Color	White Space (WS)	Thumbnail Image Location	Thumbnail Image Size	Layout
13	7	White	More WS	Left	Large	Second

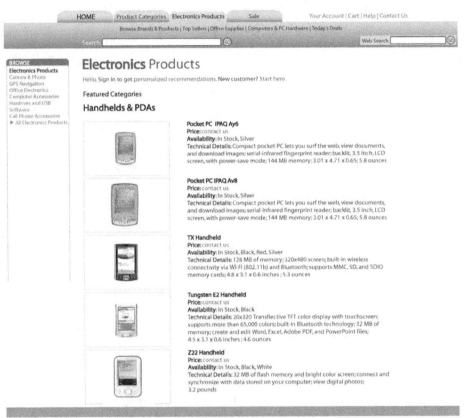

Figure 1.15. Electronics Products, Handhelds and PDAs

Prototype	Block	Back-ground Color	White Space (WS)	Thumbnail Image Location	Thumbnail Image Size	Layout
14	7	White	Less WS	Right	Small	First

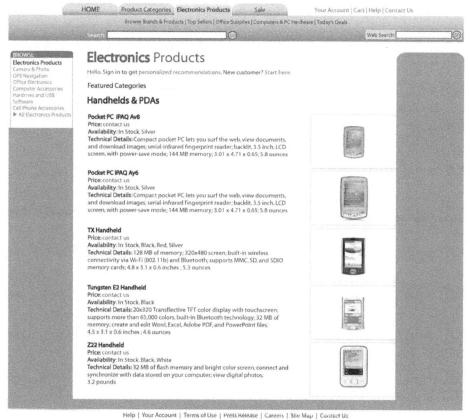

Figure 1.16. Electronics Products, Handhelds and PDAs

Prototype	Block	Background Color	White Space (WS)	Thumbnail Image Location	Thumbnail Image Size	Layout
15	8	White	Less WS	Left	Large	First

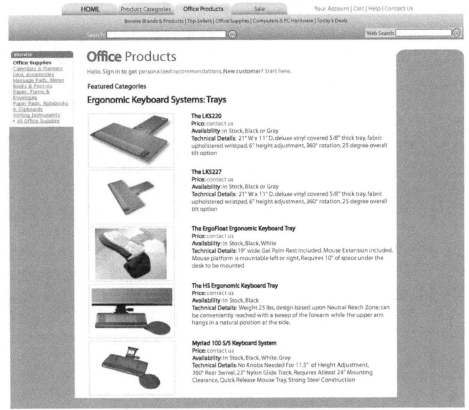

Figure 1.17. Ergonomic Office Products, Ergonomic Keyboard Trays

Prototype	Block	Back-ground Color	White Space (WS)	Thumbnail Image Location	Thumbnail Image Size	Layout
16	8	Blue	More WS	Right	Small	First

Figure 1.18. Ergonomic Office Products, Ergonomic Keyboard Trays

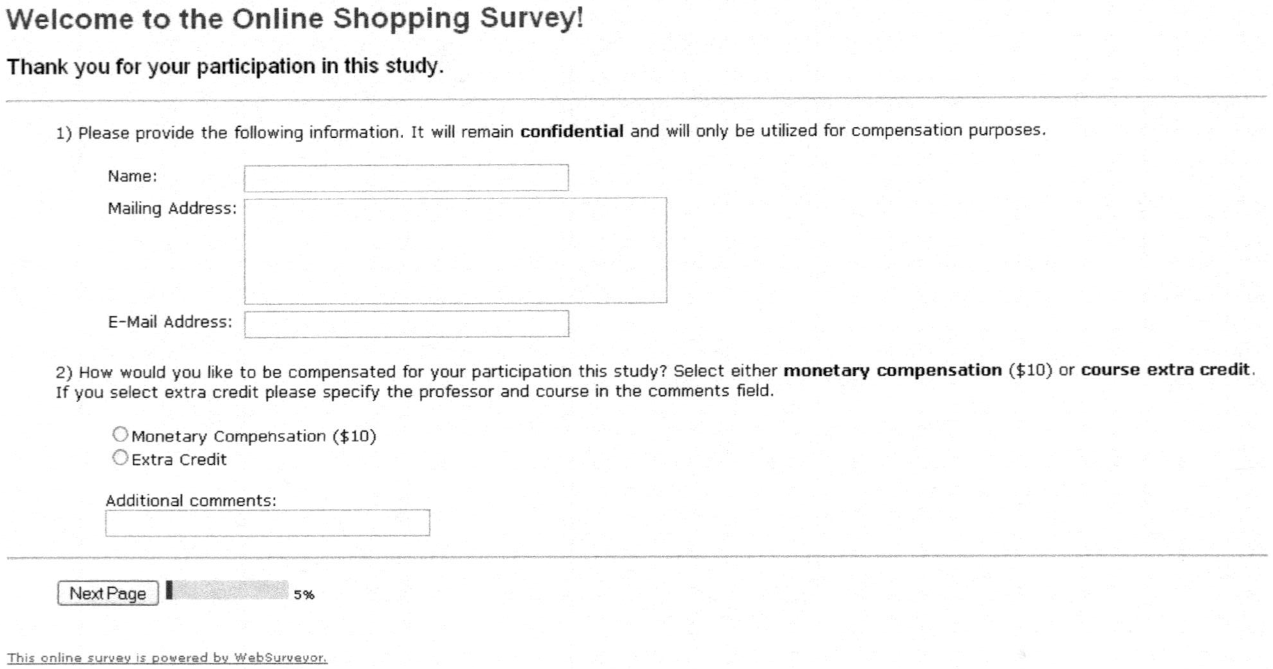

Welcome to the Online Shopping Survey!

Thank you for your participation in this study.

1) Please provide the following information. It will remain **confidential** and will only be utilized for compensation purposes.

Name:

Mailing Address:

E-Mail Address:

2) How would you like to be compensated for your participation this study? Select either **monetary compensation** ($10) or **course extra credit**. If you select extra credit please specify the professor and course in the comments field.

○ Monetary Compensation ($10)
○ Extra Credit

Additional comments:

[Next Page]   ▮ 5%

This online survey is powered by WebSurveyor.

Figure 1.19. Online Survey, Verification and Information Page

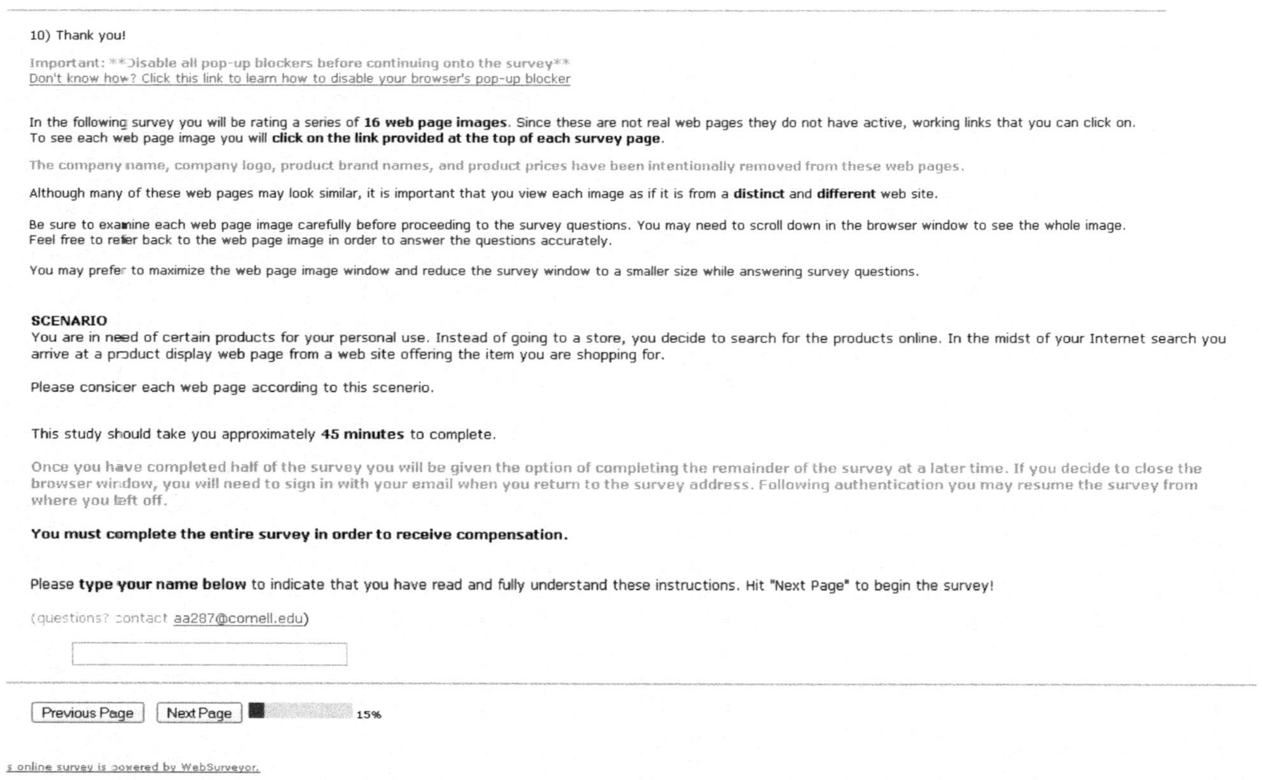

10) Thank you!

Important: **Disable all pop-up blockers before continuing onto the survey**
Don't know how? Click this link to learn how to disable your browser's pop-up blocker

In the following survey you will be rating a series of **16 web page images**. Since these are not real web pages they do not have active, working links that you can click on. To see each web page image you will **click on the link provided at the top of each survey page**.

The company name, company logo, product brand names, and product prices have been intentionally removed from these web pages.

Although many of these web pages may look similar, it is important that you view each image as if it is from a **distinct** and **different** web site.

Be sure to examine each web page image carefully before proceeding to the survey questions. You may need to scroll down in the browser window to see the whole image. Feel free to refer back to the web page image in order to answer the questions accurately.

You may prefer to maximize the web page image window and reduce the survey window to a smaller size while answering survey questions.

SCENARIO
You are in need of certain products for your personal use. Instead of going to a store, you decide to search for the products online. In the midst of your Internet search you arrive at a product display web page from a web site offering the item you are shopping for.

Please consider each web page according to this scenario.

This study should take you approximately **45 minutes** to complete.

Once you have completed half of the survey you will be given the option of completing the remainder of the survey at a later time. If you decide to close the browser window, you will need to sign in with your email when you return to the survey address. Following authentication you may resume the survey from where you left off.

You must complete the entire survey in order to receive compensation.

Please **type your name below** to indicate that you have read and fully understand these instructions. Hit **"Next Page"** to begin the survey!

(questions? contact aa2287@cornell.edu)

Previous Page   Next Page   ■ ▨ 15%

s online survey is powered by WebSurveyor.

Figure 1.20. Online Survey, Instructions Page

11) <u>Click this link to view the first web page image.</u>

Based on the **web page image** provided in the above link, please rate the following statements below on a scale from **Strongly Disagree** to **Strongly Agree**:

	Strongly Disagree	Moderately Disagree	Slightly Disagree	Neither Agree nor Disagree	Slightly Agree	Moderately Agree	Strongly Agree
The web page looks cluttered.	O	O	O	O	O	O	O
I dislike the location of the product images.	O	O	O	O	O	O	O
I would trust buying products from this web page.	O	O	O	O	O	O	O
I dislike how the web page looks.	O	O	O	O	O	O	O
It would be difficult for me to quickly find the product I wanted on this web page.	O	O	O	O	O	O	O
The web page is easy to read.	O	O	O	O	O	O	O
I dislike the color scheme of this web page.	O	O	O	O	O	O	O
I like how color is used on this web page.	O	O	O	O	O	O	O
This looks like a web page for a quality company	O	O	O	O	O	O	O
It is easy for me to see which product description goes with which image.	O	O	O	O	O	O	O
The web page looks professional.	O	O	O	O	O	O	O
This looks like a low-budget web page.	O	O	O	O	O	O	O

12) Imagine you are shopping online for one of the products shown on this web page. Please rate the following statements on a scale from **Highly Unlikely** to **Highly Likely**:

	Highly Unlikely	Moderately Unlikely	Slightly Unlikely	Neither Likely nor Unlikely	Slightly Likely	Moderately Likely	Highly Likely
If you saw this web page, how likely would you be to continue searching for other web pages that have the same products?	O	O	O	O	O	O	O
If this web page offered the product you wanted, how likely would you be to purchase a product from this web page?	O	O	O	O	O	O	O

13) Assuming the products on this web page suit your needs, which of these two products displayed would you be **more likely to purchase**: the **First** or the **Second** product shown on the above web page?

O The First: The LKS220
O The Second: The LKS227

14) **Why?** Briefly explain why you'd be more likely to purchase the product you selected in the previous question.

15) Is there anything you would change with the design of this web page?

Figure 21: Online Survey, Sample Web Page Evaluation Page

APPENDIX 2

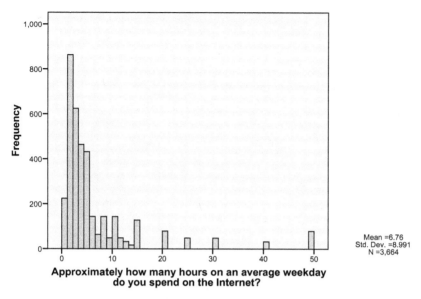

Figure 2.1. Hours spent on the internet on an average weekday

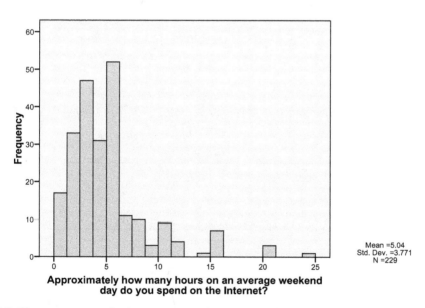

2.2. Hours spent on the internet on an average weekend day (Saturday or Sunday)

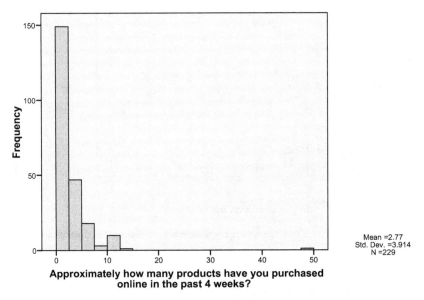

Mean =2.77
Std. Dev. =3.914
N =229

Approximately how many products have you purchased online in the past 4 weeks?

Figure 2.3. Products purchased online in the past four weeks

Table 2.4. Descriptive Statistics, Product purchase online in the past 6 months by category

Statistics

		Music (songs, CDs, etc.)	Books	Software	Office Supplies	Electronics	Computers & PC Hardware	DVDs	Kitchen & Housewares	Apparel or Accessories
N	Valid	233	233	233	233	233	233	233	233	233
	Missing	0	0	0	0	0	0	0	0	0
Mean		2.87	4.32	2.27	1.88	3.63	3.02	2.32	1.51	3.74
Median		2.00	5.00	1.00	1.00	5.00	1.00	1.00	1.00	4.00
Mode		1	5	1	1	1	1	1	1	5

200

Music (songs, CDs, etc.)

		Frequency	Percent	Valid Percent	Cumulative Percent
Valid	Never	116	49.8	49.8	49.8
	Daily	1	.4	.4	50.2
	Weekly	16	6.9	6.9	57.1
	Monthly	23	9.9	9.9	67.0
	Once Every Few Months	51	21.9	21.9	88.8
	Yearly	26	11.2	11.2	100.0
	Total	233	100.0	100.0	

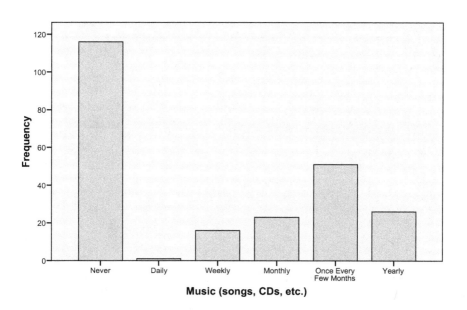

Figure 2.5. Frequencies, Online music purchase (songs, CDs, etc.) in the past 6 months

201

DVDs

		Frequency	Percent	Valid Percent	Cumulative Percent
Valid	Never	156	67.0	67.0	67.0
	Weekly	5	2.1	2.1	69.1
	Monthly	9	3.9	3.9	73.0
	Once Every Few Months	44	18.9	18.9	91.8
	Yearly	19	8.2	8.2	100.0
	Total	233	100.0	100.0	

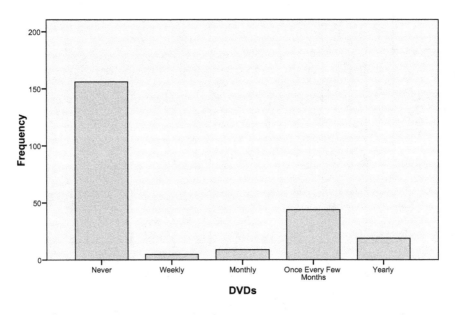

Figure 2.6. Frequencies, Online DVD purchase in the past 6 months

Books

		Frequency	Percent	Valid Percent	Cumulative Percent
Valid	Never	47	20.2	20.2	20.2
	Weekly	3	1.3	1.3	21.5
	Monthly	15	6.4	6.4	27.9
	Once Every Few Months	117	50.2	50.2	78.1
	Yearly	51	21.9	21.9	100.0
	Total	233	100.0	100.0	

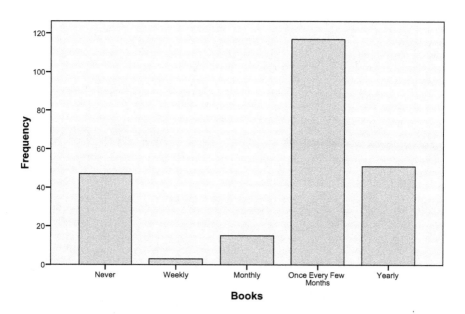

Figure 2.7. Frequencies, Online book purchase in the past 6 months

Electronics

		Frequency	Percent	Valid Percent	Cumulative Percent
Valid	Never	92	39.5	39.5	39.5
	Weekly	1	.4	.4	39.9
	Monthly	13	5.6	5.6	45.5
	Once Every Few Months	64	27.5	27.5	73.0
	Yearly	63	27.0	27.0	100.0
	Total	233	100.0	100.0	

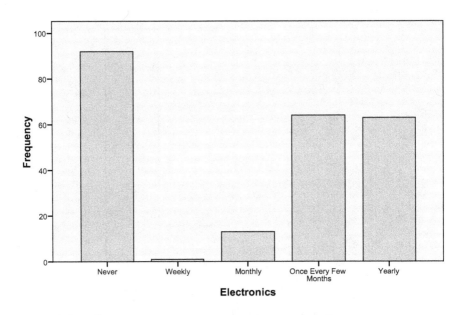

Figure 2.8. Frequencies, Online electronics purchase in the past 6 months

Computers & PC Hardware

		Frequency	Percent	Valid Percent	Cumulative Percent
Valid	Never	131	56.2	56.2	56.2
	Monthly	7	3.0	3.0	59.2
	Once Every Few Months	25	10.7	10.7	70.0
	Yearly	70	30.0	30.0	100.0
	Total	233	100.0	100.0	

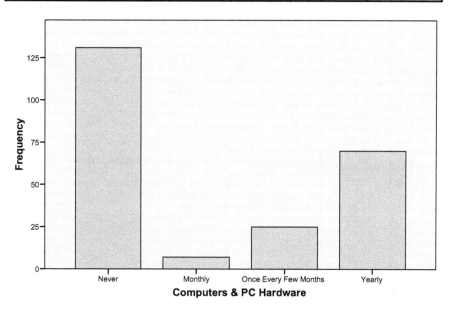

Figure 2.9. Frequencies, Online computer and pc hardware purchase in the past 6 months

Apparel or Accessories

		Frequency	Percent	Valid Percent	Cumulative Percent
Valid	Never	63	27.0	27.0	27.0
	Daily	1	.4	.4	27.5
	Weekly	10	4.3	4.3	31.8
	Monthly	49	21.0	21.0	52.8
	Once Every Few Months	79	33.9	33.9	86.7
	Yearly	31	13.3	13.3	100.0
	Total	233	100.0	100.0	

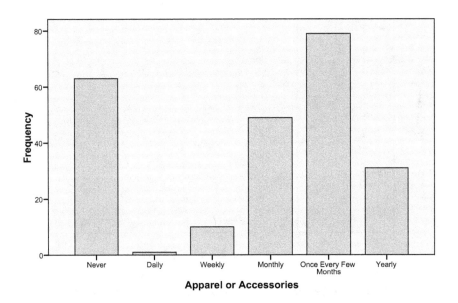

Figure 2.10. Frequencies, Online apparel or accessories purchase in the past 6 months

Software

		Frequency	Percent	Valid Percent	Cumulative Percent
Valid	Never	166	71.2	71.2	71.2
	Monthly	4	1.7	1.7	73.0
	Once Every Few Months	32	13.7	13.7	86.7
	Yearly	31	13.3	13.3	100.0
	Total	233	100.0	100.0	

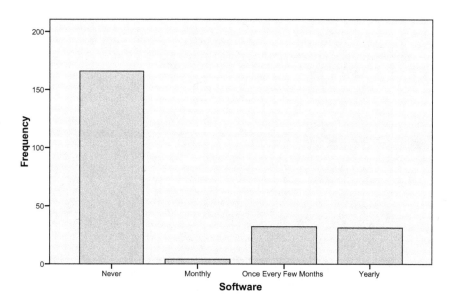

Figure 2.11. Frequencies, online software purchase in the past 6 months

Office Supplies

		Frequency	Percent	Valid Percent	Cumulative Percent
Valid	Never	183	78.5	78.5	78.5
	Weekly	1	.4	.4	79.0
	Monthly	5	2.1	2.1	81.1
	Once Every Few Months	31	13.3	13.3	94.4
	Yearly	13	5.6	5.6	100.0
	Total	233	100.0	100.0	

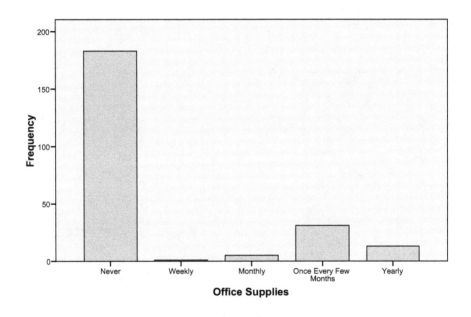

Figure 2.12. Frequencies, Online office supplies purchase in the past 6 months

208

Kitchen & Housewares

		Frequency	Percent	Valid Percent	Cumulative Percent
Valid	Never	207	88.8	88.8	88.8
	Weekly	1	.4	.4	89.3
	Monthly	1	.4	.4	89.7
	Once Every Few Months	7	3.0	3.0	92.7
	Yearly	17	7.3	7.3	100.0
	Total	233	100.0	100.0	

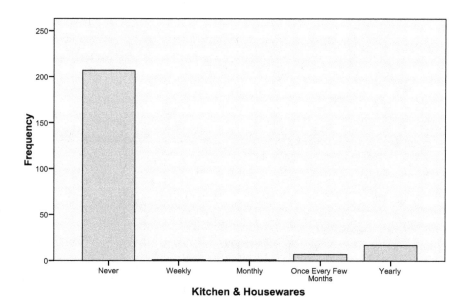

Figure 2.13. Frequencies, Online kitchen and housewares purchase in the past 6 months

I use the internet for shopping.

		Frequency	Percent	Valid Percent	Cumulative Percent
Valid	Strongly Disagree	17	7.4	7.4	7.4
	Moderately Disagree	21	9.2	9.2	16.6
	Slightly Disagree	13	5.7	5.7	22.3
	Neither Agree Nor Disagree	20	8.7	8.7	31.0
	Slightly Agree	71	31.0	31.0	62.0
	Moderately Agree	55	24.0	24.0	86.0
	Strongly Agree	32	14.0	14.0	100.0
	Total	229	100.0	100.0	

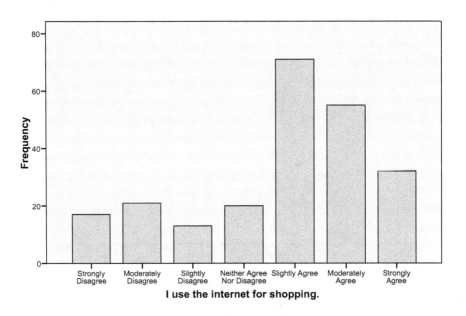

Figure 2.14. Online Shopping Attitudes, I use the internet for shopping

210

I do not like to shop online.

		Frequency	Percent	Valid Percent	Cumulative Percent
Valid	Strongly Disagree	46	20.1	20.1	20.1
	Moderately Disagree	55	24.0	24.0	44.1
	Slightly Disagree	41	17.9	17.9	62.0
	Neither Agree Nor Disagree	40	17.5	17.5	79.5
	Slightly Agree	24	10.5	10.5	90.0
	Moderately Agree	16	7.0	7.0	96.9
	Strongly Agree	7	3.1	3.1	100.0
	Total	229	100.0	100.0	

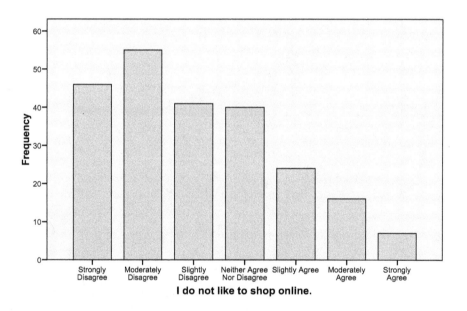

Figure 2.15. Online Shopping Attitudes, I do not like to shop online

211

I prefer shopping online to shopping in an actual store.

		Frequency	Percent	Valid Percent	Cumulative Percent
Valid	Strongly Disagree	35	15.3	15.3	15.3
	Moderately Disagree	59	25.8	25.8	41.0
	Slightly Disagree	49	21.4	21.4	62.4
	Neither Agree Nor Disagree	38	16.6	16.6	79.0
	Slightly Agree	24	10.5	10.5	89.5
	Moderately Agree	14	6.1	6.1	95.6
	Strongly Agree	10	4.4	4.4	100.0
	Total	229	100.0	100.0	

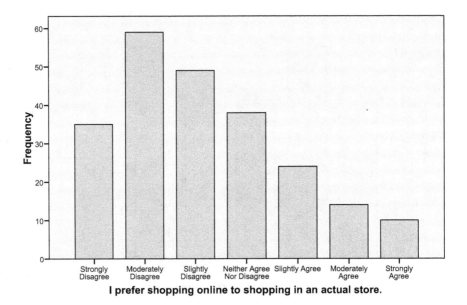

I prefer shopping online to shopping in an actual store.

Figure 2.16. Online Shopping Attitudes, I prefer shopping online to shopping in the actual store

Shopping on the internet is more risky compared to other ways of shopping.

		Frequency	Percent	Valid Percent	Cumulative Percent
Valid	Strongly Disagree	8	3.5	3.5	3.5
	Moderately Disagree	26	11.4	11.4	14.8
	Slightly Disagree	25	10.9	10.9	25.8
	Neither Agree Nor Disagree	11	4.8	4.8	30.6
	Slightly Agree	81	35.4	35.4	65.9
	Moderately Agree	61	26.6	26.6	92.6
	Strongly Agree	17	7.4	7.4	100.0
	Total	229	100.0	100.0	

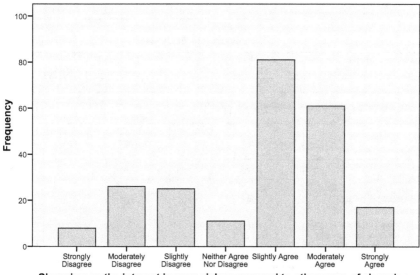

Shopping on the internet is more risky compared to other ways of shopping.

Figure 2.17. Online Shopping Attitudes, Shopping online is more risky compared to other ways of shopping

213

Table 2.18. Online Shopping Attitude Index, Reliability Analysis

Reliability Statistics

Cronbach's Alpha	Cronbach's Alpha Based on Standardized Items	N of Items
.700	.697	4

Item Statistics

	Mean	Std. Deviation	N
I use the internet for shopping.	4.7467	1.75024	3664
I prefer shopping online to shopping in an actual store.	3.1703	1.63548	3664
Shopping on the internet is less risky compared to other ways of shopping	3.3319	1.58725	3664
I like to shop online	4.9258	1.65852	3664

Summary Item Statistics

	Mean	Minimum	Maximum	Range	Maximum / Minimum	Variance	N of Items
Item Means	4.044	3.170	4.926	1.755	1.554	.847	4

Item-Total Statistics

	Scale Mean if Item Deleted	Scale Variance if Item Deleted	Corrected Item-Total Correlation	Squared Multiple Correlation	Cronbach's Alpha if Item Deleted
I use the internet for shopping.	11.4279	13.323	.530	.341	.605
I prefer shopping online to shopping in an actual store.	13.0044	14.122	.518	.318	.615
Shopping on the internet is less risky compared to other ways of shopping	12.8428	17.176	.264	.083	.759
I like to shop online	11.2489	12.714	.651	.446	.526

Scale Statistics

Mean	Variance	Std. Deviation	N of Items
16.1747	23.164	4.81286	4

I make extensive use of the internet.

		Frequency	Percent	Valid Percent	Cumulative Percent
Valid	Strongly Disagree	1	.4	.4	.4
	Moderately Disagree	3	1.3	1.3	1.7
	Slightly Disagree	14	6.1	6.1	7.9
	Neither Agree Nor Disagree	11	4.8	4.8	12.7
	Slightly Agree	46	20.1	20.1	32.8
	Moderately Agree	70	30.6	30.6	63.3
	Strongly Agree	84	36.7	36.7	100.0
	Total	229	100.0	100.0	

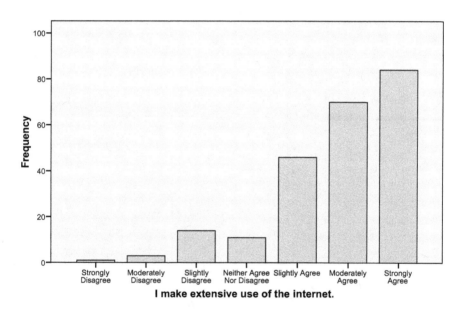

Figure 2.19. Internet Savvy/Experience, I make extensive use of the internet

215

I consider myself to be a novice internet user.

		Frequency	Percent	Valid Percent	Cumulative Percent
Valid	Strongly Disagree	66	28.8	28.8	28.8
	Moderately Disagree	65	28.4	28.4	57.2
	Slightly Disagree	29	12.7	12.7	69.9
	Neither Agree Nor Disagree	23	10.0	10.0	79.9
	Slightly Agree	29	12.7	12.7	92.6
	Moderately Agree	14	6.1	6.1	98.7
	Strongly Agree	3	1.3	1.3	100.0
	Total	229	100.0	100.0	

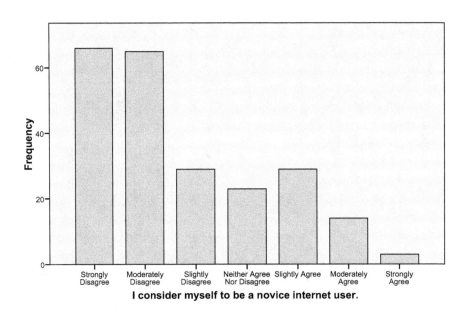

Figure 2.20. Internet Savvy/Experience, I consider myself to be a novice internet user

216

I am confident in my ability to assess trustworthiness of web sites.

		Frequency	Percent	Valid Percent	Cumulative Percent
Valid	Strongly Disagree	7	3.1	3.1	3.1
	Moderately Disagree	9	3.9	3.9	7.0
	Slightly Disagree	30	13.1	13.1	20.1
	Neither Agree Nor Disagree	29	12.7	12.7	32.8
	Slightly Agree	69	30.1	30.1	62.9
	Moderately Agree	69	30.1	30.1	93.0
	Strongly Agree	16	7.0	7.0	100.0
	Total	229	100.0	100.0	

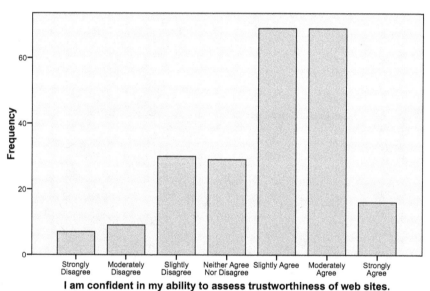

Figure 2.21. Internet Savvy/Experience, I am confident in my ability to assess trustworthiness of web sites

I am confident in my ability to assess the quality of the design of a web site.

		Frequency	Percent	Valid Percent	Cumulative Percent
Valid	Strongly Disagree	3	1.3	1.3	1.3
	Moderately Disagree	9	3.9	3.9	5.2
	Slightly Disagree	23	10.0	10.0	15.3
	Neither Agree Nor Disagree	43	18.8	18.8	34.1
	Slightly Agree	67	29.3	29.3	63.3
	Moderately Agree	61	26.6	26.6	90.0
	Strongly Agree	23	10.0	10.0	100.0
	Total	229	100.0	100.0	

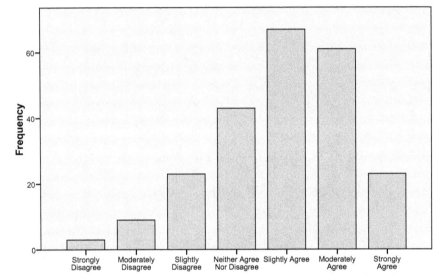

I am confident in my ability to assess the quality of the design of a web site.

Figure 2.22. Internet Savvy/Experience, I am confident in my ability to assess the quality of the design of a web site

218

Table 2.23. Internet Savvy Index, Reliability Analysis

Reliability Statistics

Cronbach's Alpha	Cronbach's Alpha Based on Standardized Items	N of Items
.596	.604	4

Item Statistics

	Mean	Std. Deviation	N
I make extensive use of the internet.	5.8122	1.26254	3664
I consider myself to be an expert internet user	5.2707	1.65255	3664
I am confident in my ability to assess trustworthiness of web sites.	4.8122	1.42812	3664
I am confident in my ability to assess the quality of the design of a web site.	4.9083	1.34649	3664

Summary Item Statistics

	Mean	Minimum	Maximum	Range	Maximum / Minimum	Variance	N of Items
Item Means	5.201	4.812	5.812	1.000	1.208	.205	4

Item-Total Statistics

	Scale Mean if Item Deleted	Scale Variance if Item Deleted	Corrected Item-Total Correlation	Squared Multiple Correlation	Cronbach's Alpha if Item Deleted
I make extensive use of the internet.	14.9913	10.326	.354	.131	.544
I consider myself to be an expert internet user	15.5328	8.880	.323	.113	.580
I am confident in my ability to assess trustworthiness of web sites.	15.9913	9.190	.411	.222	.498
I am confident in my ability to assess the quality of the design of a web site.	15.8952	9.363	.439	.240	.480

Scale Statistics

Mean	Variance	Std. Deviation	N of Items
20.8035	14.791	3.84587	4

I pay close attention to how a web site looks.

		Frequency	Percent	Valid Percent	Cumulative Percent
Valid	Strongly Disagree	1	.4	.4	.4
	Moderately Disagree	16	7.0	7.0	7.4
	Slightly Disagree	22	9.6	9.6	17.0
	Neither Agree Nor Disagree	23	10.0	10.0	27.1
	Slightly Agree	73	31.9	31.9	59.0
	Moderately Agree	59	25.8	25.8	84.7
	Strongly Agree	35	15.3	15.3	100.0
	Total	229	100.0	100.0	

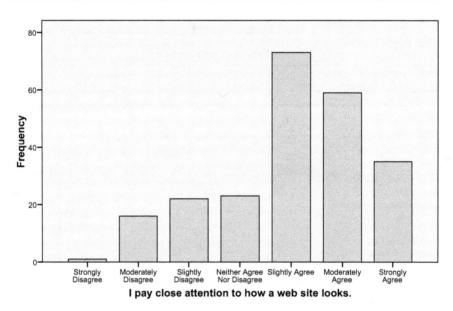

Figure 2.24. Design Mindedness, I pay close attention to how a web site looks

My feelings about a company are impacted by the visual appearance of their web site.

		Frequency	Percent	Valid Percent	Cumulative Percent
Valid	Strongly Disagree	2	.9	.9	.9
	Moderately Disagree	8	3.5	3.5	4.4
	Slightly Disagree	21	9.2	9.2	13.5
	Neither Agree Nor Disagree	23	10.0	10.0	23.6
	Slightly Agree	81	35.4	35.4	59.0
	Moderately Agree	63	27.5	27.5	86.5
	Strongly Agree	31	13.5	13.5	100.0
	Total	229	100.0	100.0	

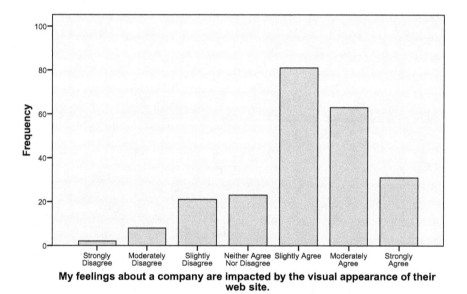

My feelings about a company are impacted by the visual appearance of their web site.

Figure 2.25. Design Mindedness, My feelings about a company are impacted by the visual appearance of their web site

If I dislike the visual appearance of a web page, I will not remain on the web site for very long.

		Frequency	Percent	Valid Percent	Cumulative Percent
Valid	Strongly Disagree	5	2.2	2.2	2.2
	Moderately Disagree	13	5.7	5.7	7.9
	Slightly Disagree	29	12.7	12.7	20.5
	Neither Agree Nor Disagree	24	10.5	10.5	31.0
	Slightly Agree	73	31.9	31.9	62.9
	Moderately Agree	63	27.5	27.5	90.4
	Strongly Agree	22	9.6	9.6	100.0
	Total	229	100.0	100.0	

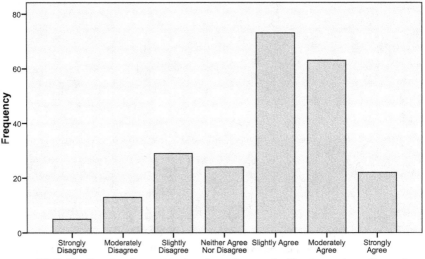

If I dislike the visual appearance of a web page, I will not remain on the web site for very long.

Figure 2.26. Design Mindedness, If I dislike the visual appearance of a web page, I will not remain on the web site for very long

222

Table 2.27. Design Mindedness Index, Reliability Analysis

Reliability Statistics

Cronbach's Alpha[a]	Cronbach's Alpha Based on Standardized Items[a]	N of Items
-.415	-.349	3

a. The value is negative due to a negative average covariance among items. This violates reliability model assumptions. You may want to check item codings.

Item Statistics

	Mean	Std. Deviation	N
If I like the visual appearance of a web page, I will remain on the web site	3.1485	1.45242	3664
I pay close attention to how a web site looks.	5.0437	1.43215	3664
My feelings about a company are impacted by the visual appearance of their web site.	5.1223	1.31283	3664

Summary Item Statistics

	Mean	Minimum	Maximum	Range	Maximum / Minimum	Variance	N of Items
Item Means	4.438	3.148	5.122	1.974	1.627	1.249	3

Item-Total Statistics

	Scale Mean if Item Deleted	Scale Variance if Item Deleted	Corrected Item-Total Correlation	Squared Multiple Correlation	Cronbach's Alpha if Item Deleted
If I like the visual appearance of a web page, I will remain on the web site	10.1659	6.158	-.507	.257	.774
I pay close attention to how a web site looks.	8.2707	2.093	.112	.439	-1.662[a]
My feelings about a company are impacted by the visual appearance of their web site.	8.1921	2.243	.164	.436	-1.710[a]

a. The value is negative due to a negative average covariance among items. This violates reliability model assumptions. You may want to check item codings.

Scale Statistics

Mean	Variance	Std. Deviation	N of Items
13.3144	4.610	2.14705	3

223

Table 3.1. Easy to Read, Mixed Model

Type III Tests of Fixed Effects

Source	Numerator df	Denominator df	F	Sig.
Intercept	1	212.000	26.036	.000
Gender	1	212.000	.493	.483
wspace	1	3428.000	1.161	.281
ImLoc	1	3428.000	43.142	.000
Color	1	3428.000	8.886	.003
Age	1	212.000	.026	.871
HoursonInternetper WeekDay	1	212.000	3.672	.057
HoursonInternetper WeekendDay	1	212.000	.000	.986
ItemsPurchased Online1M	1	212	.082	.775
InternetShopping	1	212.000	1.328	.251
LikeShop	1	212.000	3.855	.051
LessRisky	1	212.000	1.892	.170
PreferOnlineShop	1	212.000	2.675	.103
AssessTrustworthiness	1	212.000	.519	.472
AssessDesignQuality	1	212.000	.144	.704
ExpertUser	1	212.000	1.334	.249
LooksAttention	1	212.000	1.219	.271
CoVisualTrust	1	212	.511	.475
LikeStay	1	212.000	.273	.602
Imakeextensiveuseofthei nternet	1	212.000	1.922	.167
Gender * wspace	1	3428.000	.459	.498
Gender * ImLoc	1	3428.000	.685	.408
Gender * Color	1	3428.000	.233	.630
wspace * Color	1	3428.000	9.925	.002

a. Dependent Variable: etr.

224

Estimates of Fixed Effects[b]

Parameter	Estimate	Std. Error	df	t	Sig.	95% Confidence Interval	
						Lower Bound	Upper Bound
Intercept	4.275906	.837362	213.481	5.106	.000	2.625349	5.926463
[Gender=1]	-.033772	.153734	286.959	-.220	.826	-.336361	.268816
[Gender=2]	0[a]	0	.	.	.	.	.
[wspace=-1]	-.041347	.062608	3428.000	-.660	.509	-.164100	.081407
[wspace=1]	0[a]	0	.	.	.	.	.
[ImLoc=-1]	-.191456	.053985	3428.000	-3.546	.000	-.297302	-.085609
[ImLoc=1]	0[a]	0	.	.	.	.	.
[Color=-1]	.015615	.062608	3428.000	.249	.803	-.107138	.138369
[Color=1]	0[a]	0	.	.	.	.	.
Age	-.005475	.033746	212.000	-.162	.871	-.071995	.061046
HoursonInternetper WeekDay	.016415	.008567	212.000	1.916	.057	-.000471	.033302
HoursonInternetper WeekendDay	.000353	.020654	212.000	.017	.986	-.040359	.041066
ItemsPurchased Online1M	-.004740	.016587	212	-.286	.775	-.037436	.027957
InternetShopping	.053766	.046663	212.000	1.152	.251	-.038218	.145749
LikeShop	.098625	.050231	212.000	1.963	.051	-.000391	.197640
LessRisky	-.058558	.042576	212.000	-1.375	.170	-.142484	.025368
PreferOnlineShop	-.077211	.047212	212.000	-1.635	.103	-.170277	.015855
AssessTrustworthiness	.039043	.054219	212.000	.720	.472	-.067834	.145920
AssessDesignQuality	.020914	.055062	212.000	.380	.704	-.087625	.129453
ExpertUser	-.048329	.041838	212.000	-1.155	.249	-.130800	.034143
LooksAttention	.064729	.058639	212.000	1.104	.271	-.050861	.180318
CoVisualTrust	-.045487	.063620	212	-.715	.475	-.170896	.079921
LikeStay	.025540	.048904	212.000	.522	.602	-.070859	.121940
Imakeextensiveuseofthei nternet	.072472	.052278	212.000	1.386	.167	-.030579	.175522
[Gender=1] * [wspace=-1]	-.045211	.066703	3428.000	-.678	.498	-.175993	.085571
[Gender=1] * [wspace=1]	0[a]	0	.	.	.	.	.
[Gender=2] * [wspace=-1]	0[a]	0	.	.	.	.	.
[Gender=2] * [wspace=1]	0[a]	0	.	.	.	.	.
[Gender=1] * [ImLoc=-1]	-.055211	.066703	3428.000	-.828	.408	-.185993	.075571
[Gender=1] * [ImLoc=1]	0[a]	0	.	.	.	.	.
[Gender=2] * [ImLoc=-1]	0[a]	0	.	.	.	.	.
[Gender=2] * [ImLoc=1]	0[a]	0	.	.	.	.	.
[Gender=1] * [Color=-1]	-.032173	.066703	3428.000	-.482	.630	-.162955	.098609
[Gender=1] * [Color=1]	0[a]	0	.	.	.	.	.
[Gender=2] * [Color=-1]	0[a]	0	.	.	.	.	.
[Gender=2] * [Color=1]	0[a]	0	.	.	.	.	.
[wspace=-1] * [Color=-1]	.199782	.063416	3428.000	3.150	.002	.075444	.324119
[wspace=-1] * [Color=1]	0[a]	0	.	.	.	.	.
[wspace=1] * [Color=-1]	0[a]	0	.	.	.	.	.
[wspace=1] * [Color=1]	0[a]	0	.	.	.	.	.

a. This parameter is set to zero because it is redundant.

b. Dependent Variable: etr.

Table 3.2. Easy to Read, Comparison of Means

Report

Easy to Read

White Space	Thumbnail	Background Color	Mean	N	Std. Deviation
More WS - No Gray Border Present	Right	White Background Color	5.11	458	1.271
		Blue Background Color	4.85	458	1.429
		Total	4.98	916	1.357
	Left	White Background Color	5.26	458	1.186
		Blue Background Color	5.13	458	1.300
		Total	5.19	916	1.245
	Total	White Background Color	5.18	916	1.231
		Blue Background Color	4.99	916	1.372
		Total	5.09	1832	1.307
Less WS - Gray Border Present	Right	White Background Color	4.86	458	1.370
		Blue Background Color	5.02	458	1.296
		Total	4.94	916	1.335
	Left	White Background Color	5.25	458	1.261
		Blue Background Color	5.10	458	1.311
		Total	5.18	916	1.287
	Total	White Background Color	5.06	916	1.331
		Blue Background Color	5.06	916	1.303
		Total	5.06	1832	1.317
Total	Right	White Background Color	4.98	916	1.326
		Blue Background Color	4.94	916	1.366
		Total	4.96	1832	1.346
	Left	White Background Color	5.26	916	1.223
		Blue Background Color	5.12	916	1.305
		Total	5.19	1832	1.266
	Total	White Background Color	5.12	1832	1.283
		Blue Background Color	5.03	1832	1.338
		Total	5.07	3664	1.312

Estimated Marginal Means of Easy to Read

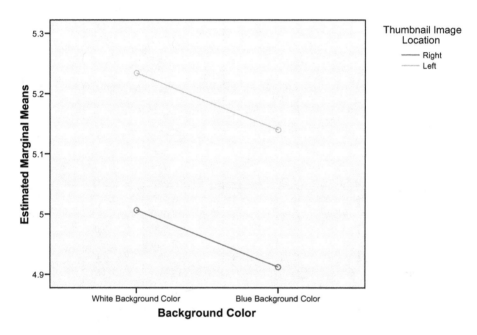

Figure 3.3. Easy to Read, Background Color versus Thumbnail Image Location

Table 3.4. Like Look, Mixed Model

Type III Tests of Fixed Effects[a]

Source	Numerator df	Denominator df	F	Sig.
Intercept	1	212.000	19.951	.000
Gender	1	212	2.127	.146
wspace	1	3428.000	.129	.719
ImLoc	1	3428.000	34.400	.000
Color	1	3428.000	25.030	.000
Age	1	212.000	.010	.921
HoursonInternetper WeekDay	1	212	7.046	.009
HoursonInternetper WeekendDay	1	212	4.482	.035
ItemsPurchased Online1M	1	212.000	.089	.766
InternetShopping	1	212.000	2.322	.129
LikeShop	1	212.000	5.859	.016
LessRisky	1	212	1.798	.181
PreferOnlineShop	1	212	2.347	.127
AssessTrustworthiness	1	212.000	1.474	.226
AssessDesignQuality	1	212.000	1.272	.261
ExpertUser	1	212.000	.020	.888
LooksAttention	1	212.000	.083	.774
CoVisualTrust	1	212.000	.023	.879
LikeStay	1	212.000	.316	.575
Imakeextensiveuseoftheinternet	1	212.000	.064	.800
Gender * wspace	1	3428.000	.621	.431
Gender * ImLoc	1	3428.000	1.498	.221
Gender * Color	1	3428.000	5.531	.019
wspace * Color	1	3428	2.297	.130

a. Dependent Variable: dislook.

Estimates of Fixed Effects[b]

Parameter	Estimate	Std. Error	df	t	Sig.	95% Confidence Interval	
						Lower Bound	Upper Bound
Intercept	3.706971	.836895	214.629	4.429	.000	2.057386	5.356556
[Gender=1]	-.013991	.161593	351.711	-.087	.931	-.331801	.303820
[Gender=2]	0[a]	0	.	.	.	.	.
[wspace=-1]	-.044877	.083195	3428.000	-.539	.590	-.207993	.118239
[wspace=1]	0[a]	0	.	.	.	.	.
[lmLoc=-1]	-.205696	.071736	3428.000	-2.867	.004	-.346346	-.065046
[lmLoc=1]	0[a]	0	.	.	.	.	.
[Color=-1]	.262085	.083195	3428.000	3.150	.002	.098969	.425201
[Color=1]	0[a]	0	.	.	.	.	.
Age	.003331	.033682	212.000	.099	.921	-.063064	.069725
HoursonInternetper WeekDay	.022697	.008550	212	2.654	.009	.005842	.039551
HoursonInternetper WeekendDay	-.043641	.020615	212	-2.117	.035	-.084277	-.003005
ItemsPurchased Online1M	.004936	.016555	212.000	.298	.766	-.027699	.037570
InternetShopping	-.070967	.046575	212.000	-1.524	.129	-.162776	.020842
LikeShop	.121351	.050135	212.000	2.420	.016	.022524	.220179
LessRisky	-.056984	.042495	212	-1.341	.181	-.140751	.026783
PreferOnlineShop	-.072197	.047123	212	-1.532	.127	-.165086	.020693
AssessTrustworthiness	.065693	.054116	212.000	1.214	.226	-.040981	.172367
AssessDesignQuality	.061979	.054957	212.000	1.128	.261	-.046354	.170312
ExpertUser	-.005909	.041758	212.000	-.142	.888	-.088224	.076406
LooksAttention	.016841	.058527	212.000	.288	.774	-.098529	.132211
CoVisualTrust	-.009654	.063499	212.000	-.152	.879	-.134824	.115517
LikeStay	.027442	.048811	212.000	.562	.575	-.068775	.123659
Imakeextensiveuseofthei nternet	.013224	.052178	212.000	.253	.800	-.089631	.116079
[Gender=1] * [wspace=-1]	-.069821	.088636	3428.000	-.788	.431	-.243605	.103964
[Gender=1] * [wspace=1]	0[a]	0	.	.	.	.	.
[Gender=2] * [wspace=-1]	0[a]	0	.	.	.	.	.
[Gender=2] * [wspace=1]	0[a]	0	.	.	.	.	.
[Gender=1] * [lmLoc=-1]	-.108470	.088636	3428.000	-1.224	.221	-.282255	.065314
[Gender=1] * [lmLoc=1]	0[a]	0	.	.	.	.	.
[Gender=2] * [lmLoc=-1]	0[a]	0	.	.	.	.	.
[Gender=2] * [lmLoc=1]	0[a]	0	.	.	.	.	.
[Gender=1] * [Color=-1]	-.208449	.088636	3428.000	-2.352	.019	-.382234	-.034665
[Gender=1] * [Color=1]	0[a]	0	.	.	.	.	.
[Gender=2] * [Color=-1]	0[a]	0	.	.	.	.	.
[Gender=2] * [Color=1]	0[a]	0	.	.	.	.	.
[wspace=-1] * [Color=-1]	.127729	.084268	3428	1.516	.130	-.037492	.292950
[wspace=-1] * [Color=1]	0[a]	0	.	.	.	.	.
[wspace=1] * [Color=-1]	0[a]	0	.	.	.	.	.
[wspace=1] * [Color=1]	0[a]	0	.	.	.	.	.

a. This parameter is set to zero because it is redundant.

b. Dependent Variable: dislook.

Table 3.5. Like Look, Comparison of Means

Report

Like Look

White Space	Thumbnail	Background Color	Mean	N	Std. Deviation
More White Space	Right	White Background Color	4.29	458	1.478
		Blue Background Color	3.93	458	1.569
		Total	4.11	916	1.534
	Left	White Background Color	4.44	458	1.506
		Blue Background Color	4.30	458	1.584
		Total	4.37	916	1.546
	Total	White Background Color	4.37	916	1.493
		Blue Background Color	4.11	916	1.587
		Total	4.24	1832	1.546
Less White Space	Right	White Background Color	4.09	458	1.540
		Blue Background Color	4.15	458	1.538
		Total	4.12	916	1.539
	Left	White Background Color	4.57	458	1.513
		Blue Background Color	4.26	458	1.541
		Total	4.41	916	1.534
	Total	White Background Color	4.33	916	1.544
		Blue Background Color	4.20	916	1.540
		Total	4.27	1832	1.543
Total	Right	White Background Color	4.19	916	1.512
		Blue Background Color	4.04	916	1.557
		Total	4.12	1832	1.536
	Left	White Background Color	4.51	916	1.510
		Blue Background Color	4.28	916	1.562
		Total	4.39	1832	1.540
	Total	White Background Color	4.35	1832	1.519
		Blue Background Color	4.16	1832	1.564
		Total	4.25	3664	1.544

Estimated Marginal Means of Like Look

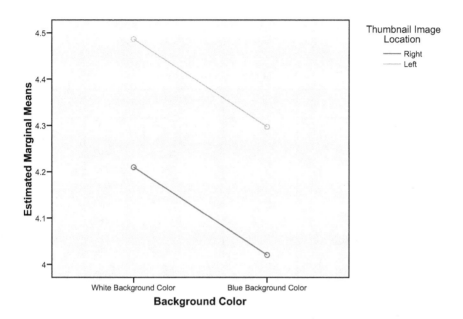

Figure 3.6. Like Look, Background Color versus Thumbnail Image Location

Table 3.7. Like Look, Comparison of Means, Gender versus Color

Descriptive Statistics

Dependent Variable: dislook

Color	Gender	Mean	Std. Deviation	N
White Background Color	Female	4.24	1.516	1200
	Male	4.56	1.502	632
	Total	4.35	1.519	1832
Blue Background Color	Female	4.12	1.555	1200
	Male	4.23	1.579	632
	Total	4.16	1.564	1832
Total	Female	4.18	1.536	2400
	Male	4.40	1.549	1264
	Total	4.25	1.544	3664

Table 3.8. Not Cluttered, Mixed Model

Type III Tests of Fixed Effects[a]

Source	Numerator df	Denominator df	F	Sig.
Intercept	1	212.000	19.350	.000
Gender	1	212.000	.446	.505
wspace	1	3428	2.624	.105
ImLoc	1	3428	48.322	.000
Color	1	3428	9.962	.002
Age	1	212.000	.006	.936
HoursonInternetper WeekDay	1	212	5.468	.020
HoursonInternetper WeekendDay	1	212	2.535	.113
ItemsPurchased Online1M	1	212.000	1.033	.311
InternetShopping	1	212.000	.128	.721
LikeShop	1	212	1.483	.225
LessRisky	1	212.000	.429	.513
PreferOnlineShop	1	212.000	.718	.398
AssessTrustworthiness	1	212	.452	.502
AssessDesignQuality	1	212	2.727	.100
ExpertUser	1	212	.113	.737
LooksAttention	1	212.000	.801	.372
CoVisualTrust	1	212.000	1.306	.254
LikeStay	1	212.000	1.916	.168
Imakeextensiveuseofthei nternet	1	212.000	.181	.671
Gender * wspace	1	3428	.181	.670
Gender * ImLoc	1	3428	1.170	.280
Gender * Color	1	3428	.570	.450
wspace * Color	1	3428	2.350	.125

a. Dependent Variable: clutter.

Estimates of Fixed Effects[b]

Parameter	Estimate	Std. Error	df	t	Sig.	95% Confidence Interval	
						Lower Bound	Upper Bound
Intercept	4.026221	.938783	213.341	4.289	.000	2.175742	5.876700
[Gender=1]	.133441	.171226	279.421	.779	.436	-.203616	.470497
[Gender=2]	0[a]	0	.	.	.	.	.
[wspace=-1]	.020929	.066796	3428	.313	.754	-.110035	.151893
[wspace=1]	0[a]	0	.	.	.	.	.
[ImLoc=-1]	-.208861	.057596	3428	-3.626	.000	-.321787	-.095934
[ImLoc=1]	0[a]	0	.	.	.	.	.
[Color=-1]	.033587	.066796	3428	.503	.615	-.097377	.164551
[Color=1]	0[a]	0	.	.	.	.	.
Age	.003025	.037839	212.000	.080	.936	-.071564	.077615
HoursonInternetper WeekDay	.022462	.009606	212	2.338	.020	.003527	.041397
HoursonInternetper WeekendDay	-.036873	.023159	212	-1.592	.113	-.082525	.008778
ItemsPurchased Online1M	-.018904	.018599	212.000	-1.016	.311	-.055567	.017758
InternetShopping	-.018729	.052324	212.000	-.358	.721	-.121870	.084413
LikeShop	.068599	.056324	212	1.218	.225	-.042427	.179626
LessRisky	-.031283	.047740	212.000	-.655	.513	-.125390	.062824
PreferOnlineShop	-.044848	.052940	212.000	-.847	.398	-.149203	.059508
AssessTrustworthiness	.040877	.060796	212	.672	.502	-.078965	.160718
AssessDesignQuality	.101965	.061741	212	1.651	.100	-.019740	.223670
ExpertUser	.015763	.046913	212	.336	.737	-.076713	.108239
LooksAttention	.058834	.065752	212.000	.895	.372	-.070777	.188444
CoVisualTrust	-.081512	.071337	212.000	-1.143	.254	-.222133	.059109
LikeStay	.075894	.054836	212.000	1.384	.168	-.032199	.183987
Imakeextensiveuseofthei nternet	-.024930	.058619	212.000	-.425	.671	-.140482	.090621
[Gender=1] * [wspace=-1]	-.030285	.071165	3428	-.426	.670	-.169815	.109245
[Gender=1] * [wspace=1]	0[a]	0	.	.	.	.	.
[Gender=2] * [wspace=-1]	0[a]	0	.	.	.	.	.
[Gender=2] * [wspace=1]	0[a]	0	.	.	.	.	.
[Gender=1] * [ImLoc=-1]	-.076973	.071165	3428	-1.082	.280	-.216503	.062557
[Gender=1] * [ImLoc=1]	0[a]	0	.	.	.	.	.
[Gender=2] * [ImLoc=-1]	0[a]	0	.	.	.	.	.
[Gender=2] * [ImLoc=1]	0[a]	0	.	.	.	.	.
[Gender=1] * [Color=-1]	.053724	.071165	3428	.755	.450	-.085806	.193254
[Gender=1] * [Color=1]	0[a]	0	.	.	.	.	.
[Gender=2] * [Color=-1]	0[a]	0	.	.	.	.	.
[Gender=2] * [Color=1]	0[a]	0	.	.	.	.	.
[wspace=-1] * [Color=-1]	.103712	.067658	3428	1.533	.125	-.028942	.236366
[wspace=-1] * [Color=1]	0[a]	0	.	.	.	.	.
[wspace=1] * [Color=-1]	0[a]	0	.	.	.	.	.
[wspace=1] * [Color=1]	0[a]	0	.	.	.	.	.

a. This parameter is set to zero because it is redundant.

b. Dependent Variable: clutter.

233

Report

Not Cluttered

White Space	Thumbnail	Background Color	Mean	N	Std. Deviation
More White Space	Right	White Background Color	4.78	458	1.410
		Blue Background Color	4.55	458	1.504
		Total	4.67	916	1.461
	Left	White Background Color	5.00	458	1.306
		Blue Background Color	4.88	458	1.377
		Total	4.94	916	1.342
	Total	White Background Color	4.89	916	1.363
		Blue Background Color	4.72	916	1.450
		Total	4.80	1832	1.409
Less White Space	Right	White Background Color	4.59	458	1.476
		Blue Background Color	4.67	458	1.454
		Total	4.63	916	1.464
	Left	White Background Color	4.98	458	1.344
		Blue Background Color	4.76	458	1.427
		Total	4.87	916	1.390
	Total	White Background Color	4.78	916	1.425
		Blue Background Color	4.72	916	1.440
		Total	4.75	1832	1.433
Total	Right	White Background Color	4.68	916	1.446
		Blue Background Color	4.61	916	1.479
		Total	4.65	1832	1.463
	Left	White Background Color	4.99	916	1.324
		Blue Background Color	4.82	916	1.403
		Total	4.91	1832	1.366
	Total	White Background Color	4.84	1832	1.395
		Blue Background Color	4.72	1832	1.445
		Total	4.78	3664	1.421

Table 3.9. Not Cluttered, Comparison of Means

Estimated Marginal Means of Not Cluttered

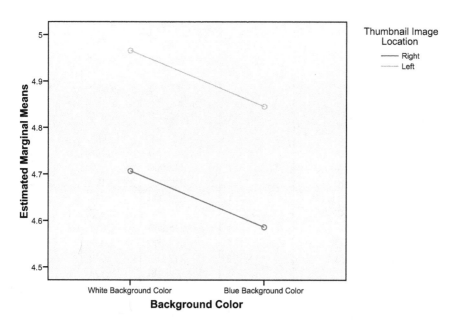

Figure 3.10. Not Cluttered, Background Color versus Thumbnail Image Location

Type III Tests of Fixed Effects[a]

Source	Numerator df	Denominator df	F	Sig.
Intercept	1	212.000	26.163	.000
Gender	1	212.000	7.694	.006
wspace	1	3428.000	.357	.550
ImLoc	1	3428.000	219.335	.000
Color	1	3428.000	4.416	.036
Age	1	212.000	1.293	.257
HoursonInternetper WeekDay	1	212.000	9.116	.003
HoursonInternetper WeekendDay	1	212.000	2.927	.089
ItemsPurchased Online1M	1	212.000	.435	.510
InternetShopping	1	212.000	.091	.764
LikeShop	1	212.000	7.104	.008
LessRisky	1	212.000	.002	.964
PreferOnlineShop	1	212.000	2.154	.144
AssessTrustworthiness	1	212.000	.244	.622
AssessDesignQuality	1	212.000	4.477	.036
ExpertUser	1	212.000	.631	.428
LooksAttention	1	212.000	1.058	.305
CoVisualTrust	1	212.000	.013	.911
LikeStay	1	212.000	.194	.660
Imakeextensiveuseofthei nternet	1	212.000	.158	.691
Gender * wspace	1	3428.000	.149	.699
Gender * ImLoc	1	3428.000	16.801	.000
Gender * Color	1	3428.000	.736	.391
wspace * Color	1	3428.000	.569	.451

a. Dependent Variable: Dslkim.

Table 3.11. Like Image Location, Regression Model

236

Estimates of Fixed Effects[b]

Parameter	Estimate	Std. Error	df	t	Sig.	95% Confidence Interval	
						Lower Bound	Upper Bound
Intercept	4.123799	.755425	215.321	5.459	.000	2.634824	5.612774
[Gender=1]	-.150467	.149996	393.352	-1.003	.316	-.445360	.144427
[Gender=2]	0[a]	0	.	.	.	.	.
[wspace=-1]	-.022712	.084303	3428.000	-.269	.788	-.188000	.142577
[wspace=1]	0[a]	0	.	.	.	.	.
[ImLoc=-1]	-.481013	.072692	3428.000	-6.617	.000	-.623536	-.338490
[ImLoc=1]	0[a]	0	.	.	.	.	.
[Color=-1]	.100706	.084303	3428.000	1.195	.232	-.064582	.265995
[Color=1]	0[a]	0	.	.	.	.	.
Age	.034538	.030379	212.000	1.137	.257	-.025344	.094421
HoursonInternetper WeekDay	.023284	.007712	212.000	3.019	.003	.008082	.038485
HoursonInternetper WeekendDay	-.031812	.018593	212.000	-1.711	.089	-.068462	.004838
ItemsPurchased Online1M	-.009843	.014932	212.000	-.659	.510	-.039277	.019590
InternetShopping	-.012640	.042007	212.000	-.301	.764	-.095445	.070164
LikeShop	.120522	.045218	212.000	2.665	.008	.031386	.209657
LessRisky	.001716	.038327	212.000	.045	.964	-.073836	.077267
PreferOnlineShop	-.062380	.042501	212.000	-1.468	.144	-.146159	.021400
AssessTrustworthiness	-.024086	.048809	212.000	-.493	.622	-.120298	.072126
AssessDesignQuality	.104874	.049568	212.000	2.116	.036	.007166	.202583
ExpertUser	-.029917	.037663	212.000	-.794	.428	-.104159	.044325
LooksAttention	-.054303	.052787	212.000	-1.029	.305	-.158358	.049753
CoVisualTrust	-.006411	.057271	212.000	-.112	.911	-.119306	.106483
LikeStay	.019391	.044024	212.000	.440	.660	-.067390	.106171
Imakeextensiveuseofthei nternet	-.018714	.047061	212.000	-.398	.691	-.111482	.074054
[Gender=1] * [wspace=-1]	.034673	.089816	3428.000	.386	.699	-.141426	.210772
[Gender=1] * [wspace=1]	0[a]	0	.	.	.	.	.
[Gender=2] * [wspace=-1]	0[a]	0	.	.	.	.	.
[Gender=2] * [wspace=1]	0[a]	0	.	.	.	.	.
[Gender=1] * [ImLoc=-1]	-.368154	.089816	3428.000	-4.099	.000	-.544253	-.192055
[Gender=1] * [ImLoc=1]	0[a]	0	.	.	.	.	.
[Gender=2] * [ImLoc=-1]	0[a]	0	.	.	.	.	.
[Gender=2] * [ImLoc=1]	0[a]	0	.	.	.	.	.
[Gender=1] * [Color=-1]	-.077078	.089816	3428.000	-.858	.391	-.253177	.099021
[Gender=1] * [Color=1]	0[a]	0	.	.	.	.	.
[Gender=2] * [Color=-1]	0[a]	0	.	.	.	.	.
[Gender=2] * [Color=1]	0[a]	0	.	.	.	.	.
[wspace=-1] * [Color=-1]	.064410	.085391	3428.000	.754	.451	-.103011	.231832
[wspace=-1] * [Color=1]	0[a]	0	.	.	.	.	.
[wspace=1] * [Color=-1]	0[a]	0	.	.	.	.	.
[wspace=1] * [Color=1]	0[a]	0	.	.	.	.	.

a. This parameter is set to zero because it is redundant.

b. Dependent Variable: Dslkim.

237

Table 3.12. Like Image Location, Comparison of Means

Report

Like Image Location

White Space	Thumbnail	Background Color	Mean	N	Std. Deviation
More White Space	Right	White Background Color	4.36	458	1.635
		Blue Background Color	4.19	458	1.657
		Total	4.27	916	1.648
	Left	White Background Color	4.99	458	1.388
		Blue Background Color	4.93	458	1.422
		Total	4.96	916	1.404
	Total	White Background Color	4.67	916	1.547
		Blue Background Color	4.56	916	1.588
		Total	4.62	1832	1.569
Less White Space	Right	White Background Color	4.15	458	1.568
		Blue Background Color	4.26	458	1.588
		Total	4.21	916	1.579
	Left	White Background Color	5.07	458	1.356
		Blue Background Color	4.86	458	1.394
		Total	4.96	916	1.379
	Total	White Background Color	4.61	916	1.536
		Blue Background Color	4.56	916	1.523
		Total	4.59	1832	1.529
Total	Right	White Background Color	4.26	916	1.605
		Blue Background Color	4.22	916	1.623
		Total	4.24	1832	1.613
	Left	White Background Color	5.03	916	1.372
		Blue Background Color	4.90	916	1.408
		Total	4.96	1832	1.391
	Total	White Background Color	4.64	1832	1.542
		Blue Background Color	4.56	1832	1.555
		Total	4.60	3664	1.549

Estimated Marginal Means of Like Image Location

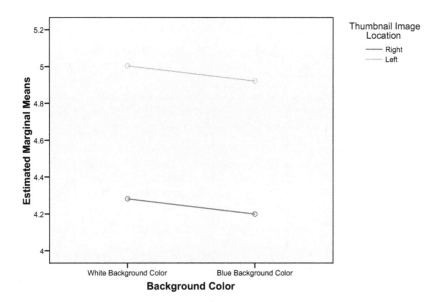

Figure 3.13. Like Image Location, Background Color versus Thumbnail Image Location

Table 3.14. Like Image Location, Comparison of Means, Gender versus Color

Descriptive Statistics

Dependent Variable: Dslkim

Gender	ImLoc	Mean	Std. Deviation	N
Female	Right	4.07	1.586	1200
	Left	4.92	1.412	1200
	Total	4.49	1.560	2400
Male	Right	4.57	1.616	632
	Left	5.05	1.349	632
	Total	4.81	1.507	1264
Total	Right	4.24	1.613	1832
	Left	4.96	1.391	1832
	Total	4.60	1.549	3664

Table 3.14. Easy to Find Product, Mixed Model

Type III Tests of Fixed Effects[a]

Source	Numerator df	Denominator df	F	Sig.
Intercept	1	212.000	15.524	.000
Gender	1	212.000	.096	.757
wspace	1	3428.000	1.025	.311
ImLoc	1	3428.000	22.891	.000
Color	1	3428.000	2.503	.114
Age	1	212.000	1.391	.240
HoursonInternetper WeekDay	1	212	4.235	.041
HoursonInternetper WeekendDay	1	212	1.179	.279
ItemsPurchased Online1M	1	212.000	.252	.616
InternetShopping	1	212.000	.197	.658
LikeShop	1	212.000	3.507	.062
LessRisky	1	212.000	.003	.954
PreferOnlineShop	1	212.000	2.455	.119
AssessTrustworthiness	1	212.000	.486	.487
AssessDesignQuality	1	212.000	1.079	.300
ExpertUser	1	212.000	.076	.783
LooksAttention	1	212.000	1.161	.282
CoVisualTrust	1	212.000	.005	.946
LikeStay	1	212.000	.546	.461
Imakeextensiveuseofthei nternet	1	212.000	.886	.348
Gender * wspace	1	3428.000	.285	.594
Gender * ImLoc	1	3428.000	13.640	.000
Gender * Color	1	3428.000	1.114	.291
wspace * Color	1	3428	4.460	.035

a. Dependent Variable: diffind.

240

Estimates of Fixed Effects[b]

Parameter	Estimate	Std. Error	df	t	Sig.	95% Confidence Interval	
						Lower Bound	Upper Bound
Intercept	3.288082	.866529	213.506	3.795	.000	1.580035	4.996128
[Gender=1]	.229513	.159270	288.289	1.441	.151	-.083966	.542993
[Gender=2]	0[a]	0	.	.	.	.	.
[wspace=-1]	-.016072	.065322	3428.000	-.246	.806	-.144146	.112003
[wspace=1]	0[a]	0	.	.	.	.	.
[ImLoc=-1]	-.037975	.056325	3428.000	-.674	.500	-.148409	.072460
[ImLoc=1]	0[a]	0	.	.	.	.	.
[Color=-1]	.021903	.065322	3428.000	.335	.737	-.106172	.149978
[Color=1]	0[a]	0	.	.	.	.	.
Age	.041184	.034920	212.000	1.179	.240	-.027651	.110020
HoursonInternetper WeekDay	.018242	.008865	212	2.058	.041	.000768	.035717
HoursonInternetper WeekendDay	-.023211	.021372	212	-1.086	.279	-.065340	.018919
ItemsPurchased Online1M	-.008613	.017164	212.000	-.502	.616	-.042448	.025221
InternetShopping	.021436	.048287	212.000	.444	.658	-.073749	.116620
LikeShop	.097338	.051979	212.000	1.873	.062	-.005123	.199799
LessRisky	-.002521	.044058	212.000	-.057	.954	-.089368	.084326
PreferOnlineShop	-.076545	.048856	212.000	-1.567	.119	-.172850	.019760
AssessTrustworthiness	.039100	.056106	212.000	.697	.487	-.071497	.149696
AssessDesignQuality	.059189	.056978	212.000	1.039	.300	-.053127	.171505
ExpertUser	-.011966	.043294	212.000	-.276	.783	-.097307	.073376
LooksAttention	-.065385	.060679	212.000	-1.078	.282	-.184998	.054227
CoVisualTrust	.004443	.065834	212.000	.067	.946	-.125330	.134216
LikeStay	.037405	.050605	212.000	.739	.461	-.062350	.137159
Imakeextensiveuseofthei nternet	.050931	.054097	212.000	.941	.348	-.055706	.157568
[Gender=1] * [wspace=-1]	-.037131	.069595	3428.000	-.534	.594	-.173582	.099321
[Gender=1] * [wspace=1]	0[a]	0	.	.	.	.	.
[Gender=2] * [wspace=-1]	0[a]	0	.	.	.	.	.
[Gender=2] * [wspace=1]	0[a]	0	.	.	.	.	.
[Gender=1] * [ImLoc=-1]	-.257025	.069595	3428.000	-3.693	.000	-.393477	-.120574
[Gender=1] * [ImLoc=1]	0[a]	0	.	.	.	.	.
[Gender=2] * [ImLoc=-1]	0[a]	0	.	.	.	.	.
[Gender=2] * [ImLoc=1]	0[a]	0	.	.	.	.	.
[Gender=1] * [Color=-1]	-.073439	.069595	3428.000	-1.055	.291	-.209890	.063013
[Gender=1] * [Color=1]	0[a]	0	.	.	.	.	.
[Gender=2] * [Color=-1]	0[a]	0	.	.	.	.	.
[Gender=2] * [Color=1]	0[a]	0	.	.	.	.	.
[wspace=-1] * [Color=-1]	.139738	.066165	3428	2.112	.035	.010011	.269465
[wspace=-1] * [Color=1]	0[a]	0	.	.	.	.	.
[wspace=1] * [Color=-1]	0[a]	0	.	.	.	.	.
[wspace=1] * [Color=1]	0[a]	0	.	.	.	.	.

a. This parameter is set to zero because it is redundant.

b. Dependent Variable: diffind.

Table 3.15. Easy to Find Product, Comparison of Means

Report

Easy to Find Product

White Space	Thumbnail	Background Color	Mean	N	Std. Deviation
More White Space	Right	White Background Color	5.05	458	1.318
		Blue Background Color	4.83	458	1.406
		Total	4.94	916	1.367
	Left	White Background Color	5.10	458	1.354
		Blue Background Color	5.09	458	1.307
		Total	5.10	916	1.330
	Total	White Background Color	5.08	916	1.335
		Blue Background Color	4.96	916	1.363
		Total	5.02	1832	1.350
Less White Space	Right	White Background Color	4.79	458	1.398
		Blue Background Color	4.93	458	1.371
		Total	4.86	916	1.385
	Left	White Background Color	5.16	458	1.321
		Blue Background Color	5.08	458	1.315
		Total	5.12	916	1.318
	Total	White Background Color	4.98	916	1.372
		Blue Background Color	5.00	916	1.344
		Total	4.99	1832	1.358
Total	Right	White Background Color	4.92	916	1.364
		Blue Background Color	4.88	916	1.389
		Total	4.90	1832	1.376
	Left	White Background Color	5.13	916	1.337
		Blue Background Color	5.08	916	1.310
		Total	5.11	1832	1.323
	Total	White Background Color	5.03	1832	1.354
		Blue Background Color	4.98	1832	1.354
		Total	5.00	3664	1.354

Figure 3.16. Easy to Find Product, Thumbnail Image Location

Estimated Marginal Means of Easy to Find Product

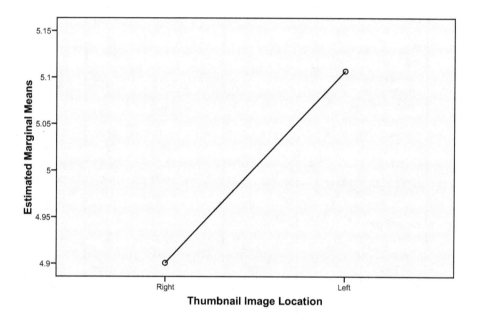

Table 3.17. Like Color Scheme, Mixed Model

Type III Tests of Fixed Effects[a]

Source	Numerator df	Denominator df	F	Sig.
Intercept	1	212.000	22.023	.000
Gender	1	212.000	1.263	.262
wspace	1	3428.000	.164	.686
ImLoc	1	3428.000	7.063	.008
Color	1	3428.000	36.949	.000
Age	1	212.000	.014	.907
HoursonInternetper WeekDay	1	212	2.906	.090
HoursonInternetper WeekendDay	1	212.000	.882	.349
ItemsPurchased Online1M	1	212.000	.396	.530
InternetShopping	1	212	6.769	.010
LikeShop	1	212.000	6.261	.013
LessRisky	1	212.000	2.171	.142
PreferOnlineShop	1	212.000	.002	.967
AssessTrustworthiness	1	212.000	.829	.364
AssessDesignQuality	1	212	1.874	.172
ExpertUser	1	212	.098	.755
LooksAttention	1	212.000	.001	.973
CoVisualTrust	1	212	.097	.756
LikeStay	1	212.000	.189	.664
Imakeextensiveuseofthei nternet	1	212.000	.112	.738
Gender * wspace	1	3428.000	.632	.427
Gender * ImLoc	1	3428.000	.216	.642
Gender * Color	1	3428.000	2.984	.084
wspace * Color	1	3428	3.134	.077

a. Dependent Variable: dslkcolor.

244

Estimates of Fixed Effects[b]

Parameter	Estimate	Std. Error	df	t	Sig.	95% Confidence Interval	
						Lower Bound	Upper Bound
Intercept	3.743469	.820541	215.303	4.562	.000	2.126146	5.360792
[Gender=1]	-.056462	.162809	392.236	-.347	.729	-.376549	.263626
[Gender=2]	0[a]	0	.	.	.	.	.
[wspace=-1]	-.062890	.091322	3428.000	-.689	.491	-.241941	.116160
[wspace=1]	0[a]	0	.	.	.	.	.
[ImLoc=-1]	-.151899	.078744	3428.000	-1.929	.054	-.306288	.002491
[ImLoc=1]	0[a]	0	.	.	.	.	.
[Color=-1]	.297869	.091322	3428.000	3.262	.001	.118819	.476919
[Color=1]	0[a]	0	.	.	.	.	.
Age	.003861	.032998	212.000	.117	.907	-.061185	.068907
HoursonInternetper WeekDay	.014280	.008377	212	1.705	.090	-.002232	.030793
HoursonInternetper WeekendDay	-.018970	.020196	212.000	-.939	.349	-.058780	.020841
ItemsPurchased Online1M	.010208	.016219	212.000	.629	.530	-.021763	.042180
InternetShopping	-.118712	.045629	212	-2.602	.010	-.208656	-.028767
LikeShop	.122900	.049117	212.000	2.502	.013	.026080	.219721
LessRisky	-.061338	.041632	212.000	-1.473	.142	-.143404	.020728
PreferOnlineShop	-.001916	.046166	212.000	-.042	.967	-.092919	.089087
AssessTrustworthiness	.048274	.053017	212.000	.911	.364	-.056233	.152782
AssessDesignQuality	.073715	.053841	212	1.369	.172	-.032418	.179847
ExpertUser	-.012786	.040910	212	-.313	.755	-.093429	.067858
LooksAttention	.001959	.057339	212.000	.034	.973	-.111068	.114986
CoVisualTrust	-.019344	.062209	212	-.311	.756	-.141972	.103285
LikeStay	-.020808	.047820	212.000	-.435	.664	-.115070	.073455
Imakeextensiveuseofthei nternet	.017135	.051119	212.000	.335	.738	-.083631	.117901
[Gender=1] * [wspace=-1]	-.077321	.097294	3428.000	-.795	.427	-.268082	.113440
[Gender=1] * [wspace=1]	0[a]	0	.	.	.	.	.
[Gender=2] * [wspace=-1]	0[a]	0	.	.	.	.	.
[Gender=2] * [wspace=1]	0[a]	0	.	.	.	.	.
[Gender=1] * [ImLoc=-1]	.045232	.097294	3428.000	.465	.642	-.145529	.235993
[Gender=1] * [ImLoc=1]	0[a]	0	.	.	.	.	.
[Gender=2] * [ImLoc=-1]	0[a]	0	.	.	.	.	.
[Gender=2] * [ImLoc=1]	0[a]	0	.	.	.	.	.
[Gender=1] * [Color=-1]	-.168080	.097294	3428.000	-1.728	.084	-.358841	.022681
[Gender=1] * [Color=1]	0[a]	0	.	.	.	.	.
[Gender=2] * [Color=-1]	0[a]	0	.	.	.	.	.
[Gender=2] * [Color=1]	0[a]	0	.	.	.	.	.
[wspace=-1] * [Color=-1]	.163755	.092500	3428	1.770	.077	-.017605	.345116
[wspace=-1] * [Color=1]	0[a]	0	.	.	.	.	.
[wspace=1] * [Color=-1]	0[a]	0	.	.	.	.	.
[wspace=1] * [Color=1]	0[a]	0	.	.	.	.	.

a. This parameter is set to zero because it is redundant.

b. Dependent Variable: dslkcolor.

245

Table 3.18. Like Color Scheme, Comparison of Means

Report

Like Color Scheme

White Space	Thumbnail	Background Color	Mean	N	Std. Deviation
More White Space	Right	White Background Color	4.26	458	1.570
		Blue Background Color	3.88	458	1.658
		Total	4.07	916	1.625
	Left	White Background Color	4.33	458	1.594
		Blue Background Color	4.01	458	1.707
		Total	4.17	916	1.658
	Total	White Background Color	4.29	916	1.581
		Blue Background Color	3.94	916	1.683
		Total	4.12	1832	1.642
Less White Space	Right	White Background Color	4.09	458	1.541
		Blue Background Color	4.06	458	1.619
		Total	4.08	916	1.579
	Left	White Background Color	4.39	458	1.604
		Blue Background Color	4.05	458	1.656
		Total	4.22	916	1.638
	Total	White Background Color	4.24	916	1.579
		Blue Background Color	4.06	916	1.636
		Total	4.15	1832	1.610
Total	Right	White Background Color	4.18	916	1.557
		Blue Background Color	3.97	916	1.640
		Total	4.07	1832	1.602
	Left	White Background Color	4.36	916	1.598
		Blue Background Color	4.03	916	1.681
		Total	4.19	1832	1.648
	Total	White Background Color	4.27	1832	1.580
		Blue Background Color	4.00	1832	1.660
		Total	4.13	3664	1.626

Estimated Marginal Means of Like Color Scheme

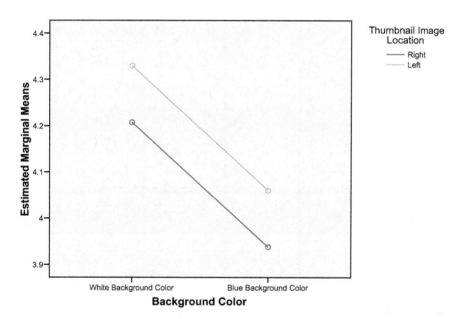

Figure 3.19. Like Color Scheme, Background Color versus Thumbnail Image Location

Table 3.20. Like Color Use, Mixed Model

Type III Tests of Fixed Effects[a]

Source	Numerator df	Denominator df	F	Sig.
Intercept	1	212.000	20.416	.000
Gender	1	212.000	1.536	.217
wspace	1	3428.000	1.105	.293
ImLoc	1	3428.000	4.705	.030
Color	1	3428.000	36.810	.000
Age	1	212.000	.417	.519
HoursonInternetper WeekDay	1	212	.770	.381
HoursonInternetper WeekendDay	1	212	.000	.998
ItemsPurchased Online1M	1	212.000	.326	.569
InternetShopping	1	212	1.279	.259
LikeShop	1	212	2.494	.116
LessRisky	1	212.000	4.657	.032
PreferOnlineShop	1	212	1.522	.219
AssessTrustworthiness	1	212	.662	.417
AssessDesignQuality	1	212	.159	.691
ExpertUser	1	212	.378	.539
LooksAttention	1	212.000	2.077	.151
CoVisualTrust	1	212.000	.315	.575
LikeStay	1	212.000	.005	.942
Imakeextensiveuseofthei nternet	1	212.000	.964	.327
Gender * wspace	1	3428.000	.671	.413
Gender * ImLoc	1	3428.000	.516	.473
Gender * Color	1	3428.000	1.961	.162
wspace * Color	1	3428	.794	.373

a. Dependent Variable: lkcolor.

Estimates of Fixed Effects[b]

Parameter	Estimate	Std. Error	df	t	Sig.	95% Confidence Interval	
						Lower Bound	Upper Bound
Intercept	3.717430	.843814	214.996	4.406	.000	2.054222	5.380638
[Gender=1]	-.106065	.165400	373.596	-.641	.522	-.431297	.219167
[Gender=2]	0[a]	0	.	.	.	.	.
[wspace=-1]	-.051469	.089498	3428.000	-.575	.565	-.226944	.124006
[wspace=1]	0[a]	0	.	.	.	.	.
[lmLoc=-1]	-.137658	.077171	3428.000	-1.784	.075	-.288965	.013648
[lmLoc=1]	0[a]	0	.	.	.	.	.
[Color=-1]	.315620	.089498	3428.000	3.527	.000	.140144	.491095
[Color=1]	0[a]	0	.	.	.	.	.
Age	-.021908	.033946	212.000	-.645	.519	-.088822	.045007
HoursonInternetper WeekDay	.007561	.008617	212	.877	.381	-.009426	.024547
HoursonInternetper WeekendDay	5.4E-005	.020776	212	.003	.998	-.040900	.041009
ItemsPurchased Online1M	.009525	.016685	212.000	.571	.569	-.023365	.042415
InternetShopping	-.053076	.046940	212	-1.131	.259	-.145605	.039452
LikeShop	.079793	.050528	212	1.579	.116	-.019809	.179395
LessRisky	-.092421	.042828	212.000	-2.158	.032	-.176844	-.007997
PreferOnlineShop	-.058600	.047492	212	-1.234	.219	-.152218	.035017
AssessTrustworthiness	.044370	.054540	212	.814	.417	-.063140	.151881
AssessDesignQuality	-.022059	.055388	212	-.398	.691	-.131241	.087123
ExpertUser	.025868	.042086	212	.615	.539	-.057092	.108828
LooksAttention	.085014	.058986	212.000	1.441	.151	-.031260	.201289
CoVisualTrust	.035919	.063997	212.000	.561	.575	-.090232	.162071
LikeStay	-.003613	.049193	212.000	-.073	.942	-.100583	.093358
Imakeextensiveuseofthei nternet	.051621	.052587	212.000	.982	.327	-.052040	.155283
[Gender=1] * [wspace=-1]	-.078091	.095352	3428.000	-.819	.413	-.265043	.108861
[Gender=1] * [wspace=1]	0[a]	0	.	.	.	.	.
[Gender=2] * [wspace=-1]	0[a]	0	.	.	.	.	.
[Gender=2] * [wspace=1]	0[a]	0	.	.	.	.	.
[Gender=1] * [lmLoc=-1]	.068492	.095352	3428.000	.718	.473	-.118460	.255444
[Gender=1] * [lmLoc=1]	0[a]	0	.	.	.	.	.
[Gender=2] * [lmLoc=-1]	0[a]	0	.	.	.	.	.
[Gender=2] * [lmLoc=1]	0[a]	0	.	.	.	.	.
[Gender=1] * [Color=-1]	-.133513	.095352	3428.000	-1.400	.162	-.320465	.053439
[Gender=1] * [Color=1]	0[a]	0	.	.	.	.	.
[Gender=2] * [Color=-1]	0[a]	0	.	.	.	.	.
[Gender=2] * [Color=1]	0[a]	0	.	.	.	.	.
[wspace=-1] * [Color=-1]	.080786	.090653	3428	.891	.373	-.096953	.258525
[wspace=-1] * [Color=1]	0[a]	0	.	.	.	.	.
[wspace=1] * [Color=-1]	0[a]	0	.	.	.	.	.
[wspace=1] * [Color=1]	0[a]	0	.	.	.	.	.

a. This parameter is set to zero because it is redundant.

b. Dependent Variable: lkcolor.

Table 3.21. Like Color Use, Mixed Model, Design Sensitivity Index

Type III Tests of Fixed Effects[a]

Source	Numerator df	Denominator df	F	Sig.
Intercept	1	223.000	25.997	.000
Gender	1	223.000	1.062	.304
wspace	1	3428	1.105	.293
lmLoc	1	3428	4.705	.030
Color	1	3428	36.810	.000
Age	1	223.000	.197	.658
onlineshopatt	1	223.000	.765	.383
intsavvy	1	223.000	.933	.335
designmind	1	223.000	5.708	.018
Gender * wspace	1	3428	.671	.413
Gender * lmLoc	1	3428	.516	.473
Gender * Color	1	3428	1.961	.162
wspace * Color	1	3428.000	.794	.373

a. Dependent Variable: lkcolor.

Estimates of Fixed Effects[b]

Parameter	Estimate	Std. Error	df	t	Sig.	95% Confidence Interval	
						Lower Bound	Upper Bound
Intercept	3.571905	.724397	227.292	4.931	.000	2.144512	4.999297
[Gender=1]	-.067939	.158577	416.059	-.428	.669	-.379652	.243774
[Gender=2]	0[a]	0	.	.	.	.	.
[wspace=-1]	-.051469	.089498	3428	-.575	.565	-.226944	.124006
[wspace=1]	0[a]	0	.	.	.	.	.
[lmLoc=-1]	-.137658	.077171	3428	-1.784	.075	-.288965	.013648
[lmLoc=1]	0[a]	0	.	.	.	.	.
[Color=-1]	.315620	.089498	3428	3.527	.000	.140144	.491095
[Color=1]	0[a]	0	.	.	.	.	.
Age	-.014090	.031765	223.000	-.444	.658	-.076689	.048508
onlineshopatt	-.041122	.047016	223.000	-.875	.383	-.133774	.051530
intsavvy	.072330	.074878	223.000	.966	.335	-.075229	.219890
designmind	.124086	.051939	223.000	2.389	.018	.021732	.226439
[Gender=1] * [wspace=-1]	-.078091	.095352	3428	-.819	.413	-.265043	.108861
[Gender=1] * [wspace=1]	0[a]	0	.	.	.	.	.
[Gender=2] * [wspace=-1]	0[a]	0	.	.	.	.	.
[Gender=2] * [wspace=1]	0[a]	0	.	.	.	.	.
[Gender=1] * [lmLoc=-1]	.068492	.095352	3428	.718	.473	-.118460	.255444
[Gender=1] * [lmLoc=1]	0[a]	0	.	.	.	.	.
[Gender=2] * [lmLoc=-1]	0[a]	0	.	.	.	.	.
[Gender=2] * [lmLoc=1]	0[a]	0	.	.	.	.	.
[Gender=1] * [Color=-1]	-.133513	.095352	3428	-1.400	.162	-.320465	.053439
[Gender=1] * [Color=1]	0[a]	0	.	.	.	.	.
[Gender=2] * [Color=-1]	0[a]	0	.	.	.	.	.
[Gender=2] * [Color=1]	0[a]	0	.	.	.	.	.
[wspace=-1] * [Color=-1]	.080786	.090653	3428.000	.891	.373	-.096953	.258525
[wspace=-1] * [Color=1]	0[a]	0	.	.	.	.	.
[wspace=1] * [Color=-1]	0[a]	0	.	.	.	.	.
[wspace=1] * [Color=1]	0[a]	0	.	.	.	.	.

a. This parameter is set to zero because it is redundant.

b. Dependent Variable: lkcolor.

Table 3.22. Like Color Use, Comparison of Means

Report

Like Color Use

White Space	Thumbnail	Background Color	Mean	N	Std. Deviation
More White Space	Right	White Background Color	4.24	458	1.567
		Blue Background Color	3.83	458	1.643
		Total	4.03	916	1.618
	Left	White Background Color	4.23	458	1.624
		Blue Background Color	4.02	458	1.675
		Total	4.12	916	1.652
	Total	White Background Color	4.23	916	1.595
		Blue Background Color	3.92	916	1.661
		Total	4.08	1832	1.635
Less White Space	Right	White Background Color	4.20	458	1.550
		Blue Background Color	3.99	458	1.624
		Total	4.09	916	1.590
	Left	White Background Color	4.31	458	1.618
		Blue Background Color	4.07	458	1.598
		Total	4.19	916	1.612
	Total	White Background Color	4.26	916	1.584
		Blue Background Color	4.03	916	1.611
		Total	4.14	1832	1.601
Total	Right	White Background Color	4.22	916	1.558
		Blue Background Color	3.91	916	1.635
		Total	4.06	1832	1.604
	Left	White Background Color	4.27	916	1.621
		Blue Background Color	4.04	916	1.636
		Total	4.16	1832	1.632
	Total	White Background Color	4.24	1832	1.589
		Blue Background Color	3.98	1832	1.636
		Total	4.11	3664	1.618

251

Estimated Marginal Means of Like Color Use

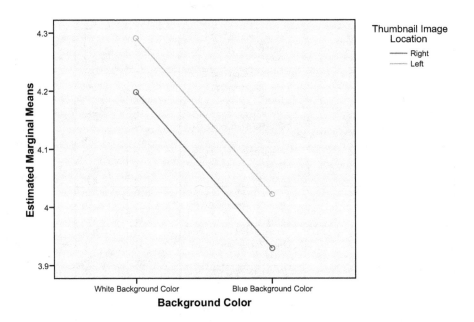

Figure 3.23. Like Color Use, Background Color versus Thumbnail Image Location

Table 3.24. Easy to See Product with Description, Mixed Model

Type III Tests of Fixed Effects[a]

Source	Numerator df	Denominator df	F	Sig.
Intercept	1	212.000	32.642	.000
Gender	1	212.000	1.513	.220
wspace	1	3428	.208	.649
ImLoc	1	3428	97.853	.000
Color	1	3428	.439	.507
Age	1	212.000	.506	.478
HoursonInternetper WeekDay	1	212	4.967	.027
HoursonInternetper WeekendDay	1	212.000	1.302	.255
ItemsPurchased Online1M	1	212.000	.298	.586
InternetShopping	1	212.000	2.072	.152
LikeShop	1	212.000	5.643	.018
LessRisky	1	212.000	1.287	.258
PreferOnlineShop	1	212.000	4.581	.033
AssessTrustworthiness	1	212.000	.002	.963
AssessDesignQuality	1	212.000	1.705	.193
ExpertUser	1	212.000	.837	.361
LooksAttention	1	212.000	.050	.823
CoVisualTrust	1	212.000	.036	.849
LikeStay	1	212.000	.974	.325
Imakeextensiveuseofthei nternet	1	212.000	3.334	.069
Gender * wspace	1	3428	.231	.631
Gender * ImLoc	1	3428	17.492	.000
Gender * Color	1	3428	.010	.919
wspace * Color	1	3428	9.241	.002

a. Dependent Variable: descimg.

Estimates of Fixed Effects[b]

Parameter	Estimate	Std. Error	df	t	Sig.	95% Confidence Interval	
						Lower Bound	Upper Bound
Intercept	4.488776	.795729	213.687	5.641	.000	2.920293	6.057260
[Gender=1]	.327521	.147476	298.143	2.221	.027	.037295	.617746
[Gender=2]	0[a]	0	.	.	.	.	.
[wspace=-1]	-.066062	.063466	3428	-1.041	.298	-.190497	.058373
[wspace=1]	0[a]	0	.	.	.	.	.
[ImLoc=-1]	-.193038	.054725	3428	-3.527	.000	-.300334	-.085742
[ImLoc=1]	0[a]	0	.	.	.	.	.
[Color=-1]	-.116695	.063466	3428	-1.839	.066	-.241130	.007740
[Color=1]	0[a]	0	.	.	.	.	.
Age	-.022806	.032060	212.000	-.711	.478	-.086004	.040392
HoursonInternetper WeekDay	.018139	.008139	212	2.229	.027	.002096	.034182
HoursonInternetper WeekendDay	-.022393	.019622	212.000	-1.141	.255	-.061072	.016286
ItemsPurchased Online1M	-.008605	.015758	212.000	-.546	.586	-.039669	.022458
InternetShopping	.063812	.044333	212.000	1.439	.152	-.023577	.151201
LikeShop	.113358	.047722	212.000	2.375	.018	.019288	.207428
LessRisky	-.045893	.040449	212.000	-1.135	.258	-.125627	.033842
PreferOnlineShop	-.096004	.044854	212.000	-2.140	.033	-.184421	-.007586
AssessTrustworthiness	.002386	.051511	212.000	.046	.963	-.099153	.103925
AssessDesignQuality	.068303	.052312	212.000	1.306	.193	-.034814	.171421
ExpertUser	-.036373	.039748	212.000	-.915	.361	-.114725	.041979
LooksAttention	.012463	.055710	212.000	.224	.823	-.097353	.122279
CoVisualTrust	.011504	.060442	212.000	.190	.849	-.107641	.130648
LikeStay	.045843	.046461	212.000	.987	.325	-.045742	.137427
Imakeextensiveuseofthei nternet	.090694	.049667	212.000	1.826	.069	-.007210	.188597
[Gender=1] * [wspace=-1]	-.032479	.067617	3428	-.480	.631	-.165053	.100095
[Gender=1] * [wspace=1]	0[a]	0	.	.	.	.	.
[Gender=2] * [wspace=-1]	0[a]	0	.	.	.	.	.
[Gender=2] * [wspace=1]	0[a]	0	.	.	.	.	.
[Gender=1] * [ImLoc=-1]	-.282795	.067617	3428	-4.182	.000	-.415369	-.150222
[Gender=1] * [ImLoc=1]	0[a]	0	.	.	.	.	.
[Gender=2] * [ImLoc=-1]	0[a]	0	.	.	.	.	.
[Gender=2] * [ImLoc=1]	0[a]	0	.	.	.	.	.
[Gender=1] * [Color=-1]	-.006846	.067617	3428	-.101	.919	-.139420	.125728
[Gender=1] * [Color=1]	0[a]	0	.	.	.	.	.
[Gender=2] * [Color=-1]	0[a]	0	.	.	.	.	.
[Gender=2] * [Color=1]	0[a]	0	.	.	.	.	.
[wspace=-1] * [Color=-1]	.195415	.064285	3428	3.040	.002	.069374	.321456
[wspace=-1] * [Color=1]	0[a]	0	.	.	.	.	.
[wspace=1] * [Color=-1]	0[a]	0	.	.	.	.	.
[wspace=1] * [Color=1]	0[a]	0	.	.	.	.	.

a. This parameter is set to zero because it is redundant.

b. Dependent Variable: descimg.

Table 3.25. Easy to See Product with Description, Comparison of Means

Easy to See Product w Description

White Space	Thumbnail	Background Color	Mean	N	Std. Deviation
More White Space	Right	White Background Color	5.21	458	1.347
		Blue Background Color	5.09	458	1.377
		Total	5.15	916	1.363
	Left	White Background Color	5.54	458	1.174
		Blue Background Color	5.52	458	1.233
		Total	5.53	916	1.203
	Total	White Background Color	5.38	916	1.273
		Blue Background Color	5.30	916	1.324
		Total	5.34	1832	1.299
Less White Space	Right	White Background Color	5.00	458	1.411
		Blue Background Color	5.28	458	1.297
		Total	5.14	916	1.362
	Left	White Background Color	5.54	458	1.239
		Blue Background Color	5.50	458	1.252
		Total	5.52	916	1.245
	Total	White Background Color	5.27	916	1.354
		Blue Background Color	5.39	916	1.279
		Total	5.33	1832	1.318
Total	Right	White Background Color	5.11	916	1.383
		Blue Background Color	5.19	916	1.341
		Total	5.15	1832	1.362
	Left	White Background Color	5.54	916	1.206
		Blue Background Color	5.51	916	1.242
		Total	5.53	1832	1.224
	Total	White Background Color	5.32	1832	1.315
		Blue Background Color	5.35	1832	1.302
		Total	5.34	3664	1.308

Estimated Marginal Means of Easy to See Product w Description

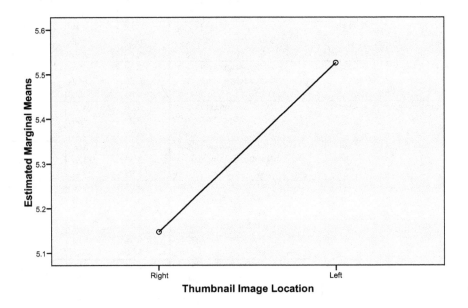

Figure 3.26. Easy to See Product with Description, Thumbnail Image Location

Table 3.27. Professional, Mixed Model

Type III Tests of Fixed Effects[a]

Source	Numerator df	Denominator df	F	Sig.
Intercept	1	212.000	27.024	.000
Gender	1	212.000	.023	.880
wspace	1	3428.000	.373	.542
ImLoc	1	3428.000	24.138	.000
Color	1	3428.000	30.796	.000
Age	1	212.000	2.042	.154
HoursonInternetper WeekDay	1	212.000	2.737	.100
HoursonInternetper WeekendDay	1	212.000	2.363	.126
ItemsPurchased Online1M	1	212.000	.177	.674
InternetShopping	1	212	.032	.859
LikeShop	1	212.000	1.562	.213
LessRisky	1	212.000	.916	.340
PreferOnlineShop	1	212	2.992	.085
AssessTrustworthiness	1	212.000	1.138	.287
AssessDesignQuality	1	212.000	2.059	.153
ExpertUser	1	212.000	1.144	.286
LooksAttention	1	212.000	.292	.590
CoVisualTrust	1	212.000	.370	.544
LikeStay	1	212.000	3.119	.079
Imakeextensiveuseofthei nternet	1	212.000	2.984	.086
Gender * wspace	1	3428.000	3.010	.083
Gender * ImLoc	1	3428.000	.281	.596
Gender * Color	1	3428.000	7.197	.007
wspace * Color	1	3428	7.882	.005

a. Dependent Variable: profess

257

Estimates of Fixed Effects[b]

Parameter	Estimate	Std. Error	df	t	Sig.	95% Confidence Interval	
						Lower Bound	Upper Bound
Intercept	4.170817	.825055	213.698	5.055	.000	2.544529	5.797105
[Gender=1]	.115551	.152991	298.778	.755	.451	-.185526	.416628
[Gender=2]	0[a]	0	.	.	.	.	.
[wspace=-1]	-.054330	.066029	3428.000	-.823	.411	-.183790	.075131
[wspace=1]	0[a]	0	.	.	.	.	.
[ImLoc=-1]	-.191456	.056935	3428.000	-3.363	.001	-.303085	-.079826
[ImLoc=1]	0[a]	0	.	.	.	.	.
[Color=-1]	.195670	.066029	3428.000	2.963	.003	.066210	.325131
[Color=1]	0[a]	0	.	.	.	.	.
Age	-.047504	.033241	212.000	-1.429	.154	-.113030	.018022
HoursonInternetper WeekDay	.013962	.008439	212.000	1.655	.100	-.002673	.030596
HoursonInternetper WeekendDay	-.031274	.020345	212.000	-1.537	.126	-.071378	.008831
ItemsPurchased Online1M	-.006874	.016339	212.000	-.421	.674	-.039082	.025333
InternetShopping	.008189	.045966	212	.178	.859	-.082420	.098797
LikeShop	.061836	.049480	212.000	1.250	.213	-.035700	.159371
LessRisky	-.040138	.041939	212.000	-.957	.340	-.122809	.042534
PreferOnlineShop	-.080441	.046507	212	-1.730	.085	-.172116	.011234
AssessTrustworthiness	.056987	.053408	212.000	1.067	.287	-.048293	.162266
AssessDesignQuality	.077832	.054239	212.000	1.435	.153	-.029084	.184749
ExpertUser	-.044089	.041212	212.000	-1.070	.286	-.125327	.037150
LooksAttention	.031192	.057762	212.000	.540	.590	-.082670	.145053
CoVisualTrust	.038123	.062669	212.000	.608	.544	-.085411	.161657
LikeStay	.085082	.048173	212.000	1.766	.079	-.009876	.180041
Imakeextensiveofthei nternet	.088959	.051496	212.000	1.727	.086	-.012551	.190470
[Gender=1] * [wspace=-1]	-.122057	.070348	3428.000	-1.735	.083	-.259984	.015870
[Gender=1] * [wspace=1]	0[a]	0	.	.	.	.	.
[Gender=2] * [wspace=-1]	0[a]	0	.	.	.	.	.
[Gender=2] * [wspace=1]	0[a]	0	.	.	.	.	.
[Gender=1] * [ImLoc=-1]	.037289	.070348	3428.000	.530	.596	-.100638	.175216
[Gender=1] * [ImLoc=1]	0[a]	0	.	.	.	.	.
[Gender=2] * [ImLoc=-1]	0[a]	0	.	.	.	.	.
[Gender=2] * [ImLoc=1]	0[a]	0	.	.	.	.	.
[Gender=1] * [Color=-1]	-.188724	.070348	3428.000	-2.683	.007	-.326651	-.050796
[Gender=1] * [Color=1]	0[a]	0	.	.	.	.	.
[Gender=2] * [Color=-1]	0[a]	0	.	.	.	.	.
[Gender=2] * [Color=1]	0[a]	0	.	.	.	.	.
[wspace=-1] * [Color=-1]	.187773	.066881	3428	2.808	.005	.056642	.318904
[wspace=-1] * [Color=1]	0[a]	0	.	.	.	.	.
[wspace=1] * [Color=-1]	0[a]	0	.	.	.	.	.
[wspace=1] * [Color=1]	0[a]	0	.	.	.	.	.

a. This parameter is set to zero because it is redundant.

b. Dependent Variable: profess.

Table 3.28. Professional, Mixed Model, Internet Savvy Index

Type III Tests of Fixed Effects[a]

Source	Numerator df	Denominator df	F	Sig.
Intercept	1	223.000	45.936	.000
Gender	1	223.000	.152	.697
wspace	1	3428	.373	.542
ImLoc	1	3428	24.138	.000
Color	1	3428	30.796	.000
Age	1	223.000	2.777	.097
onlineshopatt	1	223.000	.066	.797
intsavvy	1	223.000	4.015	.046
designmind	1	223	.792	.375
Gender * wspace	1	3428	3.010	.083
Gender * ImLoc	1	3428	.281	.596
Gender * Color	1	3428	7.197	.007
wspace * Color	1	3428.000	7.882	.005

a. Dependent Variable: profess.

Estimates of Fixed Effects[b]

Parameter	Estimate	Std. Error	df	t	Sig.	95% Confidence Interval	
						Lower Bound	Upper Bound
Intercept	4.702451	.720478	225.347	6.527	.000	3.282715	6.122188
[Gender=1]	.189315	.148053	322.308	1.279	.202	-.101957	.480588
[Gender=2]	0[a]	0	.	.	.	.	.
[wspace=-1]	-.054330	.066029	3428.000	-.823	.411	-.183790	.075131
[wspace=1]	0[a]	0	.	.	.	.	.
[ImLoc=-1]	-.191456	.056935	3428	-3.363	.001	-.303085	-.079826
[ImLoc=1]	0[a]	0	.	.	.	.	.
[Color=-1]	.195670	.066029	3428.000	2.963	.003	.066210	.325131
[Color=1]	0[a]	0	.	.	.	.	.
Age	-.052761	.031661	223.000	-1.666	.097	-.115155	.009632
onlineshopatt	-.012071	.046862	223.000	-.258	.797	-.104420	.080278
intsavvy	.149547	.074633	223.000	2.004	.046	.002470	.296624
designmind	.046057	.051769	223	.890	.375	-.055961	.148076
[Gender=1] * [wspace=-1]	-.122057	.070348	3428	-1.735	.083	-.259984	.015870
[Gender=1] * [wspace=1]	0[a]	0	.	.	.	.	.
[Gender=2] * [wspace=-1]	0[a]	0	.	.	.	.	.
[Gender=2] * [wspace=1]	0[a]	0	.	.	.	.	.
[Gender=1] * [ImLoc=-1]	.037289	.070348	3428	.530	.596	-.100638	.175216
[Gender=1] * [ImLoc=1]	0[a]	0	.	.	.	.	.
[Gender=2] * [ImLoc=-1]	0[a]	0	.	.	.	.	.
[Gender=2] * [ImLoc=1]	0[a]	0	.	.	.	.	.
[Gender=1] * [Color=-1]	-.188724	.070348	3428	-2.683	.007	-.326651	-.050796
[Gender=1] * [Color=1]	0[a]	0	.	.	.	.	.
[Gender=2] * [Color=-1]	0[a]	0	.	.	.	.	.
[Gender=2] * [Color=1]	0[a]	0	.	.	.	.	.
[wspace=-1] * [Color=-1]	.187773	.066881	3428.000	2.808	.005	.056642	.318904
[wspace=-1] * [Color=1]	0[a]	0	.	.	.	.	.
[wspace=1] * [Color=-1]	0[a]	0	.	.	.	.	.
[wspace=1] * [Color=1]	0[a]	0	.	.	.	.	.

a. This parameter is set to zero because it is redundant.

b. Dependent Variable: profess.

259

Table 3.29. Professional, Comparison of Means

Report

Professional

White Space	Thumbnail	Background Color	Mean	N	Std. Deviation
More White Space	Right	White Background Color	4.75	458	1.262
		Blue Background Color	4.36	458	1.394
		Total	4.55	916	1.343
	Left	White Background Color	4.78	458	1.311
		Blue Background Color	4.65	458	1.393
		Total	4.71	916	1.353
	Total	White Background Color	4.76	916	1.286
		Blue Background Color	4.50	916	1.400
		Total	4.63	1832	1.350
Less White Space	Right	White Background Color	4.53	458	1.331
		Blue Background Color	4.64	458	1.331
		Total	4.59	916	1.332
	Left	White Background Color	4.89	458	1.296
		Blue Background Color	4.64	458	1.349
		Total	4.76	916	1.328
	Total	White Background Color	4.71	916	1.325
		Blue Background Color	4.64	916	1.339
		Total	4.67	1832	1.332
Total	Right	White Background Color	4.64	916	1.301
		Blue Background Color	4.50	916	1.369
		Total	4.57	1832	1.337
	Left	White Background Color	4.83	916	1.304
		Blue Background Color	4.64	916	1.370
		Total	4.74	1832	1.341
	Total	White Background Color	4.74	1832	1.306
		Blue Background Color	4.57	1832	1.371
		Total	4.65	3664	1.341

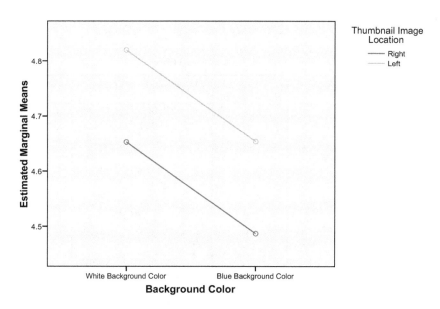

Estimated Marginal Means of Professional

Figure 3.30. Professional, Background Color versus Thumbnail Image Location

Figure 3.31. Professional, Comparison of Means, Gender versus Background Color

Descriptive Statistics

Dependent Variable: profess

Color	Gender	Mean	Std. Deviation	N
White Background Color	Female	4.69	1.300	1200
	Male	4.83	1.312	632
	Total	4.74	1.306	1832
Blue Background Color	Female	4.59	1.327	1200
	Male	4.54	1.452	632
	Total	4.57	1.371	1832
Total	Female	4.64	1.314	2400
	Male	4.68	1.391	1264
	Total	4.65	1.341	3664

Table 3.32. Quality Company, Mixed Model

Type III Tests of Fixed Effects[a]

Source	Numerator df	Denominator df	F	Sig.
Intercept	1	212.000	17.448	.000
Gender	1	212.000	.000	.996
wspace	1	3428	.965	.326
ImLoc	1	3428	12.993	.000
Color	1	3428	30.998	.000
Age	1	212.000	.467	.495
HoursonInternetper WeekDay	1	212	3.713	.055
HoursonInternetper WeekendDay	1	212	3.020	.084
ItemsPurchased Online1M	1	212.000	.765	.383
InternetShopping	1	212.000	.030	.862
LikeShop	1	212.000	.710	.400
LessRisky	1	212.000	.163	.687
PreferOnlineShop	1	212	1.852	.175
AssessTrustworthiness	1	212.000	3.987	.047
AssessDesignQuality	1	212.000	.262	.609
ExpertUser	1	212	.805	.370
LooksAttention	1	212.000	.430	.513
CoVisualTrust	1	212.000	.223	.637
LikeStay	1	212.000	3.694	.056
Imakeextensiveuseofthei nternet	1	212.000	2.985	.086
Gender * wspace	1	3428	2.233	.135
Gender * ImLoc	1	3428	.291	.590
Gender * Color	1	3428	4.876	.027
wspace * Color	1	3428.000	1.737	.188

a. Dependent Variable: qualcom.

262

Parameter	Estimate	Std. Error	df	t	Sig.	95% Confidence Interval	
						Lower Bound	Upper Bound
Intercept	3.450860	.859008	213.461	4.017	.000	1.757634	5.144085
[Gender=1]	.106777	.157561	285.881	.678	.499	-.203350	.416905
[Gender=2]	0[a]	0	.	.	.	.	.
[wspace=-1]	-.025171	.063794	3428.000	-.395	.693	-.150249	.099906
[wspace=1]	0[a]	0	.	.	.	.	.
[ImLoc=-1]	-.140823	.055007	3428	-2.560	.011	-.248673	-.032972
[ImLoc=1]	0[a]	0	.	.	.	.	.
[Color=-1]	.221664	.063794	3428.000	3.475	.001	.096586	.346742
[Color=1]	0[a]	0	.	.	.	.	.
Age	-.023662	.034619	212.000	-.683	.495	-.091904	.044580
HoursonInternetper WeekDay	.016934	.008788	212	1.927	.055	-.000389	.034258
HoursonInternetper WeekendDay	-.036819	.021188	212	-1.738	.084	-.078585	.004947
ItemsPurchased Online1M	-.014887	.017016	212.000	-.875	.383	-.048429	.018656
InternetShopping	.008342	.047871	212.000	.174	.862	-.086022	.102705
LikeShop	.043420	.051530	212.000	.843	.400	-.058157	.144997
LessRisky	-.017643	.043677	212.000	-.404	.687	-.103741	.068455
PreferOnlineShop	-.065905	.048434	212	-1.361	.175	-.161379	.029569
AssessTrustworthiness	.111056	.055622	212.000	1.997	.047	.001414	.220699
AssessDesignQuality	.028938	.056487	212.000	.512	.609	-.082410	.140285
ExpertUser	-.038519	.042920	212	-.897	.370	-.123124	.046087
LooksAttention	.039430	.060156	212.000	.655	.513	-.079151	.158010
CoVisualTrust	.030852	.065266	212.000	.473	.637	-.097801	.159505
LikeStay	.096420	.050169	212.000	1.922	.056	-.002474	.195314
Imakeextensiveuseofthei nternet	.092654	.053630	212.000	1.728	.086	-.013063	.198371
[Gender=1] * [wspace=-1]	-.101572	.067966	3428	-1.494	.135	-.234830	.031687
[Gender=1] * [wspace=1]	0[a]	0	.	.	.	.	.
[Gender=2] * [wspace=-1]	0[a]	0	.	.	.	.	.
[Gender=2] * [wspace=1]	0[a]	0	.	.	.	.	.
[Gender=1] * [ImLoc=-1]	.036656	.067966	3428	.539	.590	-.096602	.169915
[Gender=1] * [ImLoc=1]	0[a]	0	.	.	.	.	.
[Gender=2] * [ImLoc=-1]	0[a]	0	.	.	.	.	.
[Gender=2] * [ImLoc=1]	0[a]	0	.	.	.	.	.
[Gender=1] * [Color=-1]	-.150074	.067966	3428	-2.208	.027	-.283332	-.016815
[Gender=1] * [Color=1]	0[a]	0	.	.	.	.	.
[Gender=2] * [Color=-1]	0[a]	0	.	.	.	.	.
[Gender=2] * [Color=1]	0[a]	0	.	.	.	.	.
[wspace=-1] * [Color=-1]	.085153	.064617	3428.000	1.318	.188	-.041539	.211845
[wspace=-1] * [Color=1]	0[a]	0	.	.	.	.	.
[wspace=1] * [Color=-1]	0[a]	0	.	.	.	.	.
[wspace=1] * [Color=1]	0[a]	0	.	.	.	.	.

a. This parameter is set to zero because it is redundant.

b. Dependent Variable: qualcom.

263

Table 3.33. Quality Company, Mixed Model, Internet Savvy Index

Type III Tests of Fixed Effects[a]

Source	Numerator df	Denominator df	F	Sig.
Intercept	1	223.000	35.100	.000
Gender	1	223.000	.011	.918
wspace	1	3428	.965	.326
ImLoc	1	3428	12.993	.000
Color	1	3428	30.998	.000
Age	1	223.000	1.281	.259
onlineshopatt	1	223.000	.019	.891
intsavvy	1	223.000	4.285	.040
designmind	1	223.000	.400	.528
Gender * wspace	1	3428	2.233	.135
Gender * ImLoc	1	3428	.291	.590
Gender * Color	1	3428	4.876	.027
wspace * Color	1	3428	1.737	.188

a. Dependent Variable: qualcom.

Estimates of Fixed Effects[b]

Parameter	Estimate	Std. Error	df	t	Sig.	95% Confidence Interval Lower Bound	Upper Bound
Intercept	4.280801	.752207	225.008	5.691	.000	2.798529	5.763073
[Gender=1]	.121999	.152731	306.973	.799	.425	-.178533	.422531
[Gender=2]	0[a]	0	.	.	.	.	.
[wspace=-1]	-.025171	.063794	3428	-.395	.693	-.150249	.099906
[wspace=1]	0[a]	0	.	.	.	.	.
[ImLoc=-1]	-.140823	.055007	3428	-2.560	.011	-.248673	-.032972
[ImLoc=1]	0[a]	0	.	.	.	.	.
[Color=-1]	.221664	.063794	3428	3.475	.001	.096586	.346742
[Color=1]	0[a]	0	.	.	.	.	.
Age	-.037427	.033068	223.000	-1.132	.259	-.102593	.027739
onlineshopatt	-.006727	.048944	223.000	-.137	.891	-.103179	.089725
intsavvy	.161351	.077950	223.000	2.070	.040	.007739	.314963
designmind	.034191	.054069	223.000	.632	.528	-.072361	.140742
[Gender=1] * [wspace=-1]	-.101572	.067966	3428	-1.494	.135	-.234830	.031687
[Gender=1] * [wspace=1]	0[a]	0	.	.	.	.	.
[Gender=2] * [wspace=-1]	0[a]	0	.	.	.	.	.
[Gender=2] * [wspace=1]	0[a]	0	.	.	.	.	.
[Gender=1] * [ImLoc=-1]	.036656	.067966	3428	.539	.590	-.096602	.169915
[Gender=1] * [ImLoc=1]	0[a]	0	.	.	.	.	.
[Gender=2] * [ImLoc=-1]	0[a]	0	.	.	.	.	.
[Gender=2] * [ImLoc=1]	0[a]	0	.	.	.	.	.
[Gender=1] * [Color=-1]	-.150074	.067966	3428	-2.208	.027	-.283332	-.016815
[Gender=1] * [Color=1]	0[a]	0	.	.	.	.	.
[Gender=2] * [Color=-1]	0[a]	0	.	.	.	.	.
[Gender=2] * [Color=1]	0[a]	0	.	.	.	.	.
[wspace=-1] * [Color=-1]	.085153	.064617	3428	1.318	.188	-.041539	.211845
[wspace=-1] * [Color=1]	0[a]	0	.	.	.	.	.
[wspace=1] * [Color=-1]	0[a]	0	.	.	.	.	.
[wspace=1] * [Color=1]	0[a]	0	.	.	.	.	.

a. This parameter is set to zero because it is redundant.

b. Dependent Variable: qualcom.

Table 3.34. Quality Company, Comparison of Means

Report

Quality Company

White Space	Thumbnail	Background Color	Mean	N	Std. Deviation
More White Space	Right	White Background Color	4.65	458	1.287
		Blue Background Color	4.34	458	1.378
		Total	4.49	916	1.342
	Left	White Background Color	4.65	458	1.335
		Blue Background Color	4.54	458	1.398
		Total	4.59	916	1.367
	Total	White Background Color	4.65	916	1.310
		Blue Background Color	4.44	916	1.391
		Total	4.54	1832	1.355
Less White Space	Right	White Background Color	4.51	458	1.298
		Blue Background Color	4.54	458	1.323
		Total	4.53	916	1.310
	Left	White Background Color	4.79	458	1.305
		Blue Background Color	4.52	458	1.366
		Total	4.66	916	1.342
	Total	White Background Color	4.65	916	1.309
		Blue Background Color	4.53	916	1.344
		Total	4.59	1832	1.327
Total	Right	White Background Color	4.58	916	1.294
		Blue Background Color	4.44	916	1.354
		Total	4.51	1832	1.326
	Left	White Background Color	4.72	916	1.322
		Blue Background Color	4.53	916	1.381
		Total	4.63	1832	1.355
	Total	White Background Color	4.65	1832	1.309
		Blue Background Color	4.48	1832	1.368
		Total	4.57	3664	1.341

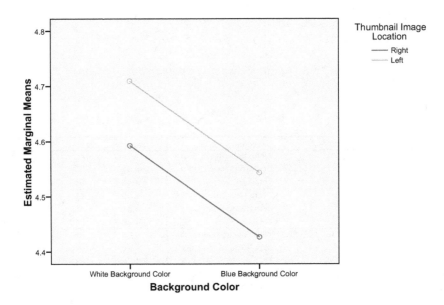

Estimated Marginal Means of Quality Company

Figure 3.35. Quality Company, Background Color versus Thumbnail Image Location

Table 3.36. Quality Company, Comparison of Means, Gender versus Background Color

Descriptive Statistics

Dependent Variable: qualcom

Color	Gender	Mean	Std. Deviation	N
White Background Color	Female	4.59	1.291	1200
	Male	4.76	1.337	632
	Total	4.65	1.309	1832
Blue Background Color	Female	4.48	1.334	1200
	Male	4.50	1.432	632
	Total	4.48	1.368	1832
Total	Female	4.53	1.314	2400
	Male	4.63	1.391	1264
	Total	4.57	1.341	3664

266

Table 3.38. High Budget, Mixed Model

Type III Tests of Fixed Effects[a]

Source	Numerator df	Denominator df	F	Sig.
Intercept	1	212.000	26.376	.000
Gender	1	212.000	.086	.769
wspace	1	3428.000	.233	.630
ImLoc	1	3428.000	5.118	.024
Color	1	3428.000	29.829	.000
Age	1	212.000	1.749	.187
HoursonInternetper WeekDay	1	212.000	1.593	.208
HoursonInternetper WeekendDay	1	212	5.841	.017
ItemsPurchased Online1M	1	212	.248	.619
InternetShopping	1	212.000	.322	.571
LikeShop	1	212.000	.844	.359
LessRisky	1	212	.198	.657
PreferOnlineShop	1	212	.313	.576
AssessTrustworthiness	1	212.000	1.395	.239
AssessDesignQuality	1	212.000	1.362	.245
ExpertUser	1	212.000	.137	.711
LooksAttention	1	212.000	.003	.953
CoVisualTrust	1	212.000	.012	.913
LikeStay	1	212.000	2.034	.155
Imakeextensiveuseofthei nternet	1	212	.151	.698
Gender * wspace	1	3428.000	.874	.350
Gender * ImLoc	1	3428.000	.345	.557
Gender * Color	1	3428.000	.006	.937
wspace * Color	1	3428.000	4.828	.028

a. Dependent Variable: lowbudg

267

Estimates of Fixed Effects[b]

Parameter	Estimate	Std. Error	df	t	Sig.	95% Confidence Interval	
						Lower Bound	Upper Bound
Intercept	4.634458	.932288	213.458	4.971	.000	2.796788	6.472128
[Gender=1]	.012381	.170978	285.714	.072	.942	-.324155	.348916
[Gender=2]	0[a]	0	.	.	.	.	.
[wspace=-1]	-.024750	.069163	3428.000	-.358	.720	-.160355	.110855
[wspace=1]	0[a]	0	.	.	.	.	.
[ImLoc=-1]	-.061709	.059637	3428.000	-1.035	.301	-.178636	.055219
[ImLoc=1]	0[a]	0	.	.	.	.	.
[Color=-1]	.127149	.069163	3428.000	1.838	.066	-.008456	.262754
[Color=1]	0[a]	0	.	.	.	.	.
Age	-.049692	.037572	212.000	-1.323	.187	-.123755	.024372
HoursonInternetper WeekDay	.012037	.009538	212.000	1.262	.208	-.006764	.030839
HoursonInternetper WeekendDay	-.055578	.022996	212	-2.417	.017	-.100907	-.010248
ItemsPurchased Online1M	-.009189	.018468	212	-.498	.619	-.045593	.027215
InternetShopping	-.029503	.051955	212.000	-.568	.571	-.131917	.072911
LikeShop	.051372	.055926	212.000	.919	.359	-.058871	.161615
LessRisky	-.021112	.047404	212	-.445	.657	-.114555	.072331
PreferOnlineShop	-.029410	.052566	212	-.559	.576	-.133030	.074209
AssessTrustworthiness	.071292	.060367	212.000	1.181	.239	-.047704	.190288
AssessDesignQuality	.071539	.061305	212.000	1.167	.245	-.049308	.192385
ExpertUser	-.017263	.046582	212.000	-.371	.711	-.109086	.074560
LooksAttention	.003852	.065288	212.000	.059	.953	-.124844	.132549
CoVisualTrust	-.007734	.070834	212.000	-.109	.913	-.147362	.131895
LikeStay	.077653	.054449	212.000	1.426	.155	-.029678	.184983
Imakeextensiveuseofthei nternet	.022621	.058206	212	.389	.698	-.092115	.137357
[Gender=1] * [wspace=-1]	-.068882	.073686	3428.000	-.935	.350	-.213356	.075592
[Gender=1] * [wspace=1]	0[a]	0	.	.	.	.	.
[Gender=2] * [wspace=-1]	0[a]	0	.	.	.	.	.
[Gender=2] * [wspace=1]	0[a]	0	.	.	.	.	.
[Gender=1] * [ImLoc=-1]	-.043291	.073686	3428.000	-.588	.557	-.187765	.101183
[Gender=1] * [ImLoc=1]	0[a]	0	.	.	.	.	.
[Gender=2] * [ImLoc=-1]	0[a]	0	.	.	.	.	.
[Gender=2] * [ImLoc=1]	0[a]	0	.	.	.	.	.
[Gender=1] * [Color=-1]	-.005781	.073686	3428.000	-.078	.937	-.150254	.138693
[Gender=1] * [Color=1]	0[a]	0	.	.	.	.	.
[Gender=2] * [Color=-1]	0[a]	0	.	.	.	.	.
[Gender=2] * [Color=1]	0[a]	0	.	.	.	.	.
[wspace=-1] * [Color=-1]	.153930	.070055	3428.000	2.197	.028	.016576	.291285
[wspace=-1] * [Color=1]	0[a]	0	.	.	.	.	.
[wspace=1] * [Color=-1]	0[a]	0	.	.	.	.	.
[wspace=1] * [Color=1]	0[a]	0	.	.	.	.	.

a. This parameter is set to zero because it is redundant.

b. Dependent Variable: lowbudg.

Table 3.39. High Budget, Comparison of Means

Report

High Budget

White Space	Thumbnail	Background Color	Mean	N	Std. Deviation
More White Space	Right	White Background Color	4.50	458	1.359
		Blue Background Color	4.09	458	1.475
		Total	4.30	916	1.433
	Left	White Background Color	4.47	458	1.443
		Blue Background Color	4.33	458	1.462
		Total	4.40	916	1.454
	Total	White Background Color	4.49	916	1.401
		Blue Background Color	4.21	916	1.472
		Total	4.35	1832	1.443
Less White Space	Right	White Background Color	4.29	458	1.391
		Blue Background Color	4.31	458	1.452
		Total	4.30	916	1.421
	Left	White Background Color	4.51	458	1.462
		Blue Background Color	4.25	458	1.433
		Total	4.38	916	1.452
	Total	White Background Color	4.40	916	1.430
		Blue Background Color	4.28	916	1.442
		Total	4.34	1832	1.437
Total	Right	White Background Color	4.40	916	1.379
		Blue Background Color	4.20	916	1.467
		Total	4.30	1832	1.426
	Left	White Background Color	4.49	916	1.452
		Blue Background Color	4.29	916	1.447
		Total	4.39	1832	1.453
	Total	White Background Color	4.44	1832	1.416
		Blue Background Color	4.24	1832	1.457
		Total	4.34	3664	1.440

Estimated Marginal Means of High Budget

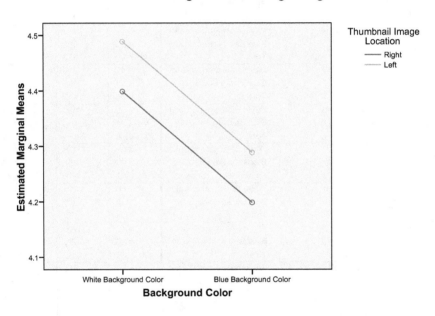

Figure 3.40. High Budget, Background Color versus Thumbnail Image Location

Table 3.41. Trust Buying Product, Mixed Model

Type III Tests of Fixed Effects[a]

Source	Numerator df	Denominator df	F	Sig.
Intercept	1	212.000	12.182	.001
Gender	1	212.000	.122	.727
wspace	1	3428	.787	.375
ImLoc	1	3428	12.333	.000
Color	1	3428	13.740	.000
Age	1	212.000	.064	.800
HoursonInternetper WeekDay	1	212.000	3.767	.054
HoursonInternetper WeekendDay	1	212.000	1.750	.187
ItemsPurchased Online1M	1	212.000	.509	.476
InternetShopping	1	212.000	.074	.786
LikeShop	1	212.000	1.325	.251
LessRisky	1	212.000	.034	.853
PreferOnlineShop	1	212.000	2.167	.143
AssessTrustworthiness	1	212.000	2.742	.099
AssessDesignQuality	1	212.000	.201	.654
ExpertUser	1	212.000	.342	.559
LooksAttention	1	212.000	.180	.671
CoVisualTrust	1	212.000	.287	.593
LikeStay	1	212.000	3.928	.049
Imakeextensiveuseofthei nternet	1	212.000	3.835	.052
Gender * wspace	1	3428.000	9.149	.003
Gender * ImLoc	1	3428.000	.230	.631
Gender * Color	1	3428.000	2.796	.095
wspace * Color	1	3428	3.212	.073

a. Dependent Variable: trust.

271

Estimates of Fixed Effects[b]

Parameter	Estimate	Std. Error	df	t	Sig.	95% Confidence Interval	
						Lower Bound	Upper Bound
Intercept	2.878921	.874808	213.277	3.291	.001	1.154543	4.603299
[Gender=1]	.219595	.159074	276.004	1.380	.169	-.093558	.532748
[Gender=2]	0[a]	0	.	.	.	.	.
[wspace=-1]	.071451	.060742	3428	1.176	.240	-.047643	.190546
[wspace=1]	0[a]	0	.	.	.	.	.
[lmLoc=-1]	-.098101	.052376	3428	-1.873	.061	-.200793	.004590
[lmLoc=1]	0[a]	0	.	.	.	.	.
[Color=-1]	.118920	.060742	3428	1.958	.050	-.000175	.238014
[Color=1]	0[a]	0	.	.	.	.	.
Age	-.008953	.035263	212.000	-.254	.800	-.078465	.060559
HoursonInternetper WeekDay	.017375	.008952	212.000	1.941	.054	-.000271	.035021
HoursonInternetper WeekendDay	-.028548	.021583	212.000	-1.323	.187	-.071092	.013996
ItemsPurchased Online1M	-.012370	.017333	212.000	-.714	.476	-.046536	.021797
InternetShopping	.013234	.048762	212.000	.271	.786	-.082886	.109355
LikeShop	.060418	.052489	212.000	1.151	.251	-.043050	.163886
LessRisky	.008227	.044490	212.000	.185	.853	-.079473	.095928
PreferOnlineShop	-.072620	.049336	212.000	-1.472	.143	-.169871	.024631
AssessTrustworthiness	.093822	.056657	212.000	1.656	.099	-.017861	.205505
AssessDesignQuality	.025799	.057538	212.000	.448	.654	-.087621	.139219
ExpertUser	-.025578	.043719	212.000	-.585	.559	-.111758	.060602
LooksAttention	.026028	.061276	212.000	.425	.671	-.094760	.146815
CoVisualTrust	.035621	.066481	212.000	.536	.593	-.095427	.166669
LikeStay	.101280	.051103	212.000	1.982	.049	.000545	.202014
Imakeextensiveuseofthei nternet	.106977	.054629	212.000	1.958	.052	-.000707	.214662
[Gender=1] * [wspace=-1]	-.195749	.064715	3428.000	-3.025	.003	-.322633	-.068865
[Gender=1] * [wspace=1]	0[a]	0	.	.	.	.	.
[Gender=2] * [wspace=-1]	0[a]	0	.	.	.	.	.
[Gender=2] * [wspace=1]	0[a]	0	.	.	.	.	.
[Gender=1] * [lmLoc=-1]	-.031065	.064715	3428.000	-.480	.631	-.157949	.095818
[Gender=1] * [lmLoc=1]	0[a]	0	.	.	.	.	.
[Gender=2] * [lmLoc=-1]	0[a]	0	.	.	.	.	.
[Gender=2] * [lmLoc=1]	0[a]	0	.	.	.	.	.
[Gender=1] * [Color=-1]	-.108217	.064715	3428.000	-1.672	.095	-.235101	.018667
[Gender=1] * [Color=1]	0[a]	0	.	.	.	.	.
[Gender=2] * [Color=-1]	0[a]	0	.	.	.	.	.
[Gender=2] * [Color=1]	0[a]	0	.	.	.	.	.
[wspace=-1] * [Color=-1]	.110262	.061526	3428	1.792	.073	-.010369	.230893
[wspace=-1] * [Color=1]	0[a]	0	.	.	.	.	.
[wspace=1] * [Color=-1]	0[a]	0	.	.	.	.	.
[wspace=1] * [Color=1]	0[a]	0	.	.	.	.	.

a. This parameter is set to zero because it is redundant.

b. Dependent Variable: trust.

272

Table 3.42. Trust Buying Product, Mixed Model, Internet Savvy Index

Type III Tests of Fixed Effects[a]

Source	Numerator df	Denominator df	F	Sig.
Intercept	1	223.000	28.053	.000
Gender	1	223.000	.222	.638
wspace	1	3428.000	.787	.375
ImLoc	1	3428.000	12.333	.000
Color	1	3428.000	13.740	.000
Age	1	223.000	.381	.538
onlineshopatt	1	223.000	.063	.802
intsavvy	1	223.000	5.625	.019
designmind	1	223.000	.024	.876
Gender * wspace	1	3428.000	9.149	.003
Gender * ImLoc	1	3428.000	.230	.631
Gender * Color	1	3428.000	2.796	.095
wspace * Color	1	3428.000	3.212	.073

a. Dependent Variable: trust.

Estimates of Fixed Effects[b]

Parameter	Estimate	Std. Error	df	t	Sig.	95% Confidence Interval Lower Bound	Upper Bound
Intercept	3.828585	.763368	224.766	5.015	.000	2.324312	5.332857
[Gender=1]	.234968	.153649	296.245	1.529	.127	-.067414	.537349
[Gender=2]	0[a]	0	.	.	.	.	.
[wspace=-1]	.071451	.060742	3428.000	1.176	.240	-.047643	.190546
[wspace=1]	0[a]	0	.	.	.	.	.
[ImLoc=-1]	-.098101	.052376	3428.000	-1.873	.061	-.200793	.004590
[ImLoc=1]	0[a]	0	.	.	.	.	.
[Color=-1]	.118920	.060742	3428.000	1.958	.050	-.000175	.238014
[Color=1]	0[a]	0	.	.	.	.	.
Age	-.020727	.033568	223.000	-.617	.538	-.086877	.045424
onlineshopatt	.012485	.049684	223.000	.251	.802	-.085425	.110394
intsavvy	.187659	.079127	223.000	2.372	.019	.031726	.343592
designmind	.008541	.054886	223.000	.156	.876	-.099620	.116702
[Gender=1] * [wspace=-1]	-.195749	.064715	3428.000	-3.025	.003	-.322633	-.068865
[Gender=1] * [wspace=1]	0[a]	0	.	.	.	.	.
[Gender=2] * [wspace=-1]	0[a]	0	.	.	.	.	.
[Gender=2] * [wspace=1]	0[a]	0	.	.	.	.	.
[Gender=1] * [ImLoc=-1]	-.031065	.064715	3428.000	-.480	.631	-.157949	.095818
[Gender=1] * [ImLoc=1]	0[a]	0	.	.	.	.	.
[Gender=2] * [ImLoc=-1]	0[a]	0	.	.	.	.	.
[Gender=2] * [ImLoc=1]	0[a]	0	.	.	.	.	.
[Gender=1] * [Color=-1]	-.108217	.064715	3428.000	-1.672	.095	-.235101	.018667
[Gender=1] * [Color=1]	0[a]	0	.	.	.	.	.
[Gender=2] * [Color=-1]	0[a]	0	.	.	.	.	.
[Gender=2] * [Color=1]	0[a]	0	.	.	.	.	.
[wspace=-1] * [Color=-1]	.110262	.061526	3428.000	1.792	.073	-.010369	.230893
[wspace=-1] * [Color=1]	0[a]	0	.	.	.	.	.
[wspace=1] * [Color=-1]	0[a]	0	.	.	.	.	.
[wspace=1] * [Color=1]	0[a]	0	.	.	.	.	.

a. This parameter is set to zero because it is redundant.

b. Dependent Variable: trust.

Table 3.43. Trust Buying Product, Comparison of Means

Report

Trust Buying Product

White Space	Thumbnail	Background Color	Mean	N	Std. Deviation
More White Space	Right	White Background Color	4.69	458	1.303
		Blue Background Color	4.40	458	1.375
		Total	4.55	916	1.347
	Left	White Background Color	4.67	458	1.280
		Blue Background Color	4.64	458	1.373
		Total	4.65	916	1.327
	Total	White Background Color	4.68	916	1.291
		Blue Background Color	4.52	916	1.378
		Total	4.60	1832	1.338
Less White Space	Right	White Background Color	4.48	458	1.293
		Blue Background Color	4.60	458	1.312
		Total	4.54	916	1.303
	Left	White Background Color	4.77	458	1.283
		Blue Background Color	4.56	458	1.304
		Total	4.67	916	1.297
	Total	White Background Color	4.63	916	1.296
		Blue Background Color	4.58	916	1.307
		Total	4.60	1832	1.301
Total	Right	White Background Color	4.58	916	1.302
		Blue Background Color	4.50	916	1.347
		Total	4.54	1832	1.325
	Left	White Background Color	4.72	916	1.282
		Blue Background Color	4.60	916	1.339
		Total	4.66	1832	1.312
	Total	White Background Color	4.65	1832	1.293
		Blue Background Color	4.55	1832	1.343
		Total	4.60	3664	1.319

Estimated Marginal Means of Trust Buying Product

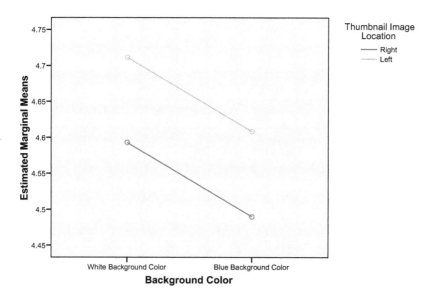

Figure 3.44. Trust Buying Product, Background Color versus Thumbnail Image Location

Table 3.45. Trust Buying Product, Comparison of Means, White Space versus Gender

Descriptive Statistics

Dependent Variable: trust

wspace	Gender	Mean	Std. Deviation	N
More White Space	Female	4.54	1.321	1200
	Male	4.71	1.363	632
	Total	4.60	1.338	1832
Less White Space	Female	4.61	1.247	1200
	Male	4.59	1.400	632
	Total	4.60	1.301	1832
Total	Female	4.58	1.285	2400
	Male	4.65	1.383	1264
	Total	4.60	1.319	3664

Table 3.46. Won't Continue Search, Mixed Model

Type III Tests of Fixed Effects[a]

Source	Numerator df	Denominator df	F	Sig.
Intercept	1	212.000	17.231	.000
Gender	1	212	.160	.690
wspace	1	3428	.050	.823
ImLoc	1	3428	1.153	.283
Color	1	3428	1.740	.187
Age	1	212.000	1.258	.263
HoursonInternetper WeekDay	1	212	.090	.764
HoursonInternetper WeekendDay	1	212	.774	.380
ItemsPurchased Online1M	1	212.000	.546	.461
InternetShopping	1	212	1.422	.234
LikeShop	1	212	.139	.710
LessRisky	1	212	.533	.466
PreferOnlineShop	1	212	.361	.548
AssessTrustworthiness	1	212.000	4.424	.037
AssessDesignQuality	1	212.000	.863	.354
ExpertUser	1	212.000	4.490	.035
LooksAttention	1	212.000	.096	.757
CoVisualTrust	1	212.000	.000	.985
LikeStay	1	212.000	.265	.607
Imakeextensiveuseofthei nternet	1	212.000	.251	.617
Gender * wspace	1	3428	.007	.933
Gender * ImLoc	1	3428	.083	.774
Gender * Color	1	3428	.155	.694
wspace * Color	1	3428	.092	.762

a. Dependent Variable: consear.

Estimates of Fixed Effects[b]

Parameter	Estimate	Std. Error	df	t	Sig.	95% Confidence Interval	
						Lower Bound	Upper Bound
Intercept	4.517996	1.104939	212.991	4.089	.000	2.339980	6.696013
[Gender=1]	-.074422	.198182	261.037	-.376	.708	-.464661	.315816
[Gender=2]	0[a]	0	.	.	.	.	.
[wspace=-1]	-.021447	.067633	3428	-.317	.751	-.154051	.111157
[wspace=1]	0[a]	0	.	.	.	.	.
[ImLoc=-1]	-.049051	.058317	3428	-.841	.400	-.163391	.065290
[ImLoc=1]	0[a]	0	.	.	.	.	.
[Color=-1]	.051338	.067633	3428	.759	.448	-.081267	.183942
[Color=1]	0[a]	0	.	.	.	.	.
Age	-.049966	.044555	212.000	-1.121	.263	-.137794	.037861
HoursonInternetper WeekDay	-.003401	.011311	212	-.301	.764	-.025697	.018895
HoursonInternetper WeekendDay	.023985	.027269	212	.880	.380	-.029769	.077738
ItemsPurchased Online1M	-.016178	.021900	212.000	-.739	.461	-.059348	.026991
InternetShopping	-.073470	.061610	212	-1.193	.234	-.194916	.047976
LikeShop	-.024690	.066320	212	-.372	.710	-.155421	.106040
LessRisky	.041054	.056213	212	.730	.466	-.069755	.151862
PreferOnlineShop	.037472	.062335	212	.601	.548	-.085404	.160347
AssessTrustworthiness	.150561	.071585	212.000	2.103	.037	.009450	.291671
AssessDesignQuality	-.067528	.072699	212.000	-.929	.354	-.210832	.075777
ExpertUser	-.117046	.055239	212.000	-2.119	.035	-.225933	-.008158
LooksAttention	.023963	.077421	212.000	.310	.757	-.128651	.176576
CoVisualTrust	.001590	.083998	212.000	.019	.985	-.163988	.167167
LikeStay	.033253	.064568	212.000	.515	.607	-.094024	.160530
Imakeextensiveuseofthei nternet	-.034574	.069023	212.000	-.501	.617	-.170632	.101484
[Gender=1] * [wspace=-1]	.006076	.072056	3428	.084	.933	-.135201	.147353
[Gender=1] * [wspace=1]	0[a]	0	.	.	.	.	.
[Gender=2] * [wspace=-1]	0[a]	0	.	.	.	.	.
[Gender=2] * [wspace=1]	0[a]	0	.	.	.	.	.
[Gender=1] * [ImLoc=-1]	.020717	.072056	3428	.288	.774	-.120560	.161995
[Gender=1] * [ImLoc=1]	0[a]	0	.	.	.	.	.
[Gender=2] * [ImLoc=-1]	0[a]	0	.	.	.	.	.
[Gender=2] * [ImLoc=1]	0[a]	0	.	.	.	.	.
[Gender=1] * [Color=-1]	-.028376	.072056	3428	-.394	.694	-.169653	.112902
[Gender=1] * [Color=1]	0[a]	0	.	.	.	.	.
[Gender=2] * [Color=-1]	0[a]	0	.	.	.	.	.
[Gender=2] * [Color=1]	0[a]	0	.	.	.	.	.
[wspace=-1] * [Color=-1]	.020742	.068505	3428	.303	.762	-.113573	.155058
[wspace=-1] * [Color=1]	0[a]	0	.	.	.	.	.
[wspace=1] * [Color=-1]	0[a]	0	.	.	.	.	.
[wspace=1] * [Color=1]	0[a]	0	.	.	.	.	.

a. This parameter is set to zero because it is redundant.

b. Dependent Variable: consear.

277

Table 3.47. Won't Continue Search, Comparison of Means

Report

Won't Continue Search

White Space	Thumbnail	Background Color	Mean	N	Std. Deviation
More White Space	Right	White Background Color	3.13	458	1.506
		Blue Background Color	3.05	458	1.593
		Total	3.09	916	1.550
	Left	White Background Color	3.12	458	1.554
		Blue Background Color	3.10	458	1.603
		Total	3.11	916	1.578
	Total	White Background Color	3.13	916	1.530
		Blue Background Color	3.07	916	1.598
		Total	3.10	1832	1.564
Less White Space	Right	White Background Color	3.10	458	1.585
		Blue Background Color	3.07	458	1.555
		Total	3.08	916	1.569
	Left	White Background Color	3.15	458	1.531
		Blue Background Color	3.11	458	1.559
		Total	3.13	916	1.545
	Total	White Background Color	3.12	916	1.558
		Blue Background Color	3.09	916	1.556
		Total	3.11	1832	1.557
Total	Right	White Background Color	3.11	916	1.545
		Blue Background Color	3.06	916	1.573
		Total	3.08	1832	1.559
	Left	White Background Color	3.14	916	1.542
		Blue Background Color	3.10	916	1.581
		Total	3.12	1832	1.561
	Total	White Background Color	3.12	1832	1.543
		Blue Background Color	3.08	1832	1.577
		Total	3.10	3664	1.560

278

Table 3.48. Purchase Likely, Mixed Model

Type III Tests of Fixed Effects[a]

Source	Numerator df	Denominator df	F	Sig.
Intercept	1	212.000	22.358	.000
Gender	1	212.000	.037	.847
wspace	1	3428.000	.037	.847
ImLoc	1	3428.000	9.443	.002
Color	1	3428.000	8.215	.004
Age	1	212.000	5.420	.021
HoursonInternetper WeekDay	1	212.000	.776	.379
HoursonInternetper WeekendDay	1	212	2.102	.149
ItemsPurchased Online1M	1	212.000	.081	.776
InternetShopping	1	212	.304	.582
LikeShop	1	212.000	2.480	.117
LessRisky	1	212	3.424	.066
PreferOnlineShop	1	212	2.946	.088
AssessTrustworthiness	1	212.000	4.189	.042
AssessDesignQuality	1	212.000	.463	.497
ExpertUser	1	212.000	1.339	.249
LooksAttention	1	212.000	.572	.450
CoVisualTrust	1	212.000	.473	.493
LikeStay	1	212.000	1.470	.227
Imakeextensiveuseofthei nternet	1	212.000	3.200	.075
Gender * wspace	1	3428.000	3.871	.049
Gender * ImLoc	1	3428.000	.088	.767
Gender * Color	1	3428.000	.075	.784
wspace * Color	1	3428	.252	.616

a. Dependent Variable: purlike

279

Estimates of Fixed Effects[b]

Parameter	Estimate	Std. Error	df	t	Sig.	95% Confidence Interval	
						Lower Bound	Upper Bound
Intercept	4.833282	1.047472	213.140	4.614	.000	2.768551	6.898014
[Gender=1]	.016630	.189236	268.807	.088	.930	-.355943	.389202
[Gender=2]	0[a]	0	.	.	.	.	.
[wspace=-1]	.061647	.068751	3428.000	.897	.370	-.073151	.196444
[wspace=1]	0[a]	0	.	.	.	.	.
[lmLoc=-1]	-.123418	.059282	3428.000	-2.082	.037	-.239649	-.007186
[lmLoc=1]	0[a]	0	.	.	.	.	.
[Color=-1]	.077469	.068751	3428.000	1.127	.260	-.057328	.212267
[Color=1]	0[a]	0	.	.	.	.	.
Age	-.098314	.042230	212.000	-2.328	.021	-.181559	-.015069
HoursonInternetper WeekDay	.009441	.010720	212.000	.881	.379	-.011691	.030574
HoursonInternetper WeekendDay	-.037472	.025846	212	-1.450	.149	-.088421	.013477
ItemsPurchased Online1M	-.005906	.020757	212.000	-.285	.776	-.046823	.035011
InternetShopping	.032213	.058395	212	.552	.582	-.082897	.147323
LikeShop	.098987	.062860	212.000	1.575	.117	-.024922	.222897
LessRisky	-.098591	.053280	212	-1.850	.066	-.203617	.006436
PreferOnlineShop	-.101412	.059083	212	-1.716	.088	-.217876	.015053
AssessTrustworthiness	.138873	.067850	212.000	2.047	.042	.005125	.272621
AssessDesignQuality	-.046870	.068905	212.000	-.680	.497	-.182698	.088957
ExpertUser	.060578	.052357	212.000	1.157	.249	-.042629	.163784
LooksAttention	.055515	.073381	212.000	.757	.450	-.089136	.200166
CoVisualTrust	-.054735	.079615	212.000	-.688	.493	-.211674	.102203
LikeStay	.074198	.061199	212.000	1.212	.227	-.046438	.194834
Imakeextensiveuseofthei nternet	.117034	.065421	212.000	1.789	.075	-.011926	.245993
[Gender=1] * [wspace=-1]	-.144114	.073248	3428.000	-1.967	.049	-.287728	-.000500
[Gender=1] * [wspace=1]	0[a]	0	.	.	.	.	.
[Gender=2] * [wspace=-1]	0[a]	0	.	.	.	.	.
[Gender=2] * [wspace=1]	0[a]	0	.	.	.	.	.
[Gender=1] * [lmLoc=-1]	.021751	.073248	3428.000	.297	.767	-.121863	.165365
[Gender=1] * [lmLoc=1]	0[a]	0	.	.	.	.	.
[Gender=2] * [lmLoc=-1]	0[a]	0	.	.	.	.	.
[Gender=2] * [lmLoc=1]	0[a]	0	.	.	.	.	.
[Gender=1] * [Color=-1]	.020063	.073248	3428.000	.274	.784	-.123550	.163677
[Gender=1] * [Color=1]	0[a]	0	.	.	.	.	.
[Gender=2] * [Color=-1]	0[a]	0	.	.	.	.	.
[Gender=2] * [Color=1]	0[a]	0	.	.	.	.	.
[wspace=-1] * [Color=-1]	.034934	.069638	3428	.502	.616	-.101602	.171471
[wspace=-1] * [Color=1]	0[a]	0	.	.	.	.	.
[wspace=1] * [Color=-1]	0[a]	0	.	.	.	.	.
[wspace=1] * [Color=1]	0[a]	0	.	.	.	.	.

a. This parameter is set to zero because it is redundant.

b. Dependent Variable: purlike.

Table 3.49. Purchase Likely, Mixed Model, Internet Savvy Index

Type III Tests of Fixed Effects[a]

Source	Numerator df	Denominator df	F	Sig.
Intercept	1	223.000	33.516	.000
Gender	1	223.000	.006	.939
wspace	1	3428	.037	.847
ImLoc	1	3428	9.443	.002
Color	1	3428	8.215	.004
Age	1	223.000	5.850	.016
onlineshopatt	1	223.000	.060	.806
intsavvy	1	223.000	6.617	.011
designmind	1	223.000	.243	.622
Gender * wspace	1	3428	3.871	.049
Gender * ImLoc	1	3428	.088	.767
Gender * Color	1	3428	.075	.784
wspace * Color	1	3428	.252	.616

a. Dependent Variable: purlike.

Estimates of Fixed Effects[b]

Parameter	Estimate	Std. Error	df	t	Sig.	95% Confidence Interval	
						Lower Bound	Upper Bound
Intercept	5.154076	.916097	224.570	5.626	.000	3.348829	6.959322
[Gender=1]	.038047	.183065	287.663	.208	.836	-.322270	.398364
[Gender=2]	0[a]	0	.	.	.	.	.
[wspace=-1]	.061647	.068751	3428	.897	.370	-.073151	.196444
[wspace=1]	0[a]	0	.	.	.	.	.
[ImLoc=-1]	-.123418	.059282	3428	-2.082	.037	-.239649	-.007186
[ImLoc=1]	0[a]	0	.	.	.	.	.
[Color=-1]	.077469	.068751	3428	1.127	.260	-.057328	.212267
[Color=1]	0[a]	0	.	.	.	.	.
Age	-.097458	.040293	223.000	-2.419	.016	-.176861	-.018056
onlineshopatt	.014630	.059637	223.000	.245	.806	-.102894	.132155
intsavvy	.244321	.094979	223.000	2.572	.011	.057149	.431493
designmind	-.032496	.065882	223.000	-.493	.622	-.162326	.097334
[Gender=1] * [wspace=-1]	-.144114	.073248	3428	-1.967	.049	-.287728	-.000500
[Gender=1] * [wspace=1]	0[a]	0	.	.	.	.	.
[Gender=2] * [wspace=-1]	0[a]	0	.	.	.	.	.
[Gender=2] * [wspace=1]	0[a]	0	.	.	.	.	.
[Gender=1] * [ImLoc=-1]	.021751	.073248	3428	.297	.767	-.121863	.165365
[Gender=1] * [ImLoc=1]	0[a]	0	.	.	.	.	.
[Gender=2] * [ImLoc=-1]	0[a]	0	.	.	.	.	.
[Gender=2] * [ImLoc=1]	0[a]	0	.	.	.	.	.
[Gender=1] * [Color=-1]	.020063	.073248	3428	.274	.784	-.123550	.163677
[Gender=1] * [Color=1]	0[a]	0	.	.	.	.	.
[Gender=2] * [Color=-1]	0[a]	0	.	.	.	.	.
[Gender=2] * [Color=1]	0[a]	0	.	.	.	.	.
[wspace=-1] * [Color=-1]	.034934	.069638	3428	.502	.616	-.101602	.171471
[wspace=-1] * [Color=1]	0[a]	0	.	.	.	.	.
[wspace=1] * [Color=-1]	0[a]	0	.	.	.	.	.
[wspace=1] * [Color=1]	0[a]	0	.	.	.	.	.

a. This parameter is set to zero because it is redundant.

b. Dependent Variable: purlike.

Table 3.50. Purchase Likely, Comparison of Means

Report

Purchase Likely

White Space	Thumbnail	Background Color	Mean	N	Std. Deviation
More White Space	Right	White Background Color	4.43	458	1.478
		Blue Background Color	4.17	458	1.560
		Total	4.30	916	1.524
	Left	White Background Color	4.40	458	1.549
		Blue Background Color	4.41	458	1.588
		Total	4.41	916	1.568
	Total	White Background Color	4.42	916	1.513
		Blue Background Color	4.29	916	1.578
		Total	4.35	1832	1.546
Less White Space	Right	White Background Color	4.24	458	1.580
		Blue Background Color	4.39	458	1.528
		Total	4.31	916	1.555
	Left	White Background Color	4.59	458	1.450
		Blue Background Color	4.26	458	1.633
		Total	4.43	916	1.552
	Total	White Background Color	4.41	916	1.526
		Blue Background Color	4.32	916	1.582
		Total	4.37	1832	1.554
Total	Right	White Background Color	4.33	916	1.532
		Blue Background Color	4.28	916	1.547
		Total	4.31	1832	1.539
	Left	White Background Color	4.50	916	1.502
		Blue Background Color	4.34	916	1.611
		Total	4.42	1832	1.560
	Total	White Background Color	4.42	1832	1.519
		Blue Background Color	4.31	1832	1.579
		Total	4.36	3664	1.550

Estimated Marginal Means of Purchase Likely

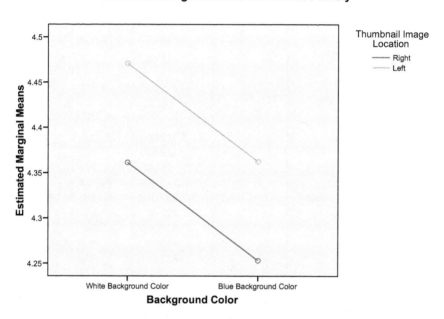

Figure 3.51. Purchase Likely, Background Color versus Thumbnail Image Location

Table 3.52. Image Size Picked, Mixed Model

Type III Tests of Fixed Effects[a]

Source	Numerator df	Denominator df	F	Sig.
Intercept	1	212.000	3.638	.058
Gender	1	212.000	.893	.346
wspace	1	3426.000	.670	.413
ImLoc	1	3426.000	112.110	.000
Color	1	3426.000	15.786	.000
Imsizedes	1	3426.000	29.953	.000
Age	1	212.000	4.833	.029
HoursonInternetper WeekDay	1	212.000	.237	.627
HoursonInternetper WeekendDay	1	212.000	1.021	.313
ItemsPurchased Online1M	1	212.000	.041	.841
InternetShopping	1	212.000	.000	.984
LikeShop	1	212.000	.009	.923
LessRisky	1	212.000	.128	.721
PreferOnlineShop	1	212.000	.121	.728
AssessTrustworthiness	1	212.000	.149	.700
AssessDesignQuality	1	212.000	1.998	.159
ExpertUser	1	212.000	.004	.951
LooksAttention	1	212.000	.057	.812
CoVisualTrust	1	212.000	.098	.754
LikeStay	1	212.000	.017	.897
Imakeextensiveuseofthei nternet	1	212.000	.014	.906
Gender * wspace	1	3426.000	.000	.983
Gender * ImLoc	1	3426.000	.203	.653
Gender * Imsizedes	1	3426.000	2.209	.137
Gender * Color	1	3426.000	.000	.989
wspace * Color	1	3426	39.992	.000

a. Dependent Variable: imsizen.

Estimates of Fixed Effects[b]

Parameter	Estimate	Std. Error	df	t	Sig.	95% Confidence Interval Lower Bound	Upper Bound
Intercept	.352236	.179903	219.378	1.958	.052	-.002323	.706795
[Gender=1]	.056110	.041183	684.409	1.362	.173	-.024749	.136969
[Gender=2]	0[a]	0	.	.	.	.	.
[wspace=-1]	.072439	.026076	3426	2.778	.005	.021313	.123565
[wspace=1]	0[a]	0	.	.	.	.	.
[lmLoc=-1]	-.140823	.022485	3426.000	-6.263	.000	-.184907	-.096738
[lmLoc=1]	0[a]	0	.	.	.	.	.
[Color=-1]	.138895	.026076	3426	5.327	.000	.087769	.190021
[Color=1]	0[a]	0	.	.	.	.	.
[lmsizedes=-1]	-.055380	.022485	3426.000	-2.463	.014	-.099464	-.011295
[lmsizedes=1]	0[a]	0	.	.	.	.	.
Age	.015830	.007201	212.000	2.198	.029	.001636	.030025
HoursonInternetper WeekDay	.000889	.001828	212.000	.486	.627	-.002714	.004492
HoursonInternetper WeekendDay	-.004453	.004407	212.000	-1.010	.313	-.013141	.004235
ItemsPurchased Online1M	-.000713	.003539	212.000	-.201	.841	-.007690	.006264
InternetShopping	.000201	.009957	212.000	.020	.984	-.019427	.019829
LikeShop	.001041	.010718	212.000	.097	.923	-.020087	.022170
LessRisky	.003251	.009085	212.000	.358	.721	-.014658	.021159
PreferOnlineShop	-.003508	.010074	212.000	-.348	.728	-.023367	.016351
AssessTrustworthiness	.004472	.011569	212.000	.387	.700	-.018334	.027278
AssessDesignQuality	.016607	.011749	212.000	1.413	.159	-.006554	.039767
ExpertUser	-.000553	.008928	212.000	-.062	.951	-.018151	.017046
LooksAttention	.002975	.012513	212.000	.238	.812	-.021690	.027640
CoVisualTrust	-.004257	.013576	212.000	-.314	.754	-.031017	.022504
LikeStay	.001359	.010435	212.000	.130	.897	-.019211	.021929
Imakeextensiveuseofthei nternet	-.001321	.011155	212.000	-.118	.906	-.023310	.020669
[Gender=1] * [wspace=-1]	-.000591	.027781	3426.000	-.021	.983	-.055061	.053879
[Gender=1] * [wspace=1]	0[a]	0	.	.	.	.	.
[Gender=2] * [wspace=-1]	0[a]	0	.	.	.	.	.
[Gender=2] * [wspace=1]	0[a]	0	.	.	.	.	.
[Gender=1] * [lmLoc=-1]	-.012511	.027781	3426.000	-.450	.653	-.066981	.041959
[Gender=1] * [lmLoc=1]	0[a]	0	.	.	.	.	.
[Gender=2] * [lmLoc=-1]	0[a]	0	.	.	.	.	.
[Gender=2] * [lmLoc=1]	0[a]	0	.	.	.	.	.
[Gender=1] * [lmsizedes=-1]	-.041287	.027781	3426.000	-1.486	.137	-.095757	.013183
[Gender=1] * [lmsizedes=1]	0[a]	0	.	.	.	.	.
[Gender=2] * [lmsizedes=-1]	0[a]	0	.	.	.	.	.
[Gender=2] * [lmsizedes=1]	0[a]	0	.	.	.	.	.
[Gender=1] * [Color=-1]	-.000380	.027781	3426.000	-.014	.989	-.054850	.054090
[Gender=1] * [Color=1]	0[a]	0	.	.	.	.	.
[Gender=2] * [Color=-1]	0[a]	0	.	.	.	.	.
[Gender=2] * [Color=1]	0[a]	0	.	.	.	.	.
[wspace=-1] * [Color=-1]	-.167031	.026412	3426	-6.324	.000	-.218816	-.115245
[wspace=-1] * [Color=1]	0[a]	0	.	.	.	.	.
[wspace=1] * [Color=-1]	0[a]	0	.	.	.	.	.
[wspace=1] * [Color=1]	0[a]	0	.	.	.	.	.

a. This parameter is set to zero because it is redundant.

b. Dependent Variable: imsizen.

285

Table 3.53. Frequencies, Image Size Picked

Image Size Picked

		Frequency	Percent	Valid Percent	Cumulative Percent
Valid	Small Image	975	26.6	26.6	26.6
	Large Image	2689	73.4	73.4	100.0
	Total	3664	100.0	100.0	

Image Size Picked

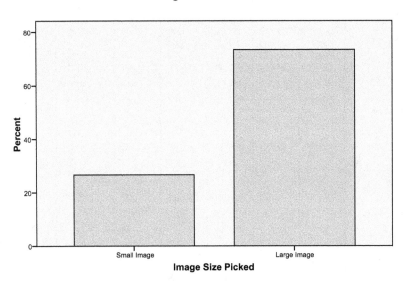

Figure 3.54. Frequencies, Histogram, Image Size Picked

Table 4.1. Web Site Design Guidelines, Compiled Guideline List

CATEGORY	SUBCATEGORY	WEB SITE DESIGN GUIDELINE	SOURCE
Prose	Brevity & Simplicity	Be succinct. Write no more than 50% of the text you would use when writing in print. Reading from computer screens is 25% slower than reading from paper.	(Nielsen, 2000)
Prose	Brevity & Simplicity	Be brief - use least number of words needed to convey meaning, avoid abbreviations.	(Cooper & Reimann, 2003)
Prose	Brevity & Simplicity	keep the content simple	(Mandel, 1997)
Prose	Structure	Write for scannability: avoid long continuous blocks of text; use short paragraphs, subheadings, highlighting, and bulleted lists. 79% of users always scanned new pages (nielsen and morkes)	(Nielsen, 2000)
Prose	Structure	Include the primary theme of a paragraph, and the scope of what it covers, in the first sentence of each paragraph. Users tend to skim the first one or two sentences of each paragraph when scanning text.	(U.S. Department of Health and Human Services, 2006)
Prose	Structure	provide overview of website	(Mandel, 1997)
Prose	Structure	To optimize reading comprehension, minimize the number of words in sentences, and the number of sentences in paragraphs. To enhance the readability of prose text, a sentence should not contain more than twenty words. A paragraph should not contain more than six sentences.	(U.S. Department of Health and Human Services, 2006)
Prose	Language	Use plain language and include topic sentences to aid scanning	(Nielsen, 2000)

287

Prose	Language	Avoid Jargon: Do not use words that typical users may not understand.	(U.S. Department of Health and Human Services, 2006)
Prose	Language	Use words that are frequently seen and heard.	(U.S. Department of Health and Human Services, 2006)
Prose	Language	Do not use unfamiliar or undefined acronyms or abbreviations. The only times to use abbreviations are when they are significantly shorter, save needed space, and will be readily understood by typical users. If users must read abbreviations, choose only common abbreviations.	(U.S. Department of Health and Human Services, 2006)
Prose	Language	Compose sentences in active rather than passive voice.	(U.S. Department of Health and Human Services, 2006)
Prose	Audience Orientation	Provide information in multiple formats if the Web site has distinct audiences who will be interested in the same information.	(U.S. Department of Health and Human Services, 2006)
Page	Citation Information	Each page should contain a title, an author, an institutional affiliation, a revision date, copyright information, and a link to the "home page" of your site.	(Lynch & Horton, 2002)
Text	Line Length	If reading speed is most important choose longer line lengths, if acceptance of the web site is most important, use shorter line lengths	(U.S. Department of Health and Human Services, 2006)
Text	Case	Avoid use of all caps,	(Cooper & Reimann, 2003)
Text	Case	Avoid use of all CAPS - ueers read 10% slower	(Nielsen, 2000)

Category	Subcategory	Guideline	Source
Text	Case	words set in all uppercase letters should generally be avoided — except perhaps for short headings — because they are difficult to scan. We recommend downstyle typing (capitalize only the first word and any proper nouns) for your headlines, subheads, and text. Downstyle is more legible because as we read we primarily scan the tops of words.	(Lynch & Horton, 2002)
Text	Case	When users must read a lot of information, use lower-case fonts and appropriate capitalization to ensure the fastest possible reading speed	(U.S. Department of Health and Human Services, 2006)
Text	Case	Display continuous (prose) text using mixed upper- and lowercase letters.	(U.S. Department of Health and Human Services, 2006)
Text	Color & Contrast	use high contrast font	(Cooper & Reimann, 2003; Weeks, 1997)
Text	Color & Contrast	Use colors with high contrast between text and background. Be wary of users with red-green colorblindness	(Nielsen, 2000)
Text	Color & Contrast	When users are expected to rapidly read and understand prose text, use black text on a plain, high-contrast, non-patterned background.	(U.S. Department of Health and Human Services, 2006)
Text	Size	use large fonts	(Cooper & Reimann, 2003)
Text	Size	make sure the text size is big enough	(Mandel, 1997)
Text	Size	Use big enough fonts - tiny fonts used only for footnotes or legal disclaimers	(Nielsen, 2000)
Text	Size	good pages use minimum font sizes of 9 pt or less for footer text	(Ivory & Hearst, 2002b)
Text	Size	Research has shown that fonts smaller than 12 points elicit slower reading performance from users. For users over age 65, it may be better to use at least fourteen-point fonts. Never use less than nine-point font on a Web site.	(U.S. Department of Health and Human Services, 2006)

Text	Justification	Long blocks of text and lists should be left justified for ease of reading	(Nielsen, 2000)
Text	Justification	Left-justified text is the most legible option for Web pages because the left margin is even and predictable and the right margin is irregular	(Lynch & Horton, 2002)
Text	Font	Any text that is really small (9pt or less) should use sans-serif typeface. Larger text can use a serif font	(Nielsen, 2000)
Text	Font	use a serif face such as Times New Roman or Georgia for body text and a sans serif face such as Verdana or Arial as a contrast for headlines (body text if printed out). Typefaces such as Georgia and Verdana were designed specifically for legibility on the computer screen; they have exaggerated x-heights and are very large compared to more traditional typefaces in the same point size. These fonts offer excellent legibility for Web pages designed to be read directly from the screen	(Lynch & Horton, 2002)
Text	Font	Use a familiar font to achieve the best possible reading speed. Research shows no reliable differences in reading speed or user preferences for twelve point Times New Roman or Georgia (serif fonts), or Arial, Helvetica, or Verdana (sans serif fonts).	(U.S. Department of Health and Human Services, 2006)
Text	Font	brief text: san serif, Paragraphs: serif	(Cooper & Reimann, 2003)
Text	Font	Visual Noise and Clutter: Use 1-2 fonts in a few sizes	(Cooper & Reimann, 2003)
Text	Emphasis	Good and average pages rarely contain italicized words within body text	(Ivory & Hearst, 2002b)

Text	Emphasis	If you include underlined text on your Web page it will certainly be confused with a hypertext link	(Lynch & Horton, 2002)
Text	Emphasis	Use bold text only when it is important to draw the user's attention to a specific piece of information.	(U.S. Department of Health and Human Services, 2006)
Text	Emphasis	Having some text and graphic items in brighter colors, and others in darker colors, helps users determine the relative importance of elements. Important attention-attracting font characteristics can include all uppercase, bolding, italics, underlining, and increased font size.	(U.S. Department of Health and Human Services, 2006)
Text	Emphasis	Do not use two (or more) different ways to highlight the same information on one page.	(U.S. Department of Health and Human Services, 2006)
Text	Emphasis	Change the font characteristics to emphasize the importance of a word or short phrase. Font characteristics that are different from the surrounding text will dominate those that are routine. Important font characteristics include bolding, italics, font style (serif vs. sans serif), font size (larger is better to gain attention), and case (upper vs. lower). The use of differing font characteristics has negative consequences as well–reading speed can decrease by almost twenty percent, and thus should be used sparingly in large blocks of prose. Do not use differing font characteristics to show emphasis for more than one or two words or a short phrase. Do not use underlining for emphasis because underlined words on the Web are generally considered to be links.	(U.S. Department of Health and Human Services, 2006)
Text	Emphasis	Make the text stand still. Moving, blinking, or zooming text is much harder to read than static words	(Nielsen, 2000)

Category	Subcategory	Description	Reference
Text	Leading - White Space	The vertical space in a text block is called leading, and it is the distance from one baseline of text to the next. We suggest generous leading to compensate for longer line lengths and the lower resolution of the computer screen, for example, 12-point type with 14 to 16 points of leading	(Lynch & Horton, 2002)
Text	Consistency	Ensure that the format of common items is consistent from one page to another.	(U.S. Department of Health and Human Services, 2006)
Multimedia	Introductory Information	Provide an introductory explanation for animation prior to it being viewed.	(U.S. Department of Health and Human Services, 2006)
Multimedia	Introductory Information	give users enough information to make an informed decision *before they click*, so that they know what to expect and are prepared to receive your materials	(Lynch & Horton, 2002)
Multimedia	Introductory Information	Include descriptive information about the materials along with previews such as still shots from the video. Include the run time for time-based media, and include the file size for materials that download. In addition, fully explain any special software requirements for accessing the materials and provide a download link	(Lynch & Horton, 2002)
Multimedia	Usage	Use video, animation, and audio only when they help to convey, or are supportive of, the Web site's message or other content.	(U.S. Department of Health and Human Services, 2006)
Multimedia	Usage	Most animation is nothing more than a distraction. If you place animation alongside primary content you will simply disrupt your readers' concentration and keep them from the objective of your site. If you require users to sit through your spiffy Flash intro every time they visit your site, you are effectively turning them away at the door	(Lynch & Horton, 2002)
Multimedia	Usage	Avoid the use of 3D - much more confusing to users	(Nielsen, 2000)

Category	Subcategory	Description	Reference
Multimedia	Usage	Minimize use of animations - makes it harder for users to concentrate on reading text on the page	(Nielsen, 2000)
Usage	Animation	do not have animations loop continuously, have them run a few times and then stop	(Nielsen, 2000)
		Use attention-attracting features with caution and only when they are highly relevant. Movement (e.g., animation or 'reveals') is the most effective attention-getting item.	(U.S. Department of Health and Human Services, 2006)
Usage	Animation	Research suggests that people cannot stop themselves from initially looking at moving items on a page. However, if the movement is not relevant or useful, it may annoy the user.	
Usage	Audio	background music should be quiet and should not compete with the information on the page for user attention	(Nielsen, 2000)
Usage	Audio	nonspeech sound effects to inform users of events should remain quiet and nonintrusive.	(Nielsen, 2000)
Multimedia	Site Architecture	High-demand content such as large multimedia files should not be part of your basic page design. These materials should appear on secondary pages that are described and can be accessed from the main pages of your site. Make the menu page a plain HTML page that loads quickly and does not require special software	(Lynch & Horton, 2002)
Multimedia	Controls	Be sure to give users status information and controls when you are presenting multimedia materials	(Lynch & Horton, 2002)
Multimedia	Controls	Should always include a user preference setting to turn audio effects off	(Nielsen, 2000)
Graphical Elements	Advertising	Good pages typically contain one graphical ad from well-known companies (i.e. Saturn). Pages with graphical ads were rated as more credible than those without graphical ads	(Ivory & Hearst, 2002b)

Graphical Elements	Images	Larger objects, particularly images, will draw users' attention before smaller ones. Users fixate on larger items first, and for longer periods of time. However, users will tend to skip certain kinds of images that they believe to be ads or decoration.	(U.S. Department of Health and Human Services, 2006)
Graphical Elements	Images	Parts of images or text that have brighter colors seem to gain focus first.	(U.S. Department of Health and Human Services, 2006)
Graphical Elements	Images	Use background images sparingly and make sure they are simple, especially if they are used behind text.	(U.S. Department of Health and Human Services, 2006)
Graphical Elements	Images	Do not make important images look like banner advertisements or gratuitous decoration	(U.S. Department of Health and Human Services, 2006)
Graphical Elements	Images	Use images only when they are critical to the success of a Web site.	(U.S. Department of Health and Human Services, 2006)
Graphical Elements	Data	Include actual data values with graphical displays of data when precise reading of the data is required.	(U.S. Department of Health and Human Services, 2006)
Graphical Elements	Images	To facilitate learning, use images rather than text whenever possible. The superiority of pictures over text in a learning situation appears to be strong.	(U.S. Department of Health and Human Services, 2006)
Links	Images	Ensure that all clickable images are either labeled or readily understood by typical users.	(U.S. Department of Health and Human Services, 2006)
Links	Images	If any part of an image is clickable, ensure that the entire image is clickable or that the clickable sections are obvious.	(U.S. Department of Health and Human Services, 2006)

Category	Subcategory	Guideline	Reference
Links	Images	Images (e.g., pushbuttons and navigation tabs) are likely to be considered as links when they are designed to emulate their real-world analogues.	(U.S. Department of Health and Human Services, 2006)
Links	Images	Use text links rather than image links: text links are more easily recognized as clickable. Text links usually download faster, are preferred by users, and should change colors after being selected. It is usually easier to convey a link's destination in text, rather than with the use of an image. Requiring users to 'minesweep' to determine what is clickable slows them down. Another benefit to using text links is that users with text-only and deactivated graphical browsers can see the navigation options.	(U.S. Department of Health and Human Services, 2006)
Links	Usage	Provide links to supportive information. Use links to provide definitions and descriptions to clarify technical concepts or jargon, so that less knowledgeable users can successfully use the Web site.	(U.S. Department of Health and Human Services, 2006)
Links	Usage	provide 'glosses' to help users select correct links - popups	(U.S. Department of Health and Human Services, 2006)
Links	Location	Keep most important links 'above the fold' - most users do not scroll	(Lynch & Horton, 2002)
Links	Location	Keep most important links 'above the fold' - most users do not scroll	(Nielsen, 2000)
Links	Number	Good pages contain significantly more links and link clusters.	(Ivory & Hearst, 2002b)
Links	Number	good pages present links multiple times in different forms (image in nav bar as well as text in footer)	(Ivory & Hearst, 2002b)
Links	Number	Ensure that important content can be accessed from more than one link.	(U.S. Department of Health and Human Services, 2006)

Links	Titles	Higher number of content words on links in good pages	(Ivory & Hearst, 2002b)
Links	Titles	Use descriptive link titles: avoid 'click here'	(Nielsen, 2000)
Links	Titles	Titles should be less than 80 characters, should not exceed 60 characters; shorter the better	(Nielsen, 2000)
Links	Titles	use meaningful link labels	(U.S. Department of Health and Human Services, 2006)
Links	Titles	Match Link Names with Their Destination Pages	(U.S. Department of Health and Human Services, 2006)
Links	Titles	When using embedded links, the link text should accurately describe the link's destination (internal or external)	(U.S. Department of Health and Human Services, 2006)
Links	Titles	Indicate to users when a link will move them to a different location on the same page or to a new page on a different Web site.	(U.S. Department of Health and Human Services, 2006)
Links		Make text links long enough to be understood, but short enough to minimize wrapping. one study found that when users scan prose text, links of nine to ten words elicit better performance than shorter or longer links.	(U.S. Department of Health and Human Services, 2006)
Links	Titles	Link title length should be 2 – 4 words	(Nielsen, 2000)
Links	Titles	Links should use 7 – 12 "useful" words that provide hints about the content of the destination page	(Sawyer & Schroeder, 2000)
Links	Clickability Cues	Avoid Misleading Cues to Click: Symbols usually must be combined with at least one other cue that suggests clickability.	(U.S. Department of Health and Human Services, 2006)

Links	Clickability Cues	Provide Consistent Clickability Cues: Be consistent in your use of underlining, bullets, arrows, and other symbols such that they always indicate clickability or never suggest clickability. Items that are in the top center of the page, or left and right panels have a high probability of being considered links.	(U.S. Department of Health and Human Services, 2006)
Links	Clickability Cues	links should be blue because of familiarity	(Nielsen, 2000)
Links	Color	Designate Used Links: Use color changes to indicate to users when a link has been visited.	(U.S. Department of Health and Human Services, 2006)
Links	Color	Designate Used Links: Use color changes to indicate to users when a link has been visited.	(Nielsen, 2000)
Navigation	Site Architecture	Provide navigational options: don't create or direct users into pages that have no navigational options (dead ends) - new windows shouldn't open as full screen	(U.S. Department of Health and Human Services, 2006)
Navigation	Site Architecture	Use a clickable list of contents on long pages that takes users directly to content	(U.S. Department of Health and Human Services, 2006)
Navigation	Site Architecture	Provide feedback to let users know where they are in the web site - path and hierarchy information (breadcrumbs)	(U.S. Department of Health and Human Services, 2006)
Navigation	Site Architecture	do not expect users to use breadcrumbs effectively	(U.S. Department of Health and Human Services, 2006)
Navigation	Site Architecture	use site maps for web sites that have many pages	(U.S. Department of Health and Human Services, 2006)
Navigation	Location	group and place navigation elements in a consistent and easy to find place on the page	(U.S. Department of Health and Human Services, 2006)

Navigation	Location	Place primary navigation menus in the left panel, and the secondary and tertiary menus together	(U.S. Department of Health and Human Services, 2006)
Navigation	Location	Ensure that navigation tabs are located at the top of the page	(U.S. Department of Health and Human Services, 2006)
Navigation	Location	feature local navigational links at the beginning and end of the page layout	(Lynch & Horton, 2002)
Navigation	Cues	cleary differentiate navigation elements	(U.S. Department of Health and Human Services, 2006)
Navigation	Cues	Ensure that navigation tabs look clickable	(U.S. Department of Health and Human Services, 2006)
Navigation	Cues	use familiar and recognizable navigational controls	(Mandel, 1997)
Navigation	Titles	ensure that tab labels are clearly descriptive of function or destination	(U.S. Department of Health and Human Services, 2006)
Navigation	Page Design	do not require users to scroll purely navigational pages	(U.S. Department of Health and Human Services, 2006)
Navigation	Page Design	use an appropriate page layout to eliminate the need for users to scroll horizontally	(U.S. Department of Health and Human Services, 2006)
Navigation	Page Design	Navigation should be kept below 20% of the space	(Nielsen, 2000)
Navigation	Page Design	'Pointing-and-clicking,' rather than mousing over, is preferred when selecting menu items from a cascading menu structure. One study found that when compared with the mouseover method, the 'point-and-click' method takes eighteen percent less time, elicits fewer errors, and is preferred by users.	(U.S. Department of Health and Human Services, 2006)

Navigation	Page Design	place consistent navigation bar on each page of web site	(Lohse & Spiller, 1998; Page & White, 2006)
Navigation	Screen-Based Controls	Distinguish clearly and consistently between required and optional data entry fields.	(U.S. Department of Health and Human Services, 2006)
Navigation	Screen-Based Controls	The label of a pushbutton should clearly indicate the action that will be applied when the pushbutton is clicked. Common pushbutton labels include 'Update,' 'Go,' 'Submit,' 'Cancel,' 'Enter,' 'Home,' 'Next,' and 'Previous.'	(U.S. Department of Health and Human Services, 2006)
Navigation	Screen-Based Controls	Ensure that data entry labels are worded consistently,	(U.S. Department of Health and Human Services, 2006)
Navigation	Screen-Based Controls	Treat upper- and lowercase letters as equivalent when users are entering codes.	(U.S. Department of Health and Human Services, 2006)
Navigation	Screen-Based Controls	Display an associated label for each data entry field to help users understand what entries are desired	(U.S. Department of Health and Human Services, 2006)
Navigation	Screen-Based Controls	Ensure that labels are close enough to their associated data entry fields so that users will recognize the label as describing the data entry field	(U.S. Department of Health and Human Services, 2006)
Navigation	Screen-Based Controls	Provide radio buttons when users need to choose one response from a list of mutually exclusive options.	(U.S. Department of Health and Human Services, 2006)
Navigation	Screen-Based Controls	Use location and highlighting to prioritize pushbuttons. One study reported that designers should place the button most likely to be clicked on the left side of a two-button set of buttons.	(U.S. Department of Health and Human Services, 2006)
Navigation	Screen-Based Controls	Ensure that double-clicking on a link will not cause undesirable or confusing results.	(U.S. Department of Health and Human Services, 2006)

Page Layout	Consistency	Place important, clickable items in the same locations, and closer to the top of the page, where their location can be better estimated (place items consistently)	(U.S. Department of Health and Human Services, 2006)
Page Layout	Consistency	Place your organization's logo in a consistent place on every page. Having a logo on each page provides a frame of reference throughout a Web site so that users can easily confirm that they have not left the site	(U.S. Department of Health and Human Services, 2006)
Page Layout	Hierarchy	Put the most important items at the top center of the Web page to facilitate users' finding the information	(U.S. Department of Health and Human Services, 2006)
Page Layout	Hierarchy	Establish a high-to-low level of importance for information and infuse this approach throughout each page (hierarchy)	(U.S. Department of Health and Human Services, 2006)
Page Layout	Hierarchy	group important choices together - hierarchy	(Mandel, 1997)
Page Layout	Site Architecture	limit number of choices at a level	(Mandel, 1997)
Page Layout	Site Architecture	Structure pages so that items can be easily compared when users must analyze those items to discern similarities, differences, trends, and relationships	(U.S. Department of Health and Human Services, 2006)
Page Layout	Site Architecture	Organize information at each level of the Web site so that it shows a clear and logical structure to typical users.	(U.S. Department of Health and Human Services, 2006)
Page Layout	Site Architecture	To allow users to efficiently find what they want, design so that the most common tasks can be successfully completed in the fewest number of clicks.	(U.S. Department of Health and Human Services, 2006)
Page Layout	Site Architecture	3 click rule: a person shouldn't have to click more than than 3 times in order to find a piece of info	(Weeks, 1997)
Page Layout	Frame Usage	Use frames when certain functions must remain visible on the screen as the user accesses other information on the site	(U.S. Department of Health and Human Services, 2006)
Page Layout	Frame Usage	Frames: "Just say no' unless used as a shortcut scroll on a page	(Nielsen, 2000)

Page Layout	Page Dimensions	Set appropriate page lengths: make page-length decisions that support the primary use of the web page	(U.S. Department of Health and Human Services, 2006)
Page Layout	Page Dimensions	creation of navigational Web pages (especially home pages and menus) that contain no more than one or two screens' worth of information and that feature local navigational links at the beginning and end of the page layout	(Lynch & Horton, 2002)
Page Layout	Page Dimensions	reduce scrolling to a minimum	(Mandel, 1997; Weeks, 1997)
Page Layout	Page Dimensions	Users don't want to scroll information - fit all on a single page	(Mandel, 1997; Weeks, 1997)
Page Layout	Page Dimensions	Use proper dimensions to prevent excess scrolling and to ensure printing is easy	(Lynch & Horton, 2002)
Page Performance	Resolution	Use a fluid layout that automatically adjusts the page size to monitor resolution settings that are 1024x768 pixels or higher	(U.S. Department of Health and Human Services, 2006)
Page Performance	Resolution	Create resolution-independent pages that adapt to whatever screen size they are displayed on	(Nielsen, 2000)
Page Performance	Resolution	never use fixed pixel width for design elements	(Nielsen, 2000)
Page Layout	Location	Avoid scroll stoppers; ensure that the location of headings and other page elements doesn't create the illusion that users have reached the top or bottom of a page when they have not	(U.S. Department of Health and Human Services, 2006)
Page Layout	Location	the header area of every Web page should contain a prominent title at or near its top. Graphics placed above the title line should not be so large that they force the title and introductory text off the page on standard office-size display screens.	(Lynch & Horton, 2002)
Page Layout	Location	emphasis on top left of the page	(Weeks, 1997)

Category	Subcategory	Description	Citation
Page Layout	Location	Put important elements in the top left and lower right parts of the screen to allow readers to skim the page	(Powell, Clark, & Clark, 1996)
Page Layout	Location	Do not fill the entire first screenful with one image if there are screensfuls of text information below the fold.	(U.S. Department of Health and Human Services, 2006)
Page Layout	Content Organization & Structure		
Content Organization & Structure	Chunking	Group all related information and functions in order to decrease time spent searching or scanning.	(U.S. Department of Health and Human Services, 2006)
Content Organization & Structure	Brevity	Limit page information only to that which is needed by users while on that page.	(U.S. Department of Health and Human Services, 2006)
Content Organization & Structure	Hierarchy	Micro/Macro Design: micro details cumulate into larger overview; Elements of the page designed to accomplish the overall goal; consistency through use of template	(Zimmermann, 1997)
Content Organization & Structure	Hierarchy	Layering and Separation: visually stratifying or ordering data to establish a proper relationship among types of info	(Zimmermann, 1997)
Content Organization & Structure	Integration	Integrating Words and Images: integrate text and figures (no appendix); focus on content of charts not on decoration	(Zimmermann, 1997)
Content Organization & Structure	Brevity	Avoid long text - use hyperlinks to shorten blocks of text and split up long information into multiple pages - Most users don't scroll.	(Nielsen, 2000)
Content Organization & Structure	Brevity	Divide the document into chunks of no more than one to two printed pages' worth of information, including inlined graphics or figures. Use the power of hypertext links	(Lynch & Horton, 2002)
Content Organization & Structure	Page Design	Page content should account for at least 50% of a page's design, preferably closer to 80%	(Nielsen, 2000)

Content Organization & Structure	Page Design	Web page content should be broken up into smaller units and distributed across multiple pages	(Nielsen, 2000)
Content Organization & Structure	Page Design	All relevant content should appear on one web page	(Landesman & Schroeder, 2000)
Content Organization & Structure	Scanning	Facilitate scanning: use clear, well-located headings; short phrases and sentences; and small readable paragraphs. place important headings high in the center section of a page	(U.S. Department of Health and Human Services, 2006)
Content Organization & Structure	Chunking	Page chunking - chunk all related information on the page	(Nielsen, 2000)
Content Organization & Structure	Headings, Titles, & Labels	Ensure that category labels, including links, clearly reflect the information and items contained within the category	(U.S. Department of Health and Human Services, 2006)
Content Organization & Structure	Headings, Titles, & Labels	Use descriptive headings liberally throughout a web site	(U.S. Department of Health and Human Services, 2006)
Content Organization & Structure	Headings, Titles, & Labels	use headings that are unique from one another and conceptually related to the content they describe	(U.S. Department of Health and Human Services, 2006)
Content Organization & Structure	Headings, Titles, & Labels	highlight important page items that require user attention, especially if those items are displayed infrequently	(U.S. Department of Health and Human Services, 2006)
Content Organization & Structure	Headings, Titles, & Labels	provide users with good ways to reduce their available options as efficiently as possible	(U.S. Department of Health and Human Services, 2006)
Content Organization & Structure	Lists	Arrange lists and tasks in an order that best facilitates efficient and successful user performance.	(U.S. Department of Health and Human Services, 2006)

Content Organization & Structure	Lists	Place a list's most important items at the top. Research indicates that users tend to stop scanning a list as soon as they see something relevant, thus illustrating the reason to place important items at the beginning of lists.	(U.S. Department of Health and Human Services, 2006)
Content Organization & Structure	Lists	Make lists easy to scan and understand: The use of meaningful labels, effective background colors, borders, and white space allow users to identify a set of items as a discrete list.	(U.S. Department of Health and Human Services, 2006)
Content Organization & Structure	Lists	Display a series of related items in a vertical list rather than as continuous text. One study indicated that users scan vertical lists more rapidly than horizontal lists.	(U.S. Department of Health and Human Services, 2006)
Content Organization & Structure	Lists	Provide an introductory heading (i.e., word or phrase) at the top of each list.	(U.S. Department of Health and Human Services, 2006)
Content Organization & Structure	Lists	Use static menus to elicit the fastest possible speed when accessing menu items.	(U.S. Department of Health and Human Services, 2006)
Content Organization & Structure	Lists	Use bullet lists to present items of equal status or value, and numbered lists if a particular order to the items is warranted.	(U.S. Department of Health and Human Services, 2006)
Content Organization & Structure	Lists	Capitalize the first letter of only the first word of a list item, a list box item, check box labels, and radio button labels.	(U.S. Department of Health and Human Services, 2006)
Page Design	Consistency	consistency in web page template, font, header size, colors	(Weeks, 1997)

Page Design	Consistency	Ensure visual consistency of Web site elements within and between Web pages: Visual consistency includes the size and spacing of characters; the colors used for labels, fonts and backgrounds; and the locations of labels, text and pictures. Earlier studies found that tasks performed on more consistent interfaces resulted in (1) a reduction in task completion times; (2) a reduction in errors; (3) an increase in user satisfaction; and (4) a reduction in learning time	(U.S. Department of Health and Human Services, 2006)
Page Design	Consistency	Micro/Macro Design: micro details cumulate into larger overview; Elements of the page designed to accomplish the overall goal; consistency through use of template	(Zimmermann, 1997)
Page Design	Consistency	Use consistency in panes and windows	(Cooper & Reimann, 2003)
Page Design	Consistency	A balanced and consistently implemented design scheme will increase readers' confidence in your site	(Lynch & Horton, 2002)
Page Design	Repetition	Small Multiples: Use slices of info to offer variations on a theme; repeat icons, symbols, menus, navigational devices	(Zimmermann, 1997)
Page Design	Simplicity	keep it simple	(Weeks, 1997; Nielsen, 2000; Cooper & Reimann, 2003; Mandel, 1997)
Page Design	Interactivity	Good pages appear to be more interactive - they contain 3 interactive objects (i.e. search button, text box, pull-down menu)	(Ivory & Hearst, 2002b)
Page Design	Density	Create pages that are not considered cluttered by users: excess items lead to degredation of performance when trying to find information	(U.S. Department of Health and Human Services, 2006)
Page Design	Density	To facilitate finding target information on a page, create pages that are not too crowded with items of information; optimize display density.	(U.S. Department of Health and Human Services, 2006)

Category	Subcategory	Guideline	Reference
Page Design	Density	Use moderate white space: limit the amount of white space on pages that are used for scanning and searching; higher density is related to faster scanning	(U.S. Department of Health and Human Services, 2006)
Page Design	Density	use lots of white space	(Mandel, 1997; Weeks, 1997)
Page Design	Density	Visual Noise and Clutter: Use simple geometric forms, minimal contours, less-saturated colors	(Cooper & Reimann, 2003)
Page Design	Alignment	be consistent in visually aligned page elements	(U.S. Department of Health and Human Services, 2006)
Page Design	Alignment	establish a layout grid and a style for handling your text and graphics; A consistent approach to layout and navigation	(Lynch & Horton, 2002)
Page Design	Alignment	Visually align page elements either vertically or horizontally, be consistent in alignments	(U.S. Department of Health and Human Services, 2006)
Page Design	Structure & Flow	Provide visual structure and flow at each level of organization: alignment, grids, symmetry, balance; spatial harmony and white space	(Cooper & Reimann, 2003)
Page Design	Visual Hierarchy	create a strong, consistent visual hierarchy in which important elements are emphasized and content is organized logically and predictably. Use contrast, visual balance, and appropriate design for your audience	(Lynch & Horton, 2002)
Page Design	Visual Hierarchy	Layering and Separation: visually stratifying or ordering data to establish a proper relationship among types of info; visual hierarchy. Separate layers using texture, weight, shape, value, size, or color.	(Zimmermann, 1997)
Page Design	Credibility	Use polished graphical design - limit amateur 'junk' ie heavy backgrounds or animated icons	(Nielsen, 2000)
Page Design	Credibility	avoid gimmicks	(Weeks, 1997)

Category	Subcategory	Guideline	Reference
Page Design	Color & Contrast	Use either plain-color backgrounds or very subtle background patterns - background graphics interfere with the eye's capability to read characters and recognize word shapes	(Nielsen, 2000)
Page Design	Color & Contrast	use color to highlight important information	(Cooper & Reimann, 2003)
Page Design	Color & Contrast	consistent use of color in signposts help users quickly navigate and find the info they need	(Cooper & Reimann, 2003)
Page Design	Color & Contrast	Avoid too many colors, use of complementary colors, excessive saturation, and inadequate contrast	(Cooper & Reimann, 2003)
Page Design	Color & Contrast	use adequate contrast	(Mandel, 1997)
Page Design	Color & Contrast	use a maximum of from 3-7 colors	(Mandel, 1997)
Page Design	Color & Contrast	use foveal and peripheral colors appropriately - red and green in the center of the field, blue is good for slide, borders, background	(Mandel, 1997)
Page Design	Color & Contrast	use colors that exhibit a minimum shift in color/size if they change in the imagery	(Mandel, 1997)
Page Design	Color & Contrast	do not use high-chroma, spectrally extreme colors simultaneously	(Mandel, 1997)
Page Design	Color & Contrast	use familiar, consistent color codings with appropriate references	(Mandel, 1997)
Page Design	Color & Contrast	use the same color for grouping related elements	(Mandel, 1997)
Page Design	Color & Contrast	use high-value, high-saturation colors to draw attention	(Mandel, 1997)
Page Design	Color & Contrast	high contrast between background and foreground	(Weeks, 1997)
Page Design	Color & Contrast	avoid black background - it doesn't print the text, harsh on eyes	(Weeks, 1997)
Page Design		Subtle pastel shades of colors typically found in nature make the best choices for background or minor elements. Avoid bold, highly saturated primary colors except in regions of maximum emphasis, and even there use them cautiously	(Lynch & Horton, 2002)
Page Design	Color & Contrast	use standard palettes and fonts	(Weeks, 1997)

Category	Subcategory	Description	Reference
Page Design	Color & Contrast	Good pages don't overuse color and tend to have at least one sparsely used accent color	(Ivory & Hearst, 2002b)
Information Design	Color & Contrast	Color and Information: use strong colors sparingly as spots against a light gray or dull background; light, bright colors adjacent to white distorts the visual field; improve screen resolution by softening background and defining lines/edges	(Zimmermann, 1997)
Page Formatting	Color & Contrast	good pages use multi-level heading schemes - headings at each level are different colors	(Ivory & Hearst, 2002b)
Page Design	Emphasis	Avoid The tools of graphic emphasis are powerful and should be used only in small doses for maximum effect. Overuse of graphic emphasis leads to a "clown's pants" effect in which everything is garish and nothing is emphasized. Ie large font, horizntal rules, graphic bullets, icons, etc.	(Lynch & Horton, 2002)
Color & Contrast	Color Coding	Color coding permits users to rapidly scan and quickly perceive patterns and relationships among items. Items that share the same color will be considered as being related to each other, while items with prominent color differences will seem to be different. People can distinguish up to ten different colors that are assigned to different categories, but it may be safer to use no more than five different colors for category coding.	(U.S. Department of Health and Human Services, 2006)
Color & Contrast	Color Coding	When using color-coding on your Web site, be sure that the coding scheme can be quickly and easily understood.	(U.S. Department of Health and Human Services, 2006)
Color & Contrast	Color Coding	When using color-coding on your Web site, be sure that the coding scheme can be quickly and easily understood.	(U.S. Department of Health and Human Services, 2006)
Repetition	Shape	use redundant coding of shape as well as color	(Mandel, 1997)

Page Design	Contrast & Layering	Contrast and Layering to distinguish and organize elements: Use 3D for manipulable controls, tonal contrast, spatial contrast, layering in color and size, figure-ground	(Cooper & Reimann, 2003)
Page Design	Icons & Symbols	Use cohesive, consistent, and contextually appropriate imagery - visually distinguish elements that behave differently	(Cooper & Reimann 2003)
Site Performance	Download Time	Minimum goal should be for users to get pages in no more than 10 seconds - the limit for keeping the user's attention focused on the web page	(Nielsen, 2000)
Site Performance	Download Time	Take steps to ensure that images on the Web site do not slow page download times unnecessarily. One study reported that users rated latencies of up to five seconds as 'good.' Delays over ten seconds were rated as 'poor.' Users rate pages with long delays as being less interesting and more difficult to scan.	(U.S. Department of Health and Human Services, 2006)
Site Performance	Download Time	incorporation of a "duration time to download" countdown, which lessens consumer uncertainty and frustration	(Page & White, 2006; Dellaert & Kahn, 1999)

REFERENCES

Aaker, D. A. (1996). *Building Strong Brands*. New York: Free Press.

Abreu, E. (2000). Consumers fight back, anonymously. *The Industry Standard:* 17 – 21.

Adams, A. S., & Edworthy, J. (1995). Quantifying and predicting the effects of basic text display variables on the perceived urgency of warning labels: Tradeoffs involving font size, border weight, and color. *Ergonomics, 38* (11): 2221 – 2237.

Alba, J., Lynch, J., Weitz, B., & Janiszewski, C. (1997). Interactive home shopping: Consumer, retailer, and manufacturer incentives to participate in electronic marketplaces. *Journal of Marketing, 61:* 38 – 53.

Anderson, N. H. (1965). Averaging versus adding as a stimulus-combination rule in impression formation. *Journal of Personality and Social Psychology*, (2): 1 – 9.

Ang, L., & Lee, B. (2000). Transacting on the internet: A qualitative and quantitative exploration of trust, brand equity, and purchase guarantee. Conference proceedings of the *Australian and New Zealand Marketing Academy: Visionary marketing for the 21st century, Facing the challenge*.

Bafail, A. O., Ishrat, S. I., Rizvi, S. A. H., & Siddiqui, T. W. (2005). Web pages of three multinational companies addressing consumer items: Are they ergonomically designed? *Proceedings of the 2005 IEEE International Communication Conference:* 300 – 307.

Barber, B. (1983). *The Logic and Limitations of Trust*. New Jersey: Rutgers University Press.

Bart, Y., Shankar, V., Sultan, F., & Urban, G. L. (2005). Are the drivers and role of online trust the same for all web sites and consumers? A large-scale exploratory empirical study. *Journal of Marketing, 69:* 133 – 152.

310

Baumeister, R. F., Bratslavsky, E., Finkenauer, C., & Vohs, K. D. (2001). Bad is stronger than good. *Review of General Psychology, 8:* 8 – 12.

Becker, S. A. & Mottay, F. E. (2001). A global perspective on web site usability. *IEEE Software, 18* (1): 54 – 61.

Bekman, S. (2006). Eye Tracking Studies for Better Ad Placement and Website Usability. Retrieved October 2nd, 2006 from http://stason.org/articles/money/passive_income/ads/more_with_less/eye_track ing_web_usability_studies.html.

Belanger, F., Hiller, J. S., & Smith, W. J. (2002). Trustworthiness in electronic commerce: The role of privacy, security, and site attributes. *The Journal of Strategic Information Systems, 11:* 245 – 270.

Bernhard, M. (2001). Criteria for optimal web design. Retrieved October 24th from: http://www.optimalweb.org.

Berry, L. (2000). Cultivating service brand equity. *Journal of the Academy of Marketing Science, 28 (1):* 128 – 137.

Bevan, N. (2004). Usability issues in web site design. *Proceedings of 6th Interactive Publishing:* 1 – 7.

Bhattacherjee, A. (2002). Individual trust in online firms: Scale development and initial test. *Journal of Management Information Systems, 19 (1):* 211 – 241.

Bloch, P.(1995). Seeking the ideal form: Product design and consumer response. *Journal of Marketing (59):* 16-29.

Bosson, J. K., Johnson, A. B., Niederhoffer, K., & Swann Jr., W. B. (2006). Interpersonal chemistry through negativity: Bonding by sharing negative attitudes about others. *Personal Relationships, 13:* 135 – 150.

Boston Consulting Group (2000). Five Key Lessons for Online Retailers. Retrieved April 10th, 2007 from: http://bcg.com.

Bucy, E. P., & Lang, A. (1999). Formal features of cyberspace: Relationships between web page complexity and site traffic. *Journal of the American Society for Information Science, 50 (13):* 1246 – 1256.

Butler, J. K. Jr. (1991). Toward understanding and measuring conditions of trust: Evolution of a conditions of trust inventory. *Journal of Management, 17* (3): 643 – 663.

Cacioppo, J. T., Marshall-Goodell, B. S., Tassinary, L. G., & Petty, R. E. (1992). Rudimentary determinants of attitudes: Classical conditioning is more effective when prior knowledge about the attitude stimulus is low than high. *Journal of Experimental Social Psychology, 28*: 207-233.

Calongne, C. M. (2001). Designing for web site usability. *Journal of Computing Sciences in Colleges, 16* (3): 39 – 45.

Card, S. K., Robertson, G. G., and Mackinlay, J. D. (1991). The information visualizer: An information workspace. *Proc. ACM CHI'91 Conf.* (New Orleans, LA, 28 April-2 May), 181-188.

Carter, R. C. (1982). Visual search with color. *Journal of Experimental Psychology: Human Perception and Performance, 8 (1):* 127 – 136.

Caudill, E. M., & Murphy, P. E. (2000). Consumer online privacy: Legal and ethical issues. *Journal of Public Policy and Marketing, 19:* 7 – 32.

Chaiken, S. (1987). *Dual Process Theories in Social Psychology.* New York: Guilford Press.

Chaudhuri, A., & Holbrook, M. B. (2001). The chain of effects from brand trust and brand affect to brand performance: The role of brand loyalty. *The Journal of Marketing, 65*: 81 – 93.

Cheung, C. M. K., & Lee, M. K. O. (2006). Understanding consumer trust in internet shopping: A multidisciplinary approach. *Journal of the American Society for Information Science and Technology, 57 (4):* 479 – 492.

Chevalier, A., & Ivory, M. Y. (2003). Web site designs: Influences of designer's experience and design constraints. *International Journal of Human Computer Studies, 58 (1):* 57 – 87.

Chevalier, A., & Kicka, M. (2006). Web designers and web users: Influence of the ergonomic quality of the web site on the information search. *International Journal of Human-Computer Studies, 64:* 1031 – 1048.

Chignell, M. H., & Hancock, P. A. (1992). Design orientation and ergonomics. *Proceedings of the IEEE International Conference on Systems, Man, and Cybernetics, 1:* 207 – 211.

Christodoulides, G., & de Chernatony, L. (2004). Dimensionalising on- and offline brands' composite equity. *Journal of Product and Brand Management, 13 (3):* 168 – 179.

*Cooper, A., & Reimann, R. (2003). *About face 2.0: The essentials of interaction design.* Indianapolis: Wiley Publishing, Inc.

Cotlier, M. (2001). Electronic catalogs: Judging a site by its home page. *Catalog Age.* Retrieved February 18th from: http://bg.catalogagemag.com/ar/marketing_electronic_catalog_judging/

Couch, L. L., Adams, J. M., & Jones, W. H. (1996). The assessment of trust orientation. *Journal of Personality Assessment, 67* (2): 305 – 323.

Dayal, S., Landesberg, H., & Zeisser, M. (1999). How to build trust online. *Marketing Management:* 64–69.

---

* Starred references were utilized in the development of the Web Site Design Guidelines Framework

DeBruin, E. N., & Van Lange, P. A. M. (2000). What people look for in others: Influences of the perceiver and the perceived on information selection. *Personality and Social Psychology Bulletin, 26*: 206 – 219.

Degeratu, A. M., Rangaswamy, A., & Wu, J. (2000). Consumer choice behavior in online and traditional supermarkets: The effects of brand name, price, and other search attributes. *International Journal of Research in Marketing, 17:* 55 – 78.

*Dellaert, B. G. C., & Kahn, B. E. (1999). How tolerable is delay? Consumer's evaluations of internet web sites after waiting. *Journal of Interactive Marketing, 13:* 41 – 54.

DeLone, W. H., & McLean, E. R. (2003). The DeLone and McLean model of information systems success: A ten year update. *Journal of Management Information Systems, 19* (4): 9 – 30.

Dholakia, U. M., & Rego, L. L. (1998). What makes commercial web pages popular? *European Journal of Marketing, 32 (7/8):* 724 – 736.

Dieli, M. (1989). The usability process: Working with iterative design principles. *IEEE Transactions of Professional Communication, 32* (4): 272 – 278.

Dijksterhuis, A., & Aarts, H. (2003). On wildebeests and humans: The preferential detection of negative stimuli. *Psychological Science, 14:* 14 – 18.

Dreze, X., & Zufryden, F. (1997). Testing web site design and promotional content. *Journal of Advertising Research, 37:* 77 – 100.

Dion, K.K., Berscheid, E., Walster, E. (1972). What is beautiful is good. *Journal of Personality and Social Psychology, 24*: 285–290.

Doney, P. M., & Cannon, J. P. (1997). An examination of the nature of trust in buyer-seller relationships. *Journal of Marketing, 61:* 35 – 51.

Driscoll, J.W. (1978). Trust and participation in organizational decision making as predictors of satisfaction. *Academy of Management Journal 21* (1): 44–56.

DTI (1999). Building confidence in electronic commerce – a consultation document. Department of Trade & Industry. Document reference: URN 99/642.

Dunn, J. (2004). Survey shows online security perception gap between experts, users. *Knight Rider Tribune Business News: 1.*

Evans, M. B. (2000). Challenges in developing research-based web design guidelines. *IEEE Transactions on Professional Communication, 43 (3):* 302 – 312.

Everard, A., & Galletta, D. F. (2006). How presentation flaws affect perceived site quality, trust, and intention to purchase from an online store. *Journal of Management Information Systems, 22 (3):* 55 – 95.

Farenc, C., Palanque, P., & Vanderdonckt, J. (1995). User interface evaluation: Is it ever usable? *Proceedings of the 6th International Conference on Human-Computer Interaction: HCI International '95:* 329 – 334.

Fernandes, G., Lindgaard, G., Dillon, R., & Wood, J. (2003). Judging the appeal of web sites. *Proceedings of the 4th World Congress on the Management of Electronic Commerce.*

Fiore, A. M., & H. Jin. (2003). Influence of image interactivity on approach responses towards an online retailer. *Internet Research: Electronic Networking Applications and Policy, 13*(1): 38 – 48.

Fiske, S. T. (1980). Attention and weight in person perception: The impact of negative and extreme behavior. *Journal of Personality and Social Psychology, 38 (6):* 889 – 906.

Fletcher, C. (2000). Getting personal online. *Catalog Age, 17:* 53 – 54.

Fogg, B. J., Marshall, J., Laraki, O., Osipovich, A., Varma, C., Fang, N., Paul, J., Rangnekar, A., Shon, J., Swani, P., & Treinen, M. (2001). What makes web sites credible? A report on a large quantitative study. *Proceedings of SIGCHI.*

Fogg, B. J., Soohoo, C., Danielson, D. R., Marable, L., Stanford, J., & Tauber, E. R. (2003). How do users evaluate the credibility of web sites? A study with over 2,500 participants. *Proceedings of the 2003 conference on Designing for User Experiences,* San Francisco, CA: 1 – 15.

Forrester Research (1999). Report January 1999. Retrieved April 7th, 2007 from: http://www.forrester.com.

Forsythe, C., Ring, L., Grose, E. Bederson, B., Hollan, J., Perlin, K., & Meyer, J. (1996). Human factors research and development for the international web at Sandia national laboratories: A review and update. *Human Factors and Ergonomics Conference Proceedings.*

Friedman, B., Kahn, P. H. Jr., & Howe, D. C. (2000). Trust online. *Communications of the ACM, 43* (12): 34 – 40.

Fu, L., & Salvendy, G. (2002). The contribution of apparent and inherent usability to a user's satisfaction in a searching and browsing task on the web. *Ergonomics, 45* (6): 415 – 424.

Ganesan, S. (1994). Determinants of long-term orientation in buyer–seller relationships. *Journal of Marketing, 58*: 1–19.

Gabarro, J.J. (1978). The development of trust influence and expectations. In A. G. Athos & J. J
Gabarro (Eds.), *Interpersonal Behavior: Communication and Understanding in Relationships* (pp. 290-303). New Jersey: Prentice Hall.

Gillan, D. J., & Bias, R. G. (2001). Usability science I: Foundations. *International Journal of Human-Computer Interaction, 13* (4): 351 – 372.

Gommans, M., Krishnan, K. S., & Scheffold, K. B. (2001). From brand loyalty to e-loyalty: A conceptual framework. *Journal of Economic and Social Research, 3 (1):* 43 – 58.

Gould, J. D. & Lewis, C. (1985). Designing for usability: Key principles and what designers think. *Communications of the ACM, 28:* 300 – 311.

Grabner-Krauter, S., & Kaluscha, E. A. (2003). Empirical research in on-line trust: A review and critical assessment. *International Journal of Human-Computer Studies, 58 (6):* 783 – 812.

Green, D., & Pearson, J. M. (2006). Development of a web site usability instrument based on ISO 9241-11. *Journal of Computer Information Systems:* 66 – 72.

Green, E. P., & Srinivasan, V. (1990). Conjoint analysis in marketing: New developments with implications for research and practice. *Journal of Marketing:* 3 – 19.

Green, E. P., & Rao, V. (1971). Conjoint measurement for quantifying judgmental data. *Journal of Marketing Research,* 1: 61 – 68.

Green, P. E., & Krieger, A. M. (1989). Recent contributions to optimal product positioning and buyer segmentation. *European Journal of Operational Research, 41*: 137 - 141.

Gustafsson, A., Ekdahl, F., & Bergman, B. (1999). Conjoint analysis: A useful tool in the design process. *Total Quality Management, 10* (3): 327 – 343.

Ha, H. (2004). Factors influencing consumer perceptions of brand trust online. *Journal of Product & Brand Management, 13*(5): 329 – 342.

Haig, M. (2002). Who still needs an e-strategy? *Computer Business Review, 10*: 45 – 48.

Halverson, T. & Hornof, A.J. (2004). Local density guides visual search: Sparse groups are first and faster. *Proceedings from the 48th Annual Human Factors and Ergonomics Meeting.*

Hamermesh, D., & Biddle, J. (2004). Beauty and the labor market. *American Economic Review (84)*: 1174 – 1194.

Hamermesh, D., & Parker, A. M. (2005). Beauty in the classroom: Professors' pulchritude and putative pedagogical productivity. *Economics of Education Review.*

Hamilton, D. L., & Zanna, M. P. (1972). Differential weighting of favorable and unfavorable attributes in impressions of personality. *Journal of Experimental Research in Personality, 6:* 204 – 212.

Hampton-Sosa, W., & Koufaris, M. (2005). The effect of web site perceptions on initial trust in the owner company. *International Journal of Electronic Commerce, 10* (1): 55 – 81.

Harris, L. C., & Goode, M. M. H. (2004). The four levels of loyalty and the pivotal role of trust: A study of online service dynamics. *Journal of Retailing, 80:* 139 – 158.

Hassenzahl, M. (2001). The Effect of Perceived Hedonic Quality on Product Appealingness. *International Journal of Human–Computer Interaction, 13* (4): 481–99.

Hassenzahl, M. (2004). The interplay of beauty, goodness and usability in interactive products. *Human-Computer Interaction, 19* (4).

Henneman, R. L. (1999). Design for usability: Process, skills, and tools. *Information Knowledge Systems Management, 1:* 133 – 144.

Henry, D., Cooke, S., Buckley, P., Dumagan, J., Gill, G., Pastore, D., & LaPorte, S. (1999). The U.S. Department of Commerce: Economics and Statistics Administration. The Emerging Digital Economy II.

Hoffman, R., & Krauss, K. (2004). A critical evaluation of literature on visual aesthetics for the web. *Proceedings of SAICSIT 2004,* 205 – 209.

Hoffman, D. L., Novak, T. P., & Peralta, M. A. (1999). Building consumer trust online. *Communications of the ACM, 42 (4):* 80 – 85.

Holzschlag, M. E. (1999). Satisfying customers with color, shape, and type. *Web Techniques, 4 (11) :* 24 – 29.

Ivory, M. Y. (2003). Automated web site evaluation: Researcher's and practitioner's perspectives. *Human-Computer Interaction Series, 4.*

Ivory, M. Y., & Hearst, M. A. (2002a). Improving web site design. *IEEE Internet Computing:* 56 – 63.

*Ivory, M. Y., & Hearst, M. A. (2002b). Statistical Profiles of Highly-Rated Web Sites. *Proceedings of SIGCHI 2002, 1*(1): 367 – 374.

Ivory, M. Y., Mankoff, J., & Le, A. (2003). Using automated tools to improve web site usage by users with diverse abilities. *IT & Society, 1 (3):* 195 – 236.

Ivory, M. Y., & Megraw, R. (2005). Evolution of web site design patterns. *ACM Transactions on Information Systems, 23 (4):* 463 – 497.

Ivory, M. Y., Sinha, R. R., & Hearst, M. A. (2001). Empirically Validated Web Page Metrics. *Proceedings of SIGCHI 2001, 3*(1): 53 – 60.

Jarvenpaa, S.L., Tractinsky, N., & Vitale, M. (2000). Consumer trust in an internet store. *Information Technology Management, 1*(1-2): 45 – 71.

Jarvenpaa, S.L., Tractinsky, N., & Vitale, M. (1999). Consumer trust in an internet store: A cross-cultural validation. *The Journal of Computer-Mediated Communication, 5*(2). Available at http://www.ascusc.org/jcmc/vol5/issue2/jarvenpaa.html.

Jevons, C., & Gabbott, M. (2000). Trust, brand equity and brand reality in internet business relationships: An interdisciplinary approach. *Journal of Marketing Management, 16:* 619 - 634.

Johnson-George, C., & Swap, W. C. (1982). Measurement of specific interpersonal trust: Construction and validation of a scale to assess trust in a specific other. *Journal of Personality and Social Psychology, 43* (6): 1306 – 1317.

Jones, S., Wilikens, M., Morris, P., & Masera, M. (2000). Trust requirements in e-business: A conceptual framework for understanding the needs and concerns of different stakeholders. *Communications of the ACM, 43 (12)*: 81 – 86.

Jordan, P. W. (2000). *Designing Pleasurable Products: An Introduction to the New Human Factors*. UK: Taylor & Francis Books Ltd.

Karat, C. (1993). Usability engineering in dollars and cents. *Interface:* 88 – 89.

Kim, J. & Moon, J. Y. (1998). Designing towards emotional usability in customer interfaces – Trustworthiness of cyber-banking system interfaces. *Interacting with Computers, 10 (1):* 1 – 29.

Kirvesoja, H., & Vayrynen, S. (2000). Comparative evaluation of the conjoint analysis and paired comparison methods applied to the design and evaluation of multipurpose chairs. *Theoretical Issues in Ergonomic Science, 1* (3): 283 – 299.

Kotler, P., & Rath A. G. (1984). Design a powerful but neglected strategic tool. *Journal of Business Strategy (5)*: 16 – 21.

Koufaris, M., Kambil, A., & P. A. LaBarbera (2001). Consumer behavior in web-based commerce: An empirical study. *International Journal of Electronic Commerce, 6*(2): 115 – 138.

Kuan, H. H., Bock, G., Vathanophas, V. (2005). Comparing the effects of usability on customer conversion and retention at e-commerce websites. *Proceedings of the 38th Hawaii International Conference on System Sciences:* 1 – 9.

Kuhfeld, W. F. (2005). *Marketing research methods in SAS: Experimental design, choice, conjoint, and graphical techniques*. Cary, NC: SAS Institute, Inc.

Kurosu, M., & Kashimura, K. (1995a). Apparent usability vs. inherent usability: Experimental analysis on the determinants of the apparent usability. *Proceedings of Computer Human Interaction Conference:* 292 – 293.

Kurosu, M. & Kashimura, K. (1995b). Determinants of apparent usability. *Proceedings of the IEEE International Conference on Systems, Man, and Cybernetics, 2:* 1509 – 1514.

Lais, S. (2002). How to stop web shopper flight. *Computerworld:* 44 – 45.

Lam, S. Y., Chau, A. W., & Wong, T. J. (2007). Thumbnails as online product displays: How consumers process them. *Journal of Interactive Marketing, 21 (1):* 36 – 59.

*Landesman, L., & Schroeder, W. (2000). Report 5: Organizing links. *Designing Information-Rich Web Sites*. Bradford: User Interface Engineering.

Lavie, T. & Tractinsky, N. (2004). Assessing dimensions of perceived visual aesthetics of web sites. *International Journal of Human-Computer Studies, 60* (3): 269-298.

Lee, M. K. O., & Turban, E. (2001). A trust model for consumer internet shopping. *International Journal of Electronic Commerce, 6 (1):* 75 – 91.

Lewis, J. R. (2001). Introduction: Current issues in usability evaluation. *International Journal of Human-Computer Interaction, 13* (4): 343 – 349.

Li, H., Kuo, C., & Russell, M. G. (1999). The impact of perceived channel utilities, shopping orientations, and demographics on the consumer's online buying behavior. *Journal of Computer-Mediated Communication.*

Liao, Z., & Cheung, M. T. (2001). Internet-based e-shopping and consumer attitudes: An empirical study. *Information and Management, 38:* 299 – 306.

Lindgaard, G., & Dudek, C. (2003). What is this evasive beast we call user satisfaction? *Interacting with Computers (15)*: 429-452.

Liu, C. & Arnett, K. P. (2000). Exploring the factors associated with web site success in the context of e-commerce. *Information and Management, 38* (1): 23 – 33.

Lippincott Mercer (1997). Strategic communications issues affecting top management. *Sense, 97:* 1 – 34.

*Lohse, G. L., & Spiller, P. (1998). "Electronic shopping: Designing stores with effective customer interfaces has a critical influence on traffic and sales." *Communications of the ACM, 41:* 81.

*Lynch, P. and Horton, S. (2002). Web Style Guide, 2nd Edition. Retrieved October 3rd, 2006 from http://www.webstyleguide.com/index.html.

Lynch, P., Kent, R., & Srinivasan, S. S. (2001). The global internet shopper: Evidence from shopping tasks in twelve countries. *Journal of Advertising Research, 41 (3):* 83 – 103.

*Mandel, T. (1997). *The Elements of User Interface Design.* United States of America: John Wiley & Sons, Inc.

Mariage, C., Vanderdonckt, J., & Chevalier, A. (2005). Using the MetroWeb tool to improve usability quality of web sites. *Proceedings of the Third Latin American Web Congress.*

Maslow, A. H. (1970). *Motivation and Personality* (2nd ed.). New York: Harper & Row.

Mayer, R. C., Davis, J. H., & Schoorman, F. D. (1995). An integrative model of organizational trust. *Academy of Management Review, 20 (3):* 709 – 734.

McKnight, D. H., Choudhury, V., & Kacmar, C. (2002a). Developing and validating trust measures for e-commerce: An integrative typology. *Information Systems Research, 3:* 334 – 359.

McKnight, D. H., Choudhury, V., & Kacmar, C. (2002b). The impact of initial consumer trust on intentions to transact with a web site: A trust building model. *Journal of Strategic Information Systems, 11:* 297–323.

McKnight, D. H., Choudhury, V., & Kacmar, C. (2000). Trust in e-commerce vendors: A two-stage model. *Proceedings of the twenty first international conference on Information systems:* 532 – 536.

McKnight, D. H., Cummings, L. L., & Chervany, N. L. (1998). Initial trust formation in new organizational relationships. *Academy of Management Review, 23 (3):* 473 – 490.

Meyerson, D., Weick, K.E., Kramer, R.M. (1996). Swift trust and temporary groups. In: Kramer,
R.M., Tyler, T.R. (Eds.). *Trust in Organizations: Frontiers of Theory And Research.* Sage, Thousand Oaks, CA: 166–195.

Miller, R. B. (1968). Response time in man-computer conversational transactions. *Proc. AFIPS Fall Joint Computer Conference, 33:* 267-277.

Miniwatts Marketing Group (2007). Internet usage statistics: The big picture. Internet World Stats Web Site. Retrieved May 7th, 2007 from http://www.internetworldstats.com/stats.htm.

Moore, W. L., Louviere, J. L., & Verma, R. (1999). Using conjoint analysis to help design product platforms. *Journal of Product Innovation Management, 16:* 27 – 39.

Moorman, C., Deshpande, R., & Zaltman, G. (1993). Factors affecting trust in market research relationships. *Journal of Marketing, 57:* 81 – 101.

Morgan, R. M., & Hunt, S. D. (1994). The commitment-trust theory of relationship marketing. *Journal of Marketing, 58:* 20 – 38.

Murayama, N., Saito, S., & Okumura, M. (2004). Are web pages characterized by color? *Proceedings from WWW2004,* May 17-22, New York: 248 – 249.

Neal, W. D. (1999). Satisfaction is nice but value drives loyalty – the most satisfied customer may not necessarily be the most loyal. *Journal of Marketing Research, 11* (1): 21 – 23.

Nelson, M. G. (2000). Fast is no longer fast enough – As competition continues to grow online, the price for not keeping your web site up to speed can be lost consumers. *Information Week:* 48 – 60.

*Nielsen, J. (2000). *Designing web usability: The practice of simplicity.* Indianapolis: New Riders Publishing.

Nielsen, J. (2001). Did poor usability kill e-commerce? (August 19th, 2001). Retrieved September 30th, 2006 from http://www.useit.com/alertbox/20010819.html.

Nielsen, J. (1994). Response times: The three important limits. Retrieved January 8th, 2007 from: http://www.useit.com/papers/responsetime.html.

Nielsen, J. (1992). The usability engineering life cycle. *Computer:* 12 – 22.

Nielsen, J. (1993). *Usability Engineering.* Boston: Academic Press.

Nielsen, J., Molich, R., Snyder, C., & Farrell, S. (2000). *E-commerce user experience: Trust.* Fremont: Nielsen Norman Group.

Norman, D. A. (2002). Emotion and design: Attractive things work better. *Interactions* 9 (4): 36-42.

Norman, D. A. (2004). *Emotional Design: Why We Love (or Hate) Everyday Things.* New York: Basic Books.

Norman, D. A. (1998). *The Invisible Computer: Why Good Products Can Fail, the Personal Computer is so Complex, and Information Appliances are the Solution.* Cambridge: The MIT Press.

Norman, K., & Chin, J. (1998). The effect of tree structure on search in a hierarchical menu selection system. *Behavior and Information Technology, 7:* 51 – 65.

Nua. (2002). Internet users still not buying online. Retrieved November 11th, 2006 from: http://www.nua.ie/surveys/index.cgi?f=VS&art_id=905358100&rel=true.

Pace, B. J. (1984). Color combinations and contrast reversals on visual display units. *Proceedings of the Human Factors Society Twenty-Eighth Annual Meeting:* 326 – 330. Santa Monica, CA.

*Page, C., & Lepkowska-White, E. (2002). Web equity: A framework for building consumer value in online companies. *Journal of Consumer Marketing, 19 (3):* 231 – 248.

Paivio, A. (1974). Pictures and words in visual search. *Memory and Cognition, 2 (3):* 515 – 521.

Palmer, J. (2002a). Designing for web site usability. *Computer, 35* (7): 102 – 103.

Palmer, J. (2002b). Web site usability, design, and performance metrics. *Information Systems Research, 13* (2): 151 – 167.

Palmer, J. W., Bailey, J. P., & Faraj, S. (2000). The role of intermediaries in the development of trust on the WWW: The use and prominence of trusted third parties and privacy statements. *Journal of Computer-Mediated Communication, 5:* 1 – 25.

Palmer, J. W., & Griffith, D. A. (1998). An emerging model of web site design for marketing. *Communications of the ACM, 41 (3):* 45 – 51.

Papadopoulou, P., Kanellis, P., & Martakos, D. (2001). Investigating trust in e-commerce: A literature review and model for its formation in customer relationships. *Seventh Americas Conference on Information Systems*: 791 – 798.

Peeters, G., & Czapinski, J. (1990). Positive-negative asymmetry in evaluations: The distinction between affective and informational negativity effects. In W. Stroebe & M. Hewstone (Eds.). *European Review of Social Psychology* (pp. 33 – 60). New York: Wiley.

Petre, M., Minocha, S., & Roberts, D. (2006). Usability beyond the website: An empirically-grounded e-commerce evaluation instrument for the total customer experience. *Behaviour & Information Technology, 25* (2): 189 – 203.

Petty, R. E., & Cacioppo, J. T. (1981). *Attitude and persuasion: Classic and contemporary approaches*. Dubuque: Wm. C. Brown Company.

Petty, R. E., & Cacioppo, J. T. (1983). The role of bodily responses in attitude measurement and change. In J. T. Cacioppo & R. E. Petty (Eds.). *Social psychophysiology: A sourcebook* (pp.51-101). New York: Guilford.

Petty, R. E., & Wegener, D. T. (1999). The elaboration likelihood model: Current status and controversies. *Dual Process Theories in Social Psychology*. New York: Guilford Press.

Pham, M. T., Cohen, J. B., Pracejus, J. W., & Hughes, G. D. Affect monitoring and the primacy of feelings in judgment. *Journal of Consumer Research (28)*:167-188.

Pitkow, J., & Kehoe, C. (1995). GVU third WWW user survey. Retrieved from: http://www.cc.gatech.edu/gvu.user_surveys.

Plath, S. (2000). *The unabridged journals* (K.V. Kukil, Ed.). New York: Anchor.

*Powell, C. C., Clark, W. R., & Clark, C. L. (1996). *Working the Web: A Student's Guide, 1st edition.* Harcourt Brace College Publishers.

Princeton Survey Research Associates. (2002). A matter of trust: What users want from web sites. Results of a National Survey of Internet Users for Consumer WebWatch. 1 – 42.

Quesenbery, W. (2004). WQUsability. Retrieved May 7th from: http://www.wqusability.com/articles/getting-started.html

Quesenbery, W. (2003). Dimensions of usability. In Aburs, M. & Mazur, B. (Eds.). *Content and Complexity.* Erlbaum.

Raganathan, C. & Ganapathy, S. (2002). Key dimensions of business-to-consumer websites. *Information and Management, 39* (6): 457 – 465.

Reichheld, F. F., Markey, R. G., & Hopton, C. (2000). E-customer loyalty – Applying the traditional rules of business for online success. *European Business Journal:* 173 – 179.

Reichheld, F. F. & Sasser, W. E. (1990). Zero defections: Quality comes to services. *Harvard Business Review:* September – October.

Reichheld, F. F. & Schefter, P. (2000). E-loyalty: Your secret weapon on the web. *Harvard Business Review, 78:* 105 – 113.

Resnick, M. L., & Montania, R. (2003). Perceptions of customer service, information privacy, and product quality from semiotic design features in an online web store. *International Journal of Human-Computer Interaction, 16* (2): 211 – 234.

Richards, A. R., & David, C. (2005). Decorative color as a rhetorical enhancement on the world wide web. *Technical Communications Quarterly, 14 (1):* 31 – 48.

Riegelsberger, J. (2006). Building Trust in Online Shopping (May 2006). Brandchannel.com. Retrieved November 17th, 2006 from http://www.brandchannel.com/papers_review.asp?sp_id=1238.

Roozenburg, N. F. M. & Eekels, J. (1995). *Product Design: Fundamentals and Methods*. Chichester, UK: Wiley.

Rosenholtz, R., Li, Y., Mansfield, J., & Jin, Z. (2005). Feature Congestion: A Measure of Display Clutter. *Proceedings of CHI 2005:* 761 – 770.

Rotter, J. B. (1967). A new scale for the measurement of interpersonal trust. *Journal of Personality, 35* (4): 651 – 665.

Rowley, J. (2004). Online branding. *Online Information Review, 28* (2): 131 – 138.

Rowley, J. (2004). Online branding: The case of McDonald's. *British Food Journal, 106* (3): 228 – 237.

Roy, M. C., Dewit, O., & Aubert, B. A. (2001). The impact of interface usability on trust in web retailers. *Internet Research: Electronic Networking Applications and Policy, 11*(5): 388-398.

Russell, J. A., & Pratt, G. A. (1980). Description of the affective quality attributed to environments. *Journal of Personality and Social Psychology 38* (2): 311 – 322.

Salam, A. F., Iyer, L., Palvia, P., & Singh, R. (2005). Trust in e-commerce. *Communications of the ACM, 48 (2):* 73 – 77.

*Sawyer, P., & Schroeder, W. (2000). Report 4: Links that give off scent. *Designing Information-Rich Web Sites*. User Interface Engineering: Bradford, MA.

Schaik, P. v. and Ling, J. (2006). The effects of graphical display and screen ratio on information retrieval in web pages. *Computers in Human Behavior, 22*: 870 – 884.

Schaik, P. v. and Ling, J. (2001). Design parameters in web pages: Frame location and differential background contrast in visual search performance. *International Journal of Cognitive Ergonomics, 5* (4): 459 – 471.

Scheleur, S., King, C. & M. Shimberg. (2006). US Census Bureau Retail Indicators Branch. Quarterly retail e-commerce sales: 2nd quarter 2006. Retrieved October 1st, 2006 from http://www.census.gov/mrts/www/data/html/06Q2.html.

Schenkman, B. N. and Jönsson, F. U. (2000). Aesthetics and preferences of web pages. *Behaviour & Information Technology, 19*(5): 367-377.

Schlosser, A. E., White, T. B., & Lloyd, S. M. (2006). Converting web site visitors into buyers: How web site investment increases consumer trusting beliefs and online purchase intentions. *Journal of Marketing, 70:* 133 – 148.

Scholl, A., Manthey, L., Helm, R., & Steiner, M. (2005). Solving multiattribute design problems with analytic hierarchy process and conjoint analysis: An empirical comparison. *European Journal of Operational Research, 164:* 760 – 777.

Schneiderman, B. (1998). *Designing the User Interface: Strategies for Effective Human-Computer Interaction.* Reading: Addison-Wesley.

Schriver, K. A. (1997). *Dynamics in document design.* New York: Wiley Computer Publishing, John Wiley & Sons, Inc.

Schwarz, N., & Clore, G.L. (1983). Mood, misattribution, and judgments of well-being: Informative and directive functions of affective states. *Journal of Personality and Social Psychology, 45*: 513-523.

Seal, W., & Vincent-Jones, P. (1997). Accounting and trust in the enabling of long-term relations. *Accounting, Auditing, and Accountability Journal, 10* (3): 406 – 431.

Shankar, V., Smith, A., & Rangaswamy, A. (2003). Customer satisfaction and loyalty in online and offline environments. *International Journal of Research in Marketing, 20* (2): 153 – 175.

Shankar, V., Urban, G. L., & Sultan, F. (2002). Online trust: A stakeholder perspective, concepts, implications, and future directions. *Journal of Strategic Information Systems, 11*: 325–344.

Shneiderman, B., & Plaisant, C. (2005). *Designing the user interface: Strategies for effective human-computer interaction.*, 4th ed. United States of America: Pearson Education, Inc.

Sillence, E., Briggs, P., Fishwick, L. (2004 April). Trust and mistrust of online health sites. *Proceedings of the Computer-Human Interaction conference,* Vienna, Austria.

Sirdeshmukh, D., Singh, J., & Sabol, B. (2002). Consumer trust, value, and loyalty in relational exchanges. *Journal of Marketing, 66:* 15 – 37.

Smith, M., Bailey, J., & Brynjolfsson, E. (2000). Understanding digital markets: review and assessment. In: Brynjolfsson, E., & Kahin, B. (Eds.). *Understanding the Digital Economy*. Cambridge: MIT Press.

Spekman, R. E. (1988). Strategic supplier selection: Understanding long-term relationships. *Business Horizons, 31:* 75 – 81.

Staats, A. W., & Staats, C. K. (1958). Attitudes established by classical conditioning. *Journal of Abnormal and Social Psychology, 57*: 37 – 40.

Steinfield, C., Adelaar, T., & F. Liu. (2005). Click and mortar strategies viewed from the web: A content analysis of features illustrating integration between retailers' online and offline presence. *Electronic Markets, 15*(3): 199 – 212.

Stephens, R. T. (2004). A framework for the identification of electronic commerce design elements that enable trust within the small hotel industry. *Proceedings of the ACM South East conference,* Huntsville, AL.

Sterne, J. (1999). *World wide web marketing: Integrating the web into your marketing strategy.*, 3rd ed. New York: John Wiley & Sons, Inc.

Stewart, K. J. (2003). Trust transfer on the World Wide Web. *Organization Science, 14 (1):* 5 – 17.

Stone, M. C. (2004). Color in information display: Principles, perception, and models. *SIGGRAPH 2004, Course 20.*

Sultan, F., Urban, G.L., Shankar, V., & Bart, I. (2002). Determinants and Consequences of Trust in e-Business. Working Paper, Sloan School of Management, MIT: Cambridge, MA.

Szymanski, D. M., & Hise, R. T. (2000). E-satisfaction: An initial examination. *Journal of Retailing, 76 (3):* 309 – 322.

Tapscott, D., Ticoll, D., & Lowy, A. (2000). Relationships Rule. *Business 2.0.* Retrieved October 12th, 2006 from http://www.business2.com/content/magazine/indepth/2000/05/01/19505

Taylor, M. J., & England, D. (2006). Internet marketing: Web site navigational design issues. *Marketing Intelligence & Planning, 24 (1):* 77 – 85.

Toms, E. G., and Taves, A. R. (2004). Measuring user perceptions of Web site reputation. *Information Processing and Management, 40:* 291 – 317.

Tractinsky, N. (1997). Aesthetics and apparent usability: Empirically assessing cultural and methodological Issues. *Proceedings of Computer-Human Interaction Conference:* 115-122.

Tractinsky, N. (2004). Towards the study of aesthetics in information technology. *Proceedings of the 25th Annual International Conference on Information Systems:* 771-780.

Tractinsky, N., Shoval-Katz A., & Ikar, D. (2000). What is beautiful is usable. *Interacting with Computers, 13*(2): 127-145.

Tull, D. S., & Hawkins, D. I. (1993). *Marketing Research, Measurement & Method.* New York: Macmillan.

Udsen, L. E., & Jorgensen, A. H. (2005). The aesthetic turn: Unravelling recent aesthetic approaches to human-computer interaction. *Digital Creativity, 16* (4): 205 – 216.

Urban, G.L., Sultan, F., & Qualls, W.J. (2000). Placing trust at the center of your internet strategy. *Sloan Management Review.* 39 – 48.

*U.S. Department of Health and Human Services (2006). *Research-based Web Usability Guidelines.* Retrieved October 1st, 2006 from http://www.usability.gov/pdfs/guidelines.html.

U.S. Department of Health and Human Services (2007). Usability.gov. Retrieved May 6th, 2007 from: http://www.usability.gov/basics/whatusa.html.

Usability Net (2006). Retrieved May 6th, 2007 from: http://www.usabilitynet.org/tools/r_international.htm

Usability Professionals Organization (UPA) (2007). UPA Website. Retrieved May 6th, 2007 from: http://www.upassoc.org/

Van Schaik, P., & Ling, J. (2001). Design parameters in web pages: Frame location and differential background contrast in visual search performance. *International Journal of Cognitive Ergonomics, 5* (4): 459 – 471.

Vassilopoulou, K., Keeling, K. A., Macaulay, L. A., & McGoldrick, P. J. (2001). Measuring purchase intentions for internet retail sites against usability attributes. *Human Computer Interaction – Interact '01.*

Venkatesh, V., & Agarwal, R. (2006). Turning visitors into customers: A usability-centric perspective on purchase behavior in electronic channels. *Management Science, 52* (3): 367 – 382.

Warden, C. A., Wu, W., & Tsai, D. (2006). Online shopping interface components: Relative importance as peripheral and central cues. *CyberPsychology and Behavior, 9* (3): 285 – 296.

Weber, L. R. & Carter, A. (1998). On constructing trust: temporality, self-disclosure, and perspective-taking. *International Journal of Sociology and Social Policy, 18* (1): 7 – 26.

*Weeks, C. E. (1997). How to design an aesthetically-pleasing, ADA-compliant website. *Proceedings of the 25th annual ACM SIGUCCS Conference on User Services:* 319 – 326.

White, J. V. (1990). *Color for the electronic age.* New York: Watson-Guptill.

"White Space (Visual Arts)." (2007). Wikipedia.com. Retrieved June 12th, 2007 from: http://en.wikipedia.org/wiki/White_space_(visual_arts).

Whitney, D. E. (1988). Manufacturing by design. *Harvard Business Review*: 83 – 90.

Wicks, A.C., Berman, S.L., Jones, T.M. (1999). The structure of optimal trust: moral and strategic implications. *Academy of Management Review 24* (1): 99–116.

Wimmer, R. D., & Dominick, J. R. (1997). Mass media research: An introduction (5th ed.). Belmont: Wadsworth.

Woodruff, A., Rosenholtz, R., Morrison, J. B., Faulring, A., & Pirolli, P. (2002). A comparison of the use of text summaries, plain thumbnails, and enhanced thumbnails for web search tasks. *Journal of the American Society for Information Science & Technology, 53 (2):* 172 – 185.

Yang, S., Hung, W., Sung, K., & Farn, C. (2006). Investigating initial trust toward e-tailers from the elaboration likelihood model perspective. *Psychology & Marketing, 23* (5): 429 – 445.

Yoon, S. (2002). The antecedents and consequences of trust in online-purchase decisions. *Journal of Interactive Marketing, 16 (2):* 47 – 63.

Yzerbyt, V., & Leyens, J. (1991). Requesting information to form an impression: The influence of valence and confirmatory status. *Journal of Experimental Social Psychology, 27:* 337 – 356.

Zaheer, A., McEvily, B., & Perrone, V. (1998). Does trust matter? Exploring the effects of interorganizational and interpersonal trust on performance. *Organization Science, 9* (2): 141-159.

Zajonc, R. B. (2001). Mere exposure: A gateway to the subliminal. *Current Directions in Psychological Science, 10* (6): 224 – 228.

Zajonc, R. B., & Markus, H. (1982). Affective and cognitive factors in preferences. *Journal of Consumer Research, 9* (2): 123-131.

Zellweger, P. (1997). Web-based sales: Defining the cognitive buyer. *Electronic Markets, 7:* 10 – 16.

Zettl, H. (1999). *Sight, sound, motion: Applied media aesthetics.* United States of America: Wadsworth Publishing Company.

*Zimmermann, B. B. (1997). Applying Tufte's principles of information design to creating effective Web sites. *Proceedings of the 15th Annual International Conference on Computer Documentation:* 309 – 317.

Zucker, L. G. (1986). Production of trust: Institutional sources of economic structure, 1840-1920. In L. L. Cummings & B. M. Staw (Eds.). *Research in Organizational Behavior* (pp. 53-111). Greenwich: JAI Press.

Wissenschaftlicher Buchverlag bietet

kostenfreie

Publikation

von

wissenschaftlichen Arbeiten

Diplomarbeiten, Magisterarbeiten, Master und Bachelor Theses
sowie Dissertationen, Habilitationen und wissenschaftliche Monographien

Sie verfügen über eine wissenschaftliche Abschlußarbeit zu aktuellen oder zeitlosen
Fragestellungen, die hohen inhaltlichen und formalen Ansprüchen genügt,
und haben **Interesse an einer honorarvergüteten Publikation**?

Dann senden Sie bitte erste Informationen über Ihre Arbeit per Email
an info@vdm-verlag.de. Unser Außenlektorat meldet sich umgehend bei Ihnen.

VDM Verlag Dr. Müller Aktiengesellschaft & Co. KG
Dudweiler Landstraße 125a
D - 66123 Saarbrücken

www.vdm-verlag.de

www.ingramcontent.com/pod-product-compliance
Lightning Source LLC
La Vergne TN
LVHW022301060326
832902LV00020B/3198